W9-BXN-143

RETHINKING EFFECTIVE SCHOOLS

RETHINKING EFFECTIVE SCHOOLS: RESEARCH AND PRACTICE

edited by

James R. Bliss
Rutgers, The State University of New Jersey

William A. Firestone
Rutgers, The State University of New Jersey

Craig E. Richards
Teachers College, Columbia University

Prentice Hall, *Englewood Cliffs, New Jersey 07632*

Library of Congress Cataloging-in-Publication Data

Rethinking effective schools : research and practice / edited by James
  R. Bliss, William A. Firestone, Craig E. Richards.
     p.   cm.—(Rutgers symposium on education)
    Includes bibliographical references and index.
    ISBN 0-13-778804-5
    1. School improvement programs—United States—Congresses.
2. School management and organization—United States—Congresses.
3. Education—Research—United States—Congresses.   4. Education—
United States—Aims and objectives.   I. Bliss, James R., 1947– .
II. Firestone, William A.   III. Richards, Craig.   IV. Series.
LB2822.82.R46   1991
371.2'00973—dc20   90-7905
                                              CIP

Editorial/production supervision, interior design,
    and page makeup: *June Sanns*
Manufacturing buyer: *Marianne Gloriande*
Prepress buyer: *Debra Kesar*

© 1991 by Prentice-Hall, Inc.
A Division of Simon & Schuster
Englewood Cliffs, New Jersey 07632

Printed in the United States of America

10 9 8 7 6 5 4 3 2 1

ISBN 0-13-778804-5

PRENTICE-HALL INTERNATIONAL (UK) LIMITED, *London*
PRENTICE-HALL OF AUSTRALIA PTY. LIMITED, *Sydney*
PRENTICE-HALL CANADA INC., *Toronto*
PRENTICE-HALL HISPANOAMERICANA, S.A., *Mexico*
PRENTICE-HALL OF INDIA PRIVATE LIMITED, *New Delhi*
PRENTICE-HALL OF JAPAN, INC., *Tokyo*
SIMON & SCHUSTER ASIA PTE. LTD., *Singapore*
EDITORA PRENTICE-HALL DO BRASIL, LTDA., *Rio de Janeiro*

RUTGERS SYMPOSIUM ON EDUCATION

Louise Cherry Wilkinson, Series Editor

Research Perspectives on the Graduate Preparation of Teachers
Anita E. Woolfolk, Editor

Assessment for Instruction in Early Literacy
Lesley Mandel Morrow and Jeffrey K. Smith, Editors

Rethinking Effective Schools: Research and Practice
James R. Bliss, William A. Firestone and Craig E. Richards, Editors

CONTENTS

SERIES FOREWORD

Within the past several years, the profession of education has been shaken to its roots as national attention focused on education and on educators. Critics and friends have raised basic questions about the profession, including whether educational professionals have successfully met the challenges that the students and the schools present and even more fundamentally, if they are able to meet those challenges. Beginning with the highly publicized *A Nation at Risk,* seemingly endless and often contradictory criticisms, analyses, and recommendations have appeared from virtually every segment of contemporary American society.

In this recent explosion of concern for educational reform, we see a need for a general and national forum in which the problems of education can be examined in light of research from a range of relevant disciplines. Too often, analyses of very complex issues and problems occur within a single discipline. Aspects of a problem that are unfamiliar to those members of the discipline are ignored, and the resulting analysis is limited in scope and unsatisfactory for that reason. Furthermore, when educational issues are investigated by members of one discipline, there is seldom an attempt to examine related issues from other fields or to apply methods developed in other fields that might prove illuminating.

The national debate on educational reform has suffered from this myopia, as problems and issues are identified and analyses and solutions often are proposed within the limited confines of a single disciplinary boundary. In the past, national discussions have been ill informed or uninformed by current research partly because there are far too few mechanisms for interdisciplinary analyses of significant issues.

The present series of volumes, the *Rutgers Symposium on Education*, attempts to address this gap. The *series will focus on timely issues and problems in education, taking an interdisciplinary perspective*. The focus of each volume will be a particular problem, such as a potential teacher shortage, the structure of schools, and the effects of cognitive psychology on how to teach mathematics. There is an accumulating corpus of high quality educational research on topics of interest to practitioners and policymakers. Each volume in the series will provide an interdisciplinary forum through which scholars can disseminate their original research and extend their work to potential applications for practice, including guides for teaching, learning, assessment, intervention, and policy formulation. We believe that this work will increase the potential for significant analysis as well as the potential for positive impact in the domains of both practice and theory.

The third volume in the series presents critical analyses of the effective schools reform movement in the United States. The editors note that effective schools was both a movement and a body of research, that was initiated in the late 1970s and blossomed throughout the succeeding decade. Initially, the movement was a reaction against the views of Coleman and others, who saw schooling as having little impact on the lives of children and their achievement levels. As the editors state succinctly; "More specifically, the effective schools movement was committed to the belief that 'children of the urban poor,' as its most eloquent spokesman put it, could succeed in school and that the school itself could help them succeed; success in school was not all up to the family."* The contribution of the work presented in this volume is, without doubt, substantial. All too often, too many rush to the most current movement, seen as the panacea for education without really understanding what was done, why it worked or did not work. By carefully reexamining one of the most significant education reform movements, the authors contribute new knowledge, so that we may learn valuable lessons from the past.

It is with great pleasure that we contribute this series of volumes on contemporary educational issues, the *Rutgers Symposium on Education*. Our expectation is that this series will serve as a seminal contribution to the literature in educational theory and practice.

Louise Cherry Wilkinson
*Dean of the Rutgers Graduate School of Education
and Professor of Educational Psychology
Rutgers, The State University of New Jersey*

*R. R. Edmonds, "Effective Schools for the Urban Poor," *Educational Leadership*, Vol. 37, no. 1 (1979), p. 15–24.

PREFACE

It is now almost a quarter century since the Coleman Report first questioned whether variations in school quality had as much impact on learning as what the student brings to school. Coleman's and related work raised fundamental questions about the schools' contribution to the national quest for equity of opportunity for children of all races and classes. In the decades that followed, some researchers and practitioners addressed the Coleman challenge by identifying the characteristics of effective schools—that is, organizational factors that contribute to student learning and help to minimize the differences between those from different backgrounds. This later work has been controversial, but it offers useful ideas about how to improve education that continue to be provocative even now that the educational agenda shifts from equity to excellence and rebuilding the nation's capacity to compete in international markets.

Since the literature on effective schools is itself two decades old, some review and assessment is in order. The chapters in this book address basic issues that need to be resolved in order to turn the writing about effective schools into useful practice: What do people mean by school effectiveness, and what should they mean? How adequate is the research base for conclusions about what makes schools successful? What new lines of research should be considered when developing blueprints for school effectiveness? How does one translate ideas about what schools should be like into transformed institutions? How do two decades of thinking about school effectiveness inform current reform efforts that use different labels and have different goals?

The authors of these chapters bring the perspectives of a variety of fields including educational administration, policy, and curriculum and such disciplines as economics, political science, psychology, and sociology to bear on these questions. Their ideas began with roots in the research they reviewed or conducted themselves and were tested and expanded through a working conference and then a series of presentations to school administrators at Rutgers University. The results help to bridge the gap between the questions about educational improvement from the 1960s and 1970s to the reform issues that will take us into the twenty-first century.

We wish to thank the many people who contributed to this project. Dean Louise Cherry Wilkinson conceived of the Rutgers Symposium in Education series and supported this effort. David Muschinske, ably assisted by Barbara Knoblock and Richard Novack, organized the conference. Linda van Vlack attended to correspondence with authors, and Kristine Spaventa prepared the manuscript. A special thanks to Diann Richards for her expertise in the final editing of the manuscript. Carol Wada, editor at Prentice Hall, supported the project and helped move it along efficiently and effectively to its rapid conclusion. Our thanks to all these friends and colleagues.

James R. Bliss
New Brunswick, New Jersey

William A. Firestone
Yardley, Pennsylvania

Craig E. Richards
Princeton, New Jersey

RETHINKING EFFECTIVE SCHOOLS

1

INTRODUCTION

William A. Firestone
Rutgers, The State University of New Jersey
Department of Educational Theory, Policy, and Administration

Reforming American education is a repetitive process. Reformers vacillate between teacher-centered and student-centered instruction, academic and practical curricula, centralizing and decentralizing authority, and using education to promote equity and productivity (Cuban, 1990). One reason for this vacillation is because Americans simply do not agree on what values they want their educational system to promote [see Miles (1981) on the goal ambiguity of education], but another is that we fail to examine and learn from our reform efforts. The attention spans of policymakers and practitioners are much shorter than the time it takes to put a reform into place (Firestone, 1989). Typically, reformers move on to the next program before the dust has settled on the last one. Postmortems are conducted in the heat of the battle, not after the dust has settled and there has been time for reflection.

This book is an effort to overcome the mindless tendency to rush from reform to reform by providing a reanalysis of the effective schools movement which took the education world by storm in the late 1970s. Indeed, "effective schools" was as much a movement as a body of research. Firmly committed to the belief that schools could make a difference in students' lives, it was a direct reaction to the work of Coleman (Coleman et al., 1966) and (Jencks et al., 1972) which discounted the contribution of schooling to student achievement and suggested that school quality (as defined at the time) did not make a difference. More specifically, the effective schools movement was committed to the belief that "children of the urban poor," as its most eloquent spokesman put it, could succeed in school and that the school itself could help them succeed; success in school was not all up to the family (Edmonds, 1979).

To buttress these beliefs, effective schools advocates had their own body of research and their own prescriptions for effectiveness. The research—often done outside the academy by private associations (Weber, 1971), federal contract shops (Wellisch et al., 1978), or state departments of education (Austin, 1978)—examined small samples of schools that were doing better than expected at educating poor and minority children. The studies identified commonalities among high-achieving schools and attributed their success to those commonalities. The lists of factors generated by this process included strong administrative leadership; a shared expectation that all students can achieve basic levels of competence at the skills taught in school; an orderly, but not repressive, climate; and regular means for monitoring student performance (Edmonds, 1979).

In the first chapter of this volume, Firestone traces the paradoxical reception this research received. Educators and policymakers hungry for new ways to improve their performance embraced it. By the end of the 1980s, two-fifths of the nation's school districts had something that could be called an effective schools program. Half the states and the federal government were also enthusiastic, incorporating effective schools ideas into programs and legislation. By contrast, the research community was ambivalent. There was a brief flurry of works critiquing—often sharply criticizing—the original research but relatively little follow-up in the form of new studies to test and expand the original findings using better research designs.

Firestone suggests two explanations for this paradoxical reception. First, researchers and educators used different standards to assess new ideas. Educators and policymakers responded positively to reform prescriptions that fit their ideas of how schools work and offered concrete guidance on how to proceed as the effective schools research did. Researchers were much more concerned with the methodological adequacy of the studies buttressing the ideas. The early effective schools studies had serious flaws although there was considerable consistency in their results. Second, the effective schools movement suggested a prescription to overcome a crisis of confidence stemming partly from the research but mostly from larger shifts in American society that afflicted the schools but had less effect on researchers themselves.

Any reassessment of the effective schools movement must deal with five questions:

- What is meant by effectiveness?
- What are the characteristics of effective schools?
- How does one change schools to make them more effective?
- How does the effective schools literature inform and relate to current movements to reform educational policy?
- How should "effective schools" be viewed as a social phenomenon?

THE MEANING OF EFFECTIVENESS

While it has connotations of rational, technical analysis, "effectiveness" is not a neutral term. Defining the effectiveness of a particular school always requires choices among competing values. Moreover, since schools—like other organizations—operate in complex environments with multiple internal and external constituencies, criteria of effectiveness will be the subject of political debate (Scott, 1981). To cope with this variety of criteria and competing constituencies, some researchers generated complex frameworks that can be used to classify divergent definitions (e.g., Hoy & Miskel, 1987). This is the strategy of the "value-free" analyst.

The effective schools literature firmly rejected this value-free approach. Instead, it intentionally took a partisan stance by advocating a specific, narrow definition. Edmonds (1979, p. 16), the movement's leading spokesperson, asserts, "I require that an effective school bring the children of the poor to those minimal masteries of basic school skills that now describe minimally successful pupil performance for children of the middle class." While not the only definition proposed, this one highlights the main themes of most of them. Unlike some researcher theories of effectiveness that focus on resources (e.g., Yuchtman & Seashore, 1967), this one emphasizes outcomes. Moreover, there are three important elements to this specification of outcomes:

- A clientele, namely poor children.
- *A subject matter to be taught*, in this case basic school skills, meaning numeracy and literacy.
- *A criterion* which in this case is comparative. Children of the poor should do as well as those of the middle class.

The comparative criterion and the stress on education of the poor makes this an equity definition of effectiveness.

One surprising aspect of reactions to the effective schools literature is that this fundamental definition which gave the movement its initial special character has received little analysis. In his chapter, Richards points out several problems with the definitions employed by effective schools writers. For instance, at various times, Edmonds proposed several criteria. In addition to the equity standard he also suggested a local one (students should meet what their district considers to be adequate mastery of basic skills) and, since local standards are likely to be low in urban districts, a national norm-referenced one. Depending on how these standards are set, students who meet them could still be underprepared for life in the adult world. Moreover, Edmonds accepted as the subject matter to be taught the basic literacy and numeracy skills measured by achievement tests, skills that may in fact be too simple for the complex jobs that will be the staple of the twenty-first century economy.

Since the early effective schools movement, Richards notes three shifts in the way effectiveness is defined. First, there has been a displacement from concern with student outcomes to the organizational characteristics said to predict those outcomes. People either assume that if the characteristics are there, the outcomes will follow or forget about outcomes entirely. Second, the original criteria have been replaced with an improvement criterion. If schools are getting better, they are considered effective even if poor students still do not achieve at levels comparable to their middle class counterparts. Finally, the biggest shift is from an equity definition to a productivity definition of excellence which broadens the clientele to include all students, broadens the subject matter to be taught to include problem-solving and higher order thinking skills, and raises the criteria above those set for the equity definition. These shifts were made partly for technical reasons; the data to apply some of the standards proposed by Edmonds are simply not available. More important, as Americans have become aware of how their economy and their children are falling behind other developed nations', pressure has built to use the educational system to help America become more competitive again.

While Richards's chapter is the only one that explicitly analyzes definitions of effectiveness, most chapters take a position on the issue at least implicitly, and these discussions illustrate both the changes that have taken place and the complexities of defining effectiveness in educational terms. While Firestone more or less uncritically accepts a general equity definition of effectiveness, most of the others take a more complex view. Peterson and Lezotte suggest that equity concerns more than issues of race and class; achievement differences based on race, disability, and family structure (e.g., single-parent families) must also be addressed.

Bliss contrasts competing themes in the effective schools literature to raise questions about the content and skills taught. The popular image emphasizes basic skills as measured by achievement tests. However, in the holistic image, effectiveness consists in helping students "experience" a wide range of content. The emphasis on experience implies not just the rote learning suggested by basic skills instruction but a more active problem-solving capacity.

Newmann argues even more explicitly for a broader conception of the content to be taught to include a wider range of subject matter and a greater sensitivity to students' depth of understanding, integration of knowledge, and ability to produce thoughtful discourse. In fact, he goes a step farther to suggest that effectiveness should be defined in terms of the presence of such behaviors and attitudes as self-esteem; racial tolerance; political efficacy; and reduced teen pregnancy, drug abuse, and gang participation. At the same time, he points out that we currently lack the technology to measure many of the criteria that he would include in his multidimensional definition of effectiveness.

Mortimore illustrates his agreement with the multidimensional view stressing student outcomes by reporting on the British effectiveness studies that in fact use several dependent variables, including achievement tests, but also delinquency, attitude toward school, attendance, and behavior.

Some of the chapters go beyond this focus on student outcomes. For instance, Berry and Ginsberg—like Newmann—criticize definitions of effectiveness that focus narrowly on basic skills instruction as reflected in current achievement tests. While they argue for a broader view of student cognition, they also introduce an organizational element. Effective schools are places where teachers are not treated like semiskilled laborers but as professionals who are the locus of the most essential knowledge about the instructional process. An effective school empowers teachers to act on that knowledge. The authors argue for this view of teaching largely as a means to achieve their cognitively complex view of what students should learn but also in part as an end in itself.

Louis and Miles share this concern for organizational characteristics. In their study of schools becoming effective, they hold to the equity criterion by focusing on urban high schools, follow what has become conventional wisdom by showing that student achievement increased in their "successful" schools, and agree with Newmann, Mortimore, and others by providing multiple indicators of excellence, including information on dropouts, attendance, and student violence. However, they are also concerned about such organizational characteristics as staff morale and the capacity to become a self-diagnosing and self-managing organization that can identify and solve problems and improve itself.

Glenn adds a different note by treating schools not just as producers of educated students but also as political institutions that embody central social values. Thus, to student-centered effectiveness criteria, he adds two others. Justice in this case essentially means equal educational opportunity regardless of race, creed, or color, not just because it facilitates the education of the urban poor, but as an end in itself for democratic society. Liberty refers to the minimization of constraint on the individual citizen. From this perspective, compulsory assignment of a student to a specific school by a governmental authority is a reduction of individual liberty that is by definition ineffective.

Together, these chapters illustrate the difficulties of reaching agreement on definitions of effectiveness. Moreover, further analysis suggests that prescriptions for how schools should become effective depend in part on these definitions of what effectiveness is.

CHARACTERISTICS OF EFFECTIVE SCHOOLS

Three chapters explicitly set out to identify characteristics of effective schools. Bliss finds two images of effective schools in the research at the elementary level. The strategic image employs an effectiveness criterion similar to Edmonds's, stressing basic reading and arithmetic skills as measured through standardized achievement tests. The instructional strategy for achieving these skills is direct instruction where teachers use a variety of rewards and punishments to manage the classroom and maximize time-on-task, that is, the attention to instruction. The teacher is the center of attention who maintains the classroom's academic focus. The strategic image requires an assertive instructional leader with strong content and pedagogical skills. This leader is typically the principal. Just as the teacher is the center of attention in the classroom, the principal is the driving force in the school.

He contrasts this image to what was initially the less popular holistic one. This image begins with a softer definition of effectiveness that stresses experiencing content. In this view the student is an active learner, and other subject areas—art, music, literature—receive importance that is closer to literacy and numeracy narrowly defined. Teachers rely on indirect instructional strategies. Since the student is an active learner, the teacher's task is to create an environment conducive to learning with an accepting climate and activities that emerge more from students' own interests. Instruction is less teacher centered and relies more on activity centers and the like. Similarly, the principal is not so much the directive leader as a facilitator who sets broad goals and provides resources but gives teachers considerable discretion in how to teach.

Newmann's review of the literature on secondary schools points to a critical, but neglected intervening variable: student engagement in academic work. Newmann defines academic work as "the tasks...that students are asked to undertake in order to master the knowledge, skills and crafts that serve as the instructional objectives of schooling." Student engagement is "the student's psychological investment in learning, understanding, or mastering the knowledge, skills or crafts that academic work is intended to promote" (p. 61). Going through the motions and being engaged in the work are two very different things. Nor is engagement always pleasant. It may involve anxiety, disagreements with others, frustration, and fatigue, but it does contribute to higher-order learning.

Newmann cites several factors that contribute to student engagement. He posits that most people have a powerful need to develop and express competence. The question is how to channel that need into academic work. At a general level, it helps if a person bonds with or feels like a member of the school. More specifically, tasks can be designed to maximize engagement. For instance, teachers can offer such extrinsic rewards as grades, social approval, special privileges, and opportunities to display one's accomplishment. Intrinsic rewards can also be enhanced. Since schooling overemphasizes abstract verbal and mathematical competence, tasks that involve aesthetic, interpersonal, kinesthetic, and other competencies can be rewarding to students who are not currently reached by schoolwork. Students' sense of ownership can be enhanced by providing more opportunities for students to design their own work rather than always responding to the teacher's assignment. Schoolwork can become more authentic by taking on characteristics of work found in the real world. Authentic work is more real, meaningful, and useful to students. Tasks can be organized to provide social support both from teachers and peers. An important element of support is reducing the public stigma of failure. Finally, and much ignored, efforts can be made to make schoolwork more fun.

Mortimore reports on a healthy tradition of effective schools research in Great Britain. In comparison with American research, British studies tend to

- Examine secondary schools
- Avoid the methodological problems that come with analysis of especially effective outlier schools
- Use larger samples of schools (as high as 140 in the extreme case)
- Use longitudinal data on students
- Employ more sophisticated mathematical techniques,
- Have a wider variety of dependent variables

These studies find that while family background continues to make a difference, so do schools. In his own work Mortimore found that in the more effective schools, students from blue-collar families achieved more than do students from white-collar families in the less effective schools. Many of the factors that contribute to school effectiveness are similar to those found in the early American studies, including leadership and school climate, but some like involving teachers in school decision making are just coming to the attention of effective schools advocates in America.

THE PROCESS OF CHANGE

One criticism of the early effective schools research is that it provided a static picture of what good schools were like but little advice on how to transform places that were not effective. By drawing on existing research on planned change, conducting original studies, and reflecting on experience, analysts have developed firmer knowledge about how to become effective.

Louis and Miles use case studies and a survey of improving urban high schools to identify strategies to make schools more effective. These cover both the leadership aspect of change—planning—and the management component or coping. Their depiction of *evolutionary planning* is a radical break from textbook theories of rational planning. Like Peters and Waterman (1982), they reject narrow operationalizable goals in favor of quick action. Action promotes learning and can build commitment. Through reflection on action, themes for change can emerge which coalesce over time into a vision of what a school should be. They also counsel that planning should not begin with mass participation but a small group of committed change agents. This group can build mass commitment over time. Although never working alone, the principal is quite central to the process of building a vision for change.

In the real world of school improvement, Louis and Miles find that planning and implementation overlap. Even as planning gets underway, the principal and other key leaders must manage, the change process. Since improvement generates many complex problems, successful change requires *deep coping*. "School change managers," they say, "...constantly search for, confront, and acknowledge serious problems when they first appear, and...act rapidly to make major adjustments to solve them" (p. 105). Coping requires assertiveness, persistence, and tenacity, but it is problem appropriate. Elephant guns are not used to shoot mice. Still a great deal of time is required to coordinate various aspects of the change effort (or efforts), to keep track of what is happening and get the right resources to the right people at the right time, and to anticipate and deal directly with the unanticipatable difficulties that will surely arise.

While Louis and Miles focus on building-level change management, Loucks-Horsley and Mundry describe a much neglected tactic to promote school effectiveness: external assistance. The outside assistor treats the school (or district) as client and helps clarify the problem to be addressed, build support for change, allocate resources, and make the changed situation more permanent, among other things.

Loucks-Horsley and Mundry identify three technical assistance models that address different aspects of the change process. The planning and capacity-building model changes school organization and classroom practices while helping individuals assess the school, improve it, and institutionalize successful changes. Its centerpiece is a school planning team of teachers and administrators who identify problems, choose courses of direction, and assess progress. Outsider assisters provide information about effective schools practices and change management and help the team work through the change process. Through several cycles of this process, the assistor gradually transfers responsibility to the team itself.

The training and follow-up assistance model helps implement a specific practice like Teacher Expectation/Student Achievement (TESA) or site-based management. The key feature here is the combination of training with follow-up assistance and coaching so the effort is more than a one-shot workshop. The assistor provides training and establishes an internal support system to offer ongoing coaching, troubleshooting, and support.

The adoption-assistance model facilitates schools helping schools. It has two layers of assistance. The first—often in a state department of education—validates that schools have improved, helps them to package their successful practices, and brokers a match between those schools and others seeking to improve. The second layer is provided by the effective schools themselves. Staff may provide presentations, model practices on their home turf, and provide follow-up and telephone assistance. Visitors may spend an extended period of time seeing how the more effective schools work. Each model fits certain situations, and they can be combined successfully. However, none of them works quickly or simply.

Peterson and Lezotte illustrate how those helping to make schools more effective have drawn on a wide variety of research advances over the last decade. These advances have been in areas like organizational theory curriculum and instruction, and planned change. These advances have helped develop a more complex, contingent view of how to help schools become more effective. Newer research has emphasized:

- The importance of context. Improvement will not take the same form in all schools.
- The importance of school culture which can be reinforced through such diverse means as ceremonies and monitoring systems.
- The need to include teachers in decisions about how to change and operate schools.
- The need for district support.
- The importance of curriculum alignment for achieving measurable success.

CURRENT POLICY DEVELOPMENTS

The work on effective schools is no longer trendy. Educators and policymakers have moved on to new "fixes" for American education. Some of these could reinforce what has been learned through effective schools research and practical experience with its use; some are unrelated or even potentially antithetical. Three of these fixes are teacher professionalization, site-based management, and choice.

Berry and Ginsberg suggest that the movements for effective schools and teacher professionalism appear to be at odds but can be mutually supportive. Certain themes in effective schools writing—most notably the emphasis on a basic skills criterion of effectiveness and strong administrative leadership—combined with other developments in research (such as direct instruction) and in American society to reinforce the first wave of reforms in the 1980s. These reforms "hyperrationalized" education (Wise, 1979) through top-down regulation and the excessive use of achievement tests for accountability. These and other developments contributed to treating teachers as semiskilled laborers and worsening working conditions for them.

Berry and Ginsberg agree with second-wave reformers like the Carnegie Commission for the Advancement of Teaching (1986) that educational improvement will require professionalizing teachers by recognizing the special knowledge about instruction they have. Professionalization will require a more complex conception of what should be taught in schools, more hospitable working conditions and supportive school cultures as well as a new breed of teachers, and their empowerment to allow them to use the knowledge and commitment they will bring to their work. According to Berry and Ginsberg, there is a subtext to the effective schools research—Bliss's holistic image—that emphasizes the need for teacher discretion and the use of teachers' professional knowledge. This subtext would argue against hyperrationalization. They question which view of the effective schools research will dominate and argue that it is time to choose the one that will professionalize teaching.

Ramirez, Webb, and Guthrie discuss recent thinking about site-based management. Since the effective schools literature asserts that the school is the logical place to begin improving instruction, it raises questions about what functions should be decentralized to the school and what central controls should be reduced to facilitate local improvement and initiative. They also point out that decentralization to the school level is not the same as inclusion of teachers in decision making. There are arguments for both, but site-based management is not the same as teacher empowerment.

While they recognize the importance of greater site-based management, especially in large urban districts, Ramirez and colleagues point out the need to strike an adequate balance between district and school interests, as well as the interests of professionals and the community. Some functions like curriculum planning, professional development, personnel, and facilities construction and site acquisition should either remain centralized or be divided so that decisions are made at the appropriate level. Certain kinds of accountability will always have to rest at the district level. Their paper provides a useful framework for considering the kind of district redesign that can facilitate building effectiveness.

Glenn suggests that parental choice can promote student achievement but also effectiveness defined in other terms. Two arguments connect choice with student learning. What he calls the "blunt weapon strategy" provides negative sanctions. In a free market situation, parents will withdraw their students from schools where children do not learn. Hence, schools must teach students to survive. A more benign argument links parental choice with teacher choice. In this argument, parental choice requires a greater diversity among schools than now exists. Schools will have to develop clear missions, and teachers will have to align their efforts with those missions. However, since there will be variety, teachers will have more choice in work situations so they can become voluntarily more committed to the schools in which they work. Comparisons of student performance in public and private schools are cited as evidence that choice will promote effectiveness.

The choice option also broadens the definition of effectiveness to include such political values as liberty—the freedom to choose one's (or one's child's) school—and justice which he defines as integration or equality of access.[1] Choice increases liberty by definition. Choice programs can also be designed to facilitate integration. As an example, he cites the choice-based desegregation program in the city of Boston which was adopted in 1989. When the program was first implemented approximately three-fifths of all first and sixth graders received their first choice school assignment, only about 15 percent were placed involuntarily, and the overall desegregation of the district increased.

"EFFECTIVE SCHOOLS" AS A SOCIAL PHENOMENON

One of the problems in rethinking effective schools, as this book sets out to do, is determining what kind of social phenomenon is the subject of interest. The difficulty is that it is both knowledge components and political components. As such it has links into distinct, but related worlds. One knowledge component is a body of research. This research is subject to all the canons of conceptual and methodological rigor that are applied to any other behavioral or social science field. In that regard, the American work in particular has been flawed and appropriately criticized as several chapters in this volume indicate. Still, although it is subject to more and less directive interpretations—see particularly Bliss and Berry and Ginsberg—there is a core of consistency to be found across a variety of studies conducted here and abroad with a range of different methodological strengths and weaknesses. Moreover, there is considerable support for the key findings in related research on organizational behavior in a variety of work settings and countries.

Another knowledge component is a body of practical understandings about how to design and operate schools. This knowledge complements and is supplemented by research and practical work on planned change in education and elsewhere as well as work on improving instruction. Firestone's and Peterson and Lezotte's chapters in particular illustrate how effective schools programs draw on and reinforce the craft knowledge about how to improve schools.

Some of the difficulty in thinking through what has been learned about effective schools arises because we are also analyzing a social movement within the field of education as several subsequent chapters indicate. The movement was initially strongly committed to a specific program of educational equity. This movement demonstrated how the search for quality and sympathy for the equity agenda can create on the one side some sensitivity about criticizing the research and on the other some impatience with what activists can see as methodological nit-picking.

Finally, over the decade, effective schools has moved from a sect to a church—that is, from a narrowly defined movement with a specific agenda to a broad panacea that seems to have applicability in a variety of settings for which it was not initially intended. As such, it has expanded its scope to encompass concerns about national productivity as well as equity and taken on a general enough form to be applicable to a wide variety of the nation's school districts. Broadening the meaning of effective schools has the advantage that it expands the scope of application of the knowledge generated about how to improve schools. The difficulty is that it discourages critical thinking about what we are trying to accomplish as educators and how we should go about doing so. Effective schools comes to mean too much and too little.

For all the rhetoric that surrounds the field, there is a core of learning about how to organize schools so that children learn more than they have before and how to help schools overcome some of the effects of poverty on student learning. But because "effective schools" combines knowledge-based and political elements, it is difficult to identify that core. This volume is an effort to sort through the methodological and conceptual issues, the political and practical complexities in order to identify what is useful for educators as we move into the twenty-first century.

REFERENCES

AUSTIN, G. R. (1978). *Process evaluation: A comprehensive study of outliers*, ED160644. Baltimore: Maryland State Dept. of Education, University of Baltimore Center of Education Research and Development.

CARNEGIE COMMISSION FOR THE ADVANCEMENT OF TEACHING. (1986). *A nation prepared: Teachers for the 21st century.* New York: Carnegie Foundation.

COLEMAN, J. S., CAMPBELL, E. Q., HOBSON, C. J., MCPARTLAND, J., MOOD, A. M., WEINFELD, F. D., & YORK, R. L. (1966). *Equality of educational opportunity.* Washington, D.C.: U.S. Office of Education, National Center for Educational Statistics.

CUBAN, L. (1990). Reforming again, again, and again. *Educational Researcher, 19*, 3–14.

EDMONDS, R. R. (1979). Effective schools for the urban poor. *Educational Leadership, 37*(1), 15–24.

FIRESTONE, W. A. (1989). Educational policy as an ecology of games. *Educational Researcher, 18*, 18–24.

HOY, W. K., & MISKEL, C. G. (1987). *Educational administration: Theory, research and practice*, 3rd ed. New York: Random House.

JENCKS, C., SMITH, M., ACLAND, H., BANE, M., COHEN, D., GINTIS, H., HEYNES, B., & MICHELSON, S. (1972). *Inequality: A reassessment of the effect of family and schooling in America.* New York: Harper & Row.

MILES, M. B. (1981). Mapping the common properties of schools. In R. Lehming & M. Kane (eds.), *Improving schools: Using what we know*. Beverly Hills, CA: Sage.

PETERS, T. J., & WATERMAN, R. H. (1982). *In search of excellence: Lessons from America's best run companies*. New York: Harper & Row.

SCOTT, W. R. (1981). *Organizations: Rational, natural and open systems*. Englewood Cliffs, NJ: Prentice Hall.

WEBER, G. (1971). *Inner-city children can be taught to read: Four successful schools*. Washington, D.C.: Council for Basic Education.

WELLISCH, J. B., ET AL. (1978). School management and organizations in successful schools (ESAA in-depth study of schools). *Sociology of Education, 51*, 21–26.

WISE, A. E. (1979). *Legislated learning*. Berkeley: University of California Press.

YUCHTMAN, E., & SEASHORE, S. E. (1967). A system resource approach to organizational effectiveness. *American Sociological Review, 32*, 214–34.

ENDNOTE

[1]The early effective schools writers implicitly defined justice in terms of equality of outcomes. They were arguing that children of the poor or of minorities could achieve in certain subjects at least at the same level as wealthier, majority children, regardless of the overall makeup of the school's student body.

2

EDUCATORS, RESEARCHERS, AND THE EFFECTIVE SCHOOLS MOVEMENT

William A. Firestone

Rutgers, The State University of New Jersey
Department of Educational Theory, Policy, and Administration

INTRODUCTION

In the late 1970s, a few people began pulling together studies indicating that some schools could help children of the urban poor achieve at levels more comparable to those in more affluent, suburban settings. At the time, this was a heretical idea, running counter to the accepted empirical wisdom that student achievement depended much more on family background than school characteristics. This new research triggered the effective schools movement. Members of the movement shared three central assumptions: "(1) schools can be identified that are unusually effective in teaching poor and minority children basic skills as measured by standardized tests; (2) these successful schools exhibit characteristics that are correlated with their success and that lie well within the domain of educators to manipulate; (3) that characteristics of successful schools provide a basis for improving schools not deemed successful" (Bickel, 1983, p. 3).

This movement triggered very different responses from educators and researchers. The phrase "school effectiveness" became part of the language of educators and policymakers, and the central findings of the early research were built into state and federal legislation. Over 40 percent of the districts in the country had effective schools programs before federal incentives for such programs became available (General Accounting Office, 1989).

The effective schools movement seemed like one of those happy occasions where research-based concepts captured the imagination of educators at many levels and became the basis for action. Yet the research community was ambivalent about the effective schools movement. Some articles criticized the effective schools research. Others suggested that the findings make sense in spite of flaws in study design. Generally, the early studies promoted a boomlet of commentary but relatively little subsequent research to extend the original ideas.

This chapter shows how the effective schools movement fits between the educator and research communities, and then describes how each community responded to that movement. Next it offers two explanations for the greater interest in the movement among educators and researchers. First, the two groups use different quality criteria, and the effective schools research met the criteria applied by educators better than those of researchers. Second, the effective schools movement was a reaction to the crisis facing educators in the 1970s. The strains experienced by educators were not felt as much by researchers. Because the movement helped resolve those strains, educators found it attractive.

To advance this view, I rely on available literature and interviews with people instrumental in applying effective schools research. After discussions with a person who studied effective schools programs and the editor of a magazine critical for the spread of the research, telephone conversations were conducted with spokespersons for five effective schools programs and a legislative aide familiar with the work. Interviews ranged from 20 minutes to 2 hours.[1]

TWO COMMUNITIES AND THE EFFECTIVE SCHOOLS MOVEMENT

While distinguishing the educator and research community seems quite easy, there are areas of ambiguity and overlap that are especially important for the rise of the effective schools movement. Thus, it is important to be precise in sorting between them.

Four criteria are especially important in this case. The first two are institutional. Generally, educators work in schools and school districts and researchers are expected to work in universities. But there are exceptions. Many university professors of education do not conduct much research, while staff of research and evaluation offices of major school districts do. Moreover, this bipolar distinction does not account for state and federal legislatures and departments of education that use research much as schools do or for the regional educational laboratories, research companies, and special interest groups that both conduct and disseminate research.

Another institutional criterion is professional association membership. This situation is not well defined on the educator side. Many belong to unions or to role-specific organizations like the American Association of School Administrators. Others belong (in addition or instead) to special interest groups like the Association for Supervision and Curriculum Development (ASCD) or associations for teaching specific subject areas. Researchers generally belong to the American Educational Research Association (AERA) or related special area organizations. Again, however, many members of AERA do not conduct much research.

A more fine-grained analysis might come from examination of individual activity. This clarifies the education side to a point; teachers and school and building administrators are pretty clearly educators. But what is a researcher? Anyone who collects and analyzes data? How important is generating theories? What about testing them? It might help to add a normative dimension. The ethic of educators stresses service, seeing children learn (Lortie, 1975). The pure research ethic emphasizes truth in some sense (M. Weber, 1962).[2] These divergent ethics allow for a continuum running from pure researchers who emphasize the value of truth to applied researchers who want accurate research but insist that it support the service concerns of educators to pure educators who concentrate on working with children. Somewhere in the middle is a "dissemination" ethic which combines respect for research and an interest in service to children with a concern to bridge the two extremes by helping educators find, interpret, and use research.

These criteria help to specify educators pretty clearly. They work in school districts teaching children or ensuring that children are taught and stress a service ethic. The research community is more ambiguous and might be thought of as a set of overlapping circles. At the center are those who spend most of their time on research, emphasize the truth ethic over service and dissemination concerns, work in universities, and are active in researchers' professional associations. However, some individuals meet two or three of these criteria, but not all four.

Somewhere in the gray area between these communities is a dissemination community consisting of people in some of the intermediate organizations—regional laboratories, state departments of education, private organizations—and large district offices who are trainers and consultants to adults. Their primary commitment is to use research to improve the quality of practice. This community lacks its own professional associations. If anything it is probably closest to the ASCD, but members belong to AERA and some other practice associations as well.

The effective schools movement grew up between the educator and research communities. Its leaders were on the margin, neither fully in the research community nor regular educators. Ronald Edmonds, the best known movement spokesman, went from Harvard to the New York school system to Michigan State University. He was involved in one research study and also started a district effective schools program. His writings suggest that his primary interest was in using research to improve practice (e.g., Edmonds, 1979). Another effective schools leader, Lawrence Lezotte, also had an atypical history. He participated in many research and action projects at Michigan State University before devoting most of his time to popularizing effective schools findings. Among the best known effective schools researchers, only Wilbur Brookover, a long-time faculty member at Michigan State, appeared to have research as a primary commitment.

The effective schools research was an advocacy literature strongly committed to education as a means to promote race and class equity in spite of evidence that strongly linked student achievement with social class (Coleman et al., 1966; Jencks et al., 1972). In one of the earliest studies, George Weber (1971) visited four inner-city schools that were unusually successful in teaching poor students to read. Just locating contradictory examples indicates that a rule can be broken. Weber went on to examine how these schools contributed to unusually high reading scores. His study was perhaps the first use of an "outlier"[3] methodology—that is, to look at schools that were "more successful than they were supposed to be." With growing sophistication, researchers sought samples of schools that deviated positively from the predicted relationship between family background and student achievement. Then through survey or case study methodology, they identified the characteristics of those schools that contributed to their unusual success (e.g., Brookover & Lezotte, 1977; Edmonds & Frederickson, 1978). Although the outlier research was supplemented with studies using other methodologies (e.g., Rutter et al., 1979), it was the predominant strategy.

Empirical studies led to a secondary industry of literature reviews that appeared primarily in the "intellectual" practitioner journals like *Educational Leadership* and

Phi Delta Kappan. Perhaps the most famous of these was Edmonds's (1979) review that identified such factors promoting high achievement of minority students in urban elementary schools as (1) strong administrative leadership; (2) high expectations for all children; (3) a safe, orderly, but not rigid environment; (4) top priority given to student acquisition of basic school skills; (5) willingness to divert energy from other tasks to this top priority; and (6) frequent monitoring of pupil progress. Later reviews followed this practice of generating lists of characteristics. These lists became the starting point for action programs.

The effective schools movement was not the only "good news" development in the late 1970s. New fine-grained classroom studies began to identify variables from time-on-task to teacher expectations that could improve student learning. This "teacher effectiveness" research was an important adjunct to the school effectiveness studies (McKenzie, 1983). So too was research on planned change. By the early 1980s, studies showed that intentional school improvement, while difficult, was possible. They suggested steps that principals, district leaders, and outside assistance agencies could take to facilitate such improvement (Fullan, 1982).

Whether the movement was more active in research or in its dissemination was always questionable. By the mid-1980s, the emphasis had definitely shifted to dissemination. In 1986 leaders of the movement founded the National Center for Effective Schools, a private nonprofit corporation that provides technical assistance not only to schools and districts, but also to state education agencies and others that are interested in using the research. Other groups contributed to this effort. The National Conference on Educating Black Children consciously used the effective schools research for their program to improve education for minority students (*Education Week,* June 21, 1989).

RESPONSES TO THE MOVEMENT

The response to the effective schools writing was positive and supportive among educators and disseminators. A major development was the rise of the "effective schools program." These were long-term technical assistance efforts to help schools understand and apply the effective schools research. They were operated by school districts but also by state departments of education and regional educational laboratories, among other agencies. One particularly strong program is operated by the Connecticut State Department of Education (1989).[4]

> Operating since 1981, this program has served 108 schools in 35 districts. The assistance offered depends on the proportion of deprived students. In the full program, state consultants first ensure that school staff agree to participate and that the superintendent promises necessary district support. An orientation to faculty stresses the need for long-range commitment, tailoring the program to unique school conditions, and their agreement on final actions. State consultants administer a questionnaire to faculty to assess their perceptions of the safety of the environment, mission clarity, instructional leadership, opportunity for student learning (including time-on-task), monitoring student progress, staff expectations for students, and parental involvement. The consultants prepare a school profile using questionnaire and student achievement data analyzed separately for low-achieving and regular students. In a two-day retreat, the school action team (the principal and seven or eight teachers) uses this profile to develop an action plan. Early plans often focus on a mission statement and discipline. Attention to

instructional issues comes later. As the school moves into implementation, the consultant helps find outside resources. As action plans are completed, results are documented and used to develop new plans. The process is considered finished when at least three annual action plans have been completed, a school-based planning process has been institutionalized, and there is evidence of significant progress towards mastery of basic skills by all students.[*]

Effective schools programs usually feature both a research base and a technology for implementing change. On the research side, 21 of the 35 programs Miles and colleagues (1983) studied specifically mentioned Edmonds's work, 17 that of Brookover or Lezotte, and 13 that of Michael Rutter. These programs also used the teaching research—most notably work on mastery learning (13 programs), classroom management (11), and time-on-task (10)—and work on change implementation (9). Miles's programs developed their own assistance configurations, but several steps were often repeated. Eighteen used their own data-collection instruments to provide feedback to schools. Most (23) worked through schoolwide planning teams, and 17 had an explicit goal-setting step. Finally, 20 programs provided intensive training or workshops, and 23 provided ongoing consulting and assistance (Miles et al., 1983).

The effective schools programs were useful because they combined the research with features conducive to its use. These included long time lines for planning and implementation, data feedback for planning, and outside technical assistance. Interviews indicate that program staff also wrestled with the issue of combining change in the effective school characteristics with the factors coming from the effective teaching research.

Use of the effective schools research spread throughout the decade. The General Accounting Office (1989) estimates that 41 percent of the nation's school districts had programs that used the effective schools research in 1988. Over half the programs started in the 1986–1988 period.

By the time of broad spread, the movement's original emphasis on helping lower class children reduce the achievement gap with their high-status peers had become less important. True, effective schools programs were slightly more prevalent in larger districts—39 of the 50 largest districts had them—but they were about as likely to be found in nonurban as in urban school districts (General Accounting Office, 1989). The programs' prevalence in large districts could simply have reflected the greater capacity of big central offices to manage such programs. There did not appear to be a strong emphasis on serving poor and minority students. Only a fifth of the districts with programs were estimated to serve a clientele where over 40 percent of the students received free or reduced-price lunches (General Accounting Office, 1989).

The effective schools programs appear to have stayed fairly close to the early conception of what constitutes school effectiveness.[5] Ninety-two percent reported that their programs emphasized instructional leadership and raising staff expectations, 88 to 89 percent monitored student achievement and stressed basic skills acquisition, and 76 percent worked on developing a safe and orderly school environment. The relatively low emphasis on safety and order may also reflect the spread of effective schools ideas beyond the inner-city neighborhoods that were the target for the movement's early leaders. The change technology that characterized the early effective schools programs was not quite so uniformly employed; only two-thirds of the districts

---

[*]The above material is the author's summary of the document cited and the interview with Dr. Joan Shoemaker, unit coordinator.

expected participating schools to use teams of teachers to develop school improvement plans (General Accounting Office, 1989).

School districts often used external assistance to design and implement their effective schools programs. Thirty-six percent of the districts were estimated to have received help from federally funded regional educational laboratories while 31 percent received university assistance. Given their greater size and frequency, university participation is particularly small. Still, the biggest source of assistance was state departments of education. About 64 percent of the district programs received state department help.

The assistance state departments offered varied considerably. Data compiled by the Council of Chief State School Officers (1988) suggests that 26 states took advantage of the effective schools research in some way. The programs deeply immersed in the original literature, like Connecticut's, seemed rare. Several states, like Maryland, included effective schools content in ongoing academies—a strategy that generated attention but did not necessarily provide the help needed for real use of the ideas. A few others, like Georgia, included effective schools characteristics among standards that all schools were required to meet.

The effective schools research also made an impact at the federal level. The ideas were built into the elementary and secondary school improvement amendments of 1988. Chapter 1 was modified so schools where 75 percent or more of students were achieving at extremely low levels could stop targeting funds on specific students and develop schoolwide programs. These schools were required to consider the effective schools research when designing their programs. Furthermore, state education agencies were required to set aside 20 percent of their Chapter 2 funds to develop school-based assistance programs based on the effective schools research. That research was defined in terms of Edmonds's factors.

In contrast to the slowly growing interest among educators and state and federal policymakers, researchers' interest developed quickly, peaked early, and died out fast without spreading widely. After the early literature reviews drew attention to effective schools thinking, researchers responded with a boomlet of writing on the topic. The apex of interest was a special issue on effective schools in the April 1983 issue of *Educational Researcher*, a journal of the American Educational Research Association (AERA). This was an unprecedented development. However, a review of the programs for AERA's annual meetings suggests that research interest began in 1980 and peaked in 1984 when 14 sessions and 43 papers were devoted to the topic. Four years later, the boom was over. No papers dealt explicitly with effective schools themes in 1988 and only 2 did in 1989. These programs also suggest that interest was strongest in the applied parts of the association. Of the 21 division-sponsored sessions on effective schools research at AERA between 1983 and 1987, 16 were presented by Division H which is the subgroup for district and state department of education evaluators—that is, researchers especially close to the educator world. Only 5 sessions were reported by more university-based divisions (A and G).

Contributions in books and research journals appeared more slowly, and new empirical work was rather limited. There is a small second generation of studies (e.g., Mortimore in this volume; Teddlie, Kirby, & Stringfield, 1989) as well as a round of revisionist reviews and interpretations (e.g., Rosenholtz, 1985). Research did spread into related issues, like examinations of the process of applying effective schools research (Louis & Miles, in this volume), but few papers reported new work on how organizational characteristics helped overcome the achievement differential between richer and poorer students.

EXPLANATIONS FOR DIVERGENT RESPONSES

Two factors help explain why educators and policymakers were so much more receptive to the message of the effective schools movement than researchers: the standards these different groups used to assess research and the crisis that permeated education at the time.

Truth and Utility Tests

In a study of how policymakers assess research, Weiss (1980) finds that they apply two criteria: truth tests and utility tests. Truth tests judge the believability of the work. They include but, are not limited to, estimates of theoretical and methodological adequacy. Users also compare research findings to their own expectations and past experience. Utility tests are also important. Users ask whether research challenges existing assumptions, suggests new courses of action, contains explicit recommendations, and identifies independent variables that can be manipulated in practice. Research that is both accurate (truth) and suggests directions for action (utility) is the most likely to be used.

The truth test is most critical for researchers who noted serious methodological and conceptual problems with the studies. As presented by Rowan and colleagues (1983) and Ralph and Fennessey (1983), these fall into two groups. First, the effective schools studies did not adequately prove that they had identified unusually effective schools. Perhaps the most serious concern is that most studies did not adequately control for the effects of student family background. This was a necessary step since family background was by far the strongest predictor of achievement, and the intent of this research was to show that the background-achievement relationship could be broken. Moreover, these critics suggested that when all was said and done, very little variation in student achievement—only from 3 to 5 percent—could be attributed to schoolwide characteristics as opposed to individual or classroom characteristics or chance.

Rowan and colleagues (1983) listed four different ways to identify effective schools: (1) setting an absolute criterion like the percentage of students above the national median in achievement, (2) trend analysis showing that scores in a particular grade had gone up over time, (3) gain scores for a cohort, and (4) true outlier studies that look at the regression-based residuals from what a school's score would be predicted based on student background. These criteria correlated poorly with each other and with expert judgment suggesting that there was no sure way to identify effective schools. Moreover, what might be the technically soundest way—the true outlier approach—was unstable since it was difficult to disentangle error from the "true score" when looking at residuals.

The second problem was that the designs used could not explain what made the schools unusually effective. Many studies compared effective and ineffective schools. (Others looked only at effective schools and had no way to identify the characteristics that differentiated them from less effective schools.) Hypotheses were then tested singly through the use of t-tests or analysis of variance. This strategy did not indicate the size of the effect of a given characteristic, nor did it control for the contribution of other school characteristics or student background.

To compound the problem, most studies used cross-sectional designs that created chicken-and-egg problems. Since student achievement was measured at the same time as such key variables as leadership and high expectations, it was difficult to know if those variables contributed to student achievement or vice versa. Certainly it is as reasonable for a teacher to expect more of students when they have a history of high performance as it is for the teacher's expectations to promote that achievement. Finally, the effective schools research typically operated at the school level without examining internal processes. It neither proposed nor tested any explanation that linked school characteristics like leadership to instruction or other classroom processes. Nor did it offer any credible explanation about how one could change schoolwide factors even if one understood how they operated.

The critics were not uniformly negative about the research. Some suggested that while individual studies were flawed, there was great consistency across reports. Others pointed out that the findings agreed with previous research and past experience. After conducting one of the most thorough methodological critiques of this research, Purkey and Smith (1983, pp. 439–40) concluded that in spite of substantial problems, the line of reasoning made considerable sense:

> ...we nevertheless find a substantive case emerging from the literature. There is a good deal of common sense to the notion that a school is more likely to have relatively high reading or math scores if the staff agree to emphasize those subjects, are serious and purposeful about the task of teaching, expect students to learn, and create a safe and comfortable environment in which students accurately perceive the school's expectations for academic success and come to share them. Such a mixture of characteristics creates a climate that would encourage...success in any endeavor, from teaching dance to building a winning football team....

Other observers stressed the similarity in findings across studies. Some also buttressed their conclusions from research they considered sounder. Clark, Lotto, and Astuto (1984) used similarities in the findings of the effective schools and the planned change research to buttress the credibility of the former.

Educators and effective schools program managers applied the truth test in a different way. Personal experience played a major role, particularly in rejecting the conclusion that family background rather than school characteristics affected student learning:

> I knew things weren't right. In _____, one school had a lot of poor and minority students just like all the others, but the kids were achieving so well that the Director of Title I said not to break the achievement data out by school. We'd lose Title I money, the principal was so good.
>
> My own sixteen years in the system working with disadvantaged kids led me to believe the research. I'd been a teacher in tough schools that got results. Eventually, I was teaching French to disadvantaged kids. They were below grade-level in reading. I knew if you expected a lot of kids and gave them an honest shot, they'd learn.

This respondent explained how he sold his program to recalcitrant principals:

> What really helped was a couple of years of success. Our demonstrable statistics of success. Principals from other schools we worked with were our greatest weapon.

For these people the experience of seeing students learn who "weren't supposed to" was what counted.

Program managers were not purists who relied on a single line of research to design their programs. Instead, they borrowed eclectically not only from the effective schools research but also from work on effective teaching and planned change. As one program spokesperson reported,

> The program is all built on the effective schools research, (but) effective schools is any practice from R&D that equitably affects learning. Not necessarily achievement. We used the curriculum alignment literature nine years ago.... We used the classroom research of Brophy, Block, Bloom, Slavin, and Rosenshine. Now I need to know about whole language instruction.... We used the building level research. The older stuff by Brookover, Lezotte, Edmonds. Now we use the newer stuff by Andrews and the new climate stuff from England.... We also included a lot of change literature. The RAND study. We had Susan (Loucks) do a 3-day thing on CBAM. Change management was always big. Matt's (Miles) stuff.

As time went on, there were fewer pure effective schools programs and more that took eclectically from many lines of research to design their programs.

The program spokespeople still had to deal with criticisms of the research. Their responses were colored by their research sophistication. Those with greater experience agreed that the effective schools studies were atheoretical and conceptually flawed, but they maintained reason to agree with the general line of conclusions. One, like Clark and colleagues, pointed out convergence among lines of research. This person argued that the effective schools studies were less competent versions of the quality-of-work-life research that had been conducted for many years in Europe. He believed American work was close enough to the European studies for him to accept that basic line of thinking. Another argued that in spite of the flaws, there was enough consistency across the studies to give them credibility.

Others were less sophisticated about research. In fact some of them were impatient with it as they went about their own business:

> The research is important but somewhat irrelevant. They should continue the research, but meanwhile back at the ranch, we'll continue our work.
>
> You AERA folk can argue that out all you want. What is there for kids?... We ought to do more research and report it, but that's not what happens. (Question: What happens?) Nothing, just dialogue about design adequacy!

They preferred personal experience or that of trusted others to methodological considerations:

> I don't think research has truth in it, but if you mix it all together, there are patterns that have truth. There are always qualifiers in research.... What's more important are the patterns. Is there other support like our good common sense about teaching and learning?

Moreover, the program spokespersons found a tension between the truth tests as applied by researchers and their concern for utility:

> We should do better studies, but from the practical side, there's nothing better out there. We're on a roll. There are things to learn, and its working. There's no reason to turn back.

This comment illustrates the different normative orientations of researchers and educators. Generally, researchers are more concerned with the truth test. If research is flawed, their commitment is to doing whatever is necessary to get the most accurate possible assessment of how variables are related. Ideally, educators are committed to doing the best they can with the students they have. When research findings are ambiguous, they cannot wait for the resolution. They must combine the imperfect truth available to them with concerns for utility.

The effective schools research did pass the utility test. In an interview, Miles points to the relative concreteness of the research. Comparing it to both organizational development and the progressive movement, he suggests that it offered a useful vision of what improved schools should look like that could be combined with the organizational development technology. Much of this concreteness stems from the lists of specific school factors or characteristics that researchers found especially simplistic. Thus, program spokespeople report that

> [The effective schools research] didn't need translation. It was good common sense. This is just the way good businesses are run.
>
> [The lists of criteria help] very definitely. We have to be careful. We say it looks like common sense. That's deceiving. Its not common sense at all, but its definitely practical.

Where the research was not presented in a clearly practical form, pressure was applied to give it one:

> It sounds like something you can grab. My initial study was more complex. [A colleague] forced us to use a simpler form. The Connecticut people did it that way. It became manageable. I had used a path model.

The Educators' Crisis

Differences in how researchers and educators applied truth and utility tests was only part of the story. The effective schools movement appeared at the end of a period when American education underwent something like a regime crisis (McAdam, McCarthy, & Zald, 1988). Such crises occur in periods of political instability when previously dominant groups are unable to maintain their hegemony due to some combination of reduced political strength and challenges to the legitimation of the existing order. It can be argued that such a situation existed in American education in the 1960s and 1970s. The specific aspects of this crisis to which the effective schools movement responded were not felt as strongly by researchers, so they were less attracted than educators to the effective schools movement as a way to restore a legitimate order and respond to the issues raised by that crisis.

As it affected American education, this crisis had at least three elements: loss of belief in education as an instrument to promote equity, loss of educators' authority with the public, and the intervention of arms of the central government. The legitimacy of the American educational system was based partly on the idea that it could help everyone succeed (Cohen & Neufeld, 1981). The civil rights movement showed how thoroughly African-Americans were denied that opportunity and was an attempt to redress that problem. By suggesting that educational achievement depends on the family, not what schools do, the research by Coleman and colleagues (1966) and others undermined basic beliefs about the legitimacy of the educational enterprise and the efficacy of educators.

At the same time, the authority of American educators declined. According to Ravitch (1983, p. 251),

> The extraordinary stress in the society outside the schools had created nearly intolerable strains within many schools in terms of student resistance to traditional authority. As authority in the larger society eroded, authority in the schools came under attack; discipline problems increased, as did truancy and vandalism.

Observers have documented how in response to declining authority, teachers reduced academic demands and traded less demanding expectations for peace in the classroom. Grant (1988) describes how these changes shook the confidence of teachers and drove many of them out of the field.

A contributing factor was the increasing role of central government in the conduct of education. The volume of legislation, regulation, and court activity affecting schooling increased dramatically (Ravitch, 1983). While these programs provided new resources to promote equal opportunity for the poor, minority groups, and the handicapped, they also placed new constraints on regular educational activities. In some situations, teachers and administrators found that their authority to control student behavior had become severely limited (Grant, 1988). It was no longer clear what they could or should do with regard to basic tasks of instruction and classroom management.

These forces created great strain among American educators in the form of questions about whether the American education system could meet its goals and ambiguity about how to proceed. This ambiguity was felt deeply by those involved. In times of crisis, widespread strain frequently leads to social movements to either overpower or restore the existing order. Such movements only arise when a number of conditions are present. When strain is not too great, it can generate a will to believe that something can be done about the situation. This generalized willingness must then be accompanied by a code specifying what to believe for the movement to take off (Smelser, 1962; Wallace, 1970).

The effective schools movement spoke explicitly to the strains related to the equity agenda. Much of that writing (e.g., Edmonds, 1979; Lezotte, 1989) follows a standard story that begins with the challenge of the Coleman Report and then shows how the effective schools research overcame that challenge and led to action to promote equal educational opportunity. This same concern with equity is apparent in interviews with observers and program people. Miles points to "race as a dynamic [in the movement]. The ideas were taken up by blacks and liberals interested in improving equity."[6] Program spokespeople universally agreed with this point. One said, "I'd worked in urban schools after Coleman.... There were differential expectations after Coleman. There seemed to be no answers."

Yet the program spokespeople would not give up the equity concern. They maintained a will to believe:

> Coleman bothered me a lot, that schools don't matter. Something seemed amiss.... I wanted to look at organizational variables that make a difference. Structure and process variables.
>
> I'd been tuned into the problems of urban schools. I started teaching in urban schools in _____. I taught low sections, the black kids no one expected to learn. I went into counseling cause I thought they needed help. When I worked in suburban schools, I decided it was not the kids but the system.

The new code or belief system is often developed by one or a very few people (Smelser, 1962; Wallace, 1970). It specifies the ends for the new movement and tells how members of that movement can get from the present stressful situation to a preferred future. The literature reviews helped develop the effective schools code; Edmonds's work especially crystalized the new way of thinking. He established the new goal statement that spoke clearly to the equity concern: "Specifically, I require that an effective school bring the children of the poor to those minimal masteries of basic school skills that now describe minimally successful pupil performance for the children of the middle class" (Edmonds, 1979, 16).

His factors and similar lists generated by others were a first step in describing how to move to this new condition. It seems unlikely that the movement would have spread as extensively as it did, however, if it only spoke to the equity agenda. The factors generated by Edmonds and others described how to respond not only to the equity concerns but also the fears and doubts generated by lost authority. The message was that things would be better if administrators led schools, order was maintained, and an academic emphasis reinstated all suggested that things would get better if people reasserted previously held values that had been under attack. Moreover, the school-specific emphasis of the research suggested that local educators could still persevere in spite of the divided control structure in which they now operated.

The success of the movement depends partly on the charisma of its leader but also on the movement's organization and means to spread the message (McAdam et al., 1988; Smelser, 1962; Wallace, 1970). Edmonds was certainly charismatic:

> I was mesmerized. He had a way of expressing himself that was poetic. Not like Martin Luther King. He was softspoken, not educated in a school of education.... We all realized there was no substitute for him.

At least three means were used to spread the effective schools movement. The written word, especially in the form of unpublished papers and articles in practitioner journals, was important. So was personal contact with the leadership of the movement. In some settings, people had Lezotte or Edmonds in to talk about their ideas. Finally, the effective schools programs themselves became a very powerful means to get the ideas out. These programs amplified an interest that was already present in the field:

> We got interested [in the effective schools literature] because of requests from people in the field. People were asking how did you do it. We read it and said it fit our mission.

Researchers were less affected by the crisis in the schools, and some resented what they saw as an effort to use the mantle of research to justify a line of reasoning that in their view was not well substantiated. Those most critical of the research emphasized the irrational elements in the spread of this new way of thinking. Ralph and Fennessey (1983, p. 693) concluded that "the significance of the effective schools research lies more in the ideology underlying it than in the validity of the empirical support for the idea that schools can lessen the effects of race and social class on academic achievement." In an article on "shamanistic rituals in effective schools," Rowan (1984) suggested that symbolic aspects of this work that led to magical thinking—rather than a careful analysis of the evidence—explained the speed with which it was accepted. Others who emphasized the similarities among study findings and the fit of the new research with work in other areas believed with Purkey and Smith (1983) that it provided a useful provisional way for American schools to address the equity issue.

CONCLUSION

The effective schools movement grew up in the gaps between the educator and research communities and received a very different reaction in each. Educators and policymakers, especially those concerned with equity issues, embraced the movement and accepted its teachings. By now these ideas have been built into federal legislation, and half the states make use of them either in assistance programs or mandated reforms. Moreover, two-fifths of the nation's school districts have some kind of effective schools program. Some of these programs take advantage of the best knowledge about educational change and are likely to promote real modification in practice. By contrast, researchers were always skeptical about this line of thinking. Their interest peaked early, many were critical, and there have been relatively few follow-up studies.

This tendency for educators to be much more enthusiastic about new developments in educational practice than researchers is not limited to the effective schools movement. Slavin (1989) suggests that this pattern recurs often in American education. Fads of unproven worth spread quickly through the educational world because educators do not wait for research to show their effectiveness. Yet, he also points out that few studies actually assess the value of the new practices to which educators gravitate.

The story of the effective schools movement suggests reasons for the different reactions of educators and researchers. Educators face strains from which researchers are protected. They must serve their students in spite of research that provides little practical guidance and social forces that undermine their authority. The first converts to the effective schools movement persisted in seeking ways to address the equity agenda in spite of research that questioned their ability to make a contribution. Their commitment was based on their personal experience that things were being done to help these students. The effective schools literature provided comfort for their determination to continue addressing that agenda. Later users may have been more attracted to aspects of the effective schools message that reinforced educators' normal authority. This pattern of educators gravitating to flawed research offering hope for progress and a clear direction for action may be quite common.

The factors that are so troubling to educators are not nearly as disturbing to educational researchers. The decline in central authority took a form in universities that was rarely connected to the disorder in the schools. While concerned about the Coleman/Jencks work, researchers generally accepted it after much scrutiny because it met their truth tests. Those less concerned about utility had few incentives to do the work that would offer the guidance educators sought. The researchers most critical of educators' susceptibility to unproven fads fail to recognize that educators must combine truth tests with utility tests and that much research fails to meet the utility test, at least in the short run.

The critics of educators who accept unproven change proposals also ignore the variation in efforts to apply research. Some of those on the forefront form an articulate, well-informed, and fairly reflective dissemination intelligentsia. These people exist between the worlds of researchers and educators in a poorly documented realm that is important for linking research and practice, what Fullan (1982) calls the innovation establishment. They are opinion leaders who mediate between the two worlds because of their interests and the resources at their disposal. Where this intelligentsia encountered the effective schools literature, it was firm in its commitment to equity, but it did not engage in the rigid orthodoxy associated with some social movements. Instead, individuals applied their own truth and utility tests, borrowing from several strands of research to design programs that fit with their "good common sense." If they made mistakes, it may have been in part because the research they needed was not available.

REFERENCES

BICKEL, W. E. (1983).   Effective schools: Knowledge, dissemination, inquiry. *Educational Researcher, 12*(4), 3–5.

BROOKOVER, W. B., & LEZOTTE, L. W. (1977).   *Changes in school characteristics coincident with changes in student achievement.* East Lansing: Michigan State University, College of Urban Development.

CLARK, D. L., LOTTO, L. S., & ASTUTO, T. A. (1984).   Effective schools and school improvement: A comparative analysis of two lines of inquiry. *Educational Administration Quarterly, 20*(3), 41–68.

COHEN, D. K., & NEUFELD, B. (1981).   The failure of high schools and the progress of education. *Daedalus, 110*(3), 69–90.

COLEMAN, J. S., CAMPBELL, E. Q., HOBSON, C. J., MCPARTLAND, J., MOOD, A. M., WEINFELD, F. D., & YORK, R. L. (1966).   *Equality of educational opportunity.* Washington, D.C.: U.S. Office of Education, National Center for Educational Statistics.

CONNECTICUT STATE DEPARTMENT OF EDUCATION. (1989).   *The school effectiveness report: History, current status, future directions.* Middletown, CT: Author.

COUNCIL OF CHIEF STATE SCHOOL OFFICERS. (1988).   *State education indicators: CCSSOC, Washington, D.C.*

EDMONDS, R. R. (1979).   Effective schools for the urban poor. *Educational Leadership, 37*(1), 15–24.

EDMONDS R. R., & FREDERICKSON, J. R. (1978).   *Search for effective schools: The identification and analysis of city schools that are instructionally effective for the urban poor.* Cambridge, MA: Center for Urban Studies.

EDUCATION WEEK (June 21, 1989).   Black educators hail rapid progress of their "effective schools" blueprint, p. 7.

FULLAN, M. G. (1982).   *The meaning of educational change.* New York: Teachers College Press.

GENERAL ACCOUNTING OFFICE. (1989).   *Effective schools programs: Their extent and characteristics.* Washington, D.C.: Author.

GRANT, G. (1988).   *The world we created at Hamilton High.* Cambridge, MA: Harvard University Press.

JENCKS, C. L., SMITH, M., ACLAND, H., BANE, M. J., COHEN, D. K., GINTIS, H., HEYNS, B. L., & MICHAELSON, S. (1972).   *Inequality: A reassessment of the effects of family and schooling in America.* New York: Basic Books.

LEZOTTE, L. W. (1989).   School improvement based on the effective schools research. In D. K. Lipsky & A. Garnter (Eds.), *Beyond separate education: Quality education for all.* Baltimore, MD: Paul H. Brookes.

LORTIE, D. C. (1975).   *Schoolteacher: A sociological analysis.* Chicago: University of Chicago Press.

MCADAM, D., MCCARTHY, J. D., & ZALD, M. N. (1988).   Social movements. In M. Smelser (Ed.), *Handbook of sociology,* pp. 695–738. Newbury Park, CA: Sage.

MCKENZIE, D. E. (1983).   Research for school improvement: An appraisal of some recent trends. *Educational researcher, 12*(4), 5–17.

MILES, M. B., FARRAR, E., & NEUFELD, B. (1983).   *Review of effective schools programs.* Vol. II, *The extent of adoption of effective schools programs,* ED 228242. Cambridge, MA: Huron Institute.

PURKEY, S. C., & SMITH, M. S. (1983).   Effective schools: A review. *Elementary School Journal, 83,* 427–47.

RALPH, J. R., & FENNESSEY, J. (1983).   Science or reform: Some questions about the effective schools model. *Phi Delta Kappan, 63,* 689–94.

RAVITCH, D. (1983).   *The troubled crusade: American education, 1945–1980.* New York: Basic Books.

ROSENHOLTZ, S. J. (1985).   Effective schools: Interpreting the evidence. *American Journal of Education, 93*(3), 352–88.

ROWAN, B. (1984).   Shamanistic rituals in effective schools. *Issues in Education, 2,* 76–87.

ROWAN, B., BOSSERT, S. T., & DWYER, D. C. (1983).   Research on effective schools: A cautionary note. *Educational Researcher, 12*(4), 24–31.

RUTTER, M., MAUGHAM, B., MORTIMORE, P., OUSTON, J., & SMITH, A. (1979).   *Fifteen thousand hours: Secondary schools and their effects on children.* Cambridge, MA: Harvard University Press, 1979.

SLAVIN, R. (1989).   PET and the pendulum: Faddism in education and how to stop it. *Phi Delta Kappan, 70,* 752–58.

SMELSER, N. J. (1962).   *Theory of collective behavior.* New York: Free Press.

TEDDLIE, C., KIRBY, P. C., & STRINGFIELD, S. (1989).   Effective versus ineffective schools: Observable differences in the classroom. *American Journal of Education, 97,* 221–36.

WALLACE, A. F. C. (1970).   *Culture and personality,* 2nd ed. New York: Random House.

WEBER, G. (1971).   *Inner-city children can be taught to read: Four successful schools.* Washington, D.C.: Council for Basic Education.

WEBER, M. (1962).   Science as a vocation. In B. Barber & W. Hirsch (Eds.), *The sociology of science,* pp. 569–89. New York: Free Press.

WEISS, C. H. (1980).   Knowledge creep and decision accretion. *Knowledge: Creation Diffusion, Utilization, 1*(3), 381–404.

ENDNOTES

[1]Those interviewed included Jan Azumi, Newark Board of Education; Ronald Brandt, editor, *Educational Leadership;* Thomas Corcoran, private consultant; Susan Everson, Mid-continent Regional Educational Laboratory (McREL); Matthew Miles, Center for Policy

Research; Joan Shoemaker, Connecticut State Department of Education; John Smith, House Committee on Education and Labor; and Anthony Spina, New York Board of Education.

[2]Since truth cannot be established with certainty, there is now a debate between postpositivist researchers who aspire to approximating understanding of what the world is like and interpretivists or constructivists who seek only to understand how different groups make sense of the world. Even this latter group, however, must provide an accurate portrayal of the interpretations of the groups it studies.

[3]The term "outlier" was used to refer to most of these studies of unusually effective schools even though in a technical sense it should only be used to describe studies selecting schools that deviated by a specific amount from the line regressing test scores on student background. I follow the casual rather than the technical sense of the term in what follows.

[4]Further information comes from an interview with Dr. Joan Shoemaker, unit coordinator.

[5]The study methodology—using superintendent reports—may overestimate this fit. More direct examination would probably show greater variation.

[6]Personal interview.

3

THE MEANING AND MEASURE
OF SCHOOL EFFECTIVENESS[1]

Craig E. Richards
Teachers College, Columbia University

INTRODUCTION

What we mean by "effective schools" and how we measure them has been dominated by two related research and policy preoccupations. The first has been a typological preoccupation: Could two or more independent observers agree that John Adams Elementary School was effective while agreeing that George Washington Elementary School was not?

While researchers attempted to resolve this first issue, another group began to investigate the policy side of the problem: Could two or more independent observers agree upon which, if any, particular antecedent conditions (inputs and processes) would transform Washington from an ineffective school into an effective one?

Thus from the beginning, the academic research on effective schools was preoccupied with a focus on policy responsive strategies for school improvement. The effective schools research agenda—to simplify somewhat—pursued the following utilitarian strategy:

- Select a valid and reliable set of indicators and norm-referenced achievement tests to verify effectiveness outcomes.
- Identify the "critical core" of characteristics essential to effective schooling and distinguish them from others which are detrimental or indicative but not essential.
- Determine the appropriate policies and implementation strategies necessary to transform ineffective schools into effective schools.

This triad of stratagems floundered on at least two accounts. The most serious reason it did so was that researchers did not have prior agreement on the definition of an effective school. That is, research failed to develop a consensus on the first leg of the triad: the definitions that emerged suffered from a lack of operational specificity, internal agreement, and logical consistency. Second, even with a workable definition of effective schooling, the accountability system necessary to provide schools with useful comparative data was not available. This chapter seeks to establish agreement on these two points and then to offer some policy prescriptions that would contribute to the goals of the effective schools movement.

DEFINING SCHOOL EFFECTIVENESS

School effectiveness leaders like Ron Edmonds were arguing that schools did make a difference and they did so for reasons that could be traced directly back to alterable organizational characteristics of the school: a focus on basic education, directive leadership, high academic expectations, orderliness, and a positive school climate were argued to distinguish effective from ineffective schools. In short, the observed variation in student achievement outcomes among common elementary schools was attributable to organizational variables and not to undetected differences in student ability, family background, or social class.

The conclusions of Coleman (Coleman et al., 1966), Mosteler and Moynihan (1972), and Jencks (1972) that family background and not schooling accounted for most of the differences in student achievement motivated the work of effective schools researchers. (Edmonds 1979, 1983; Brookover & Lezotte 1977; Weber 1971; Rutter 1987; and National Center 1989). The policy consequences of the Coleman and colleagues work could have been interpreted to mean that schools did not make much of a difference in influencing the life chances of low-income and minority youth. It became politically imperative to provide a policy-useful argument for effective schooling. That political imperative quickly demarcated the terrain within which the meaning and measure of effective schooling would subsequently be articulated.[2] However, as the politics of that policy imperative confronted a shifting political agenda in education, the definition shifted along with it.

In order to find effective schools, an operational definition of effectiveness was critical. While Ron Edmonds provided differing definitions over the years before his death, his last is probably the most carefully articulated definition of an effective school:[3]

My own work began in 1973. Initially it was an attempt to determine whether schools existed anywhere in the United States that did not have a familial effect. Was it possible to find schools with a significant low-income pupil population (or a homogeneously low-income pupil population) in which those pupils were clearly demonstrating academic mastery? In this work, mastery is defined as performance on standardized measures of achievement that permits two reports: Report No. 1 is that this level meets the requirements for mastery in the local school district. Report No. 2 is that this level allows us to predict that the student would be academically successful next year anywhere in the United States, that is, even if they didn't go to the school district in which they performed on the achievement test. We also use a particular definition of an "effective school": it is one where the proportion of low-income children demonstrating academic mastery is virtually identical to the proportion of middle-class children who do so. If a school fails that test, nothing else will qualify it as effective. Suppose that a school is 50% middle class and 50% poor, and that 96% of the middle-class students annually demonstrate academic mastery: that school would be nominated as effective only if 96% of the lower-class students annually demonstrate academic mastery. This does not mean that the schools necessarily get both groups of children to perform identically. Even in effective schools, the middle-class children as a group still outperform the poor children as a group. This does not violate our standard, because we require only that the proportion of those who exceed the minimum must be approximately the same. It turns out that the extent to which the minimum is exceeded is still highly associated with the social class character of the groups with which we are working. (1986, p. 95)[4]*

Ron Edmonds was not particularly expectant about finding large numbers of schools that met his definition of effectiveness. In fact, he states, "the proportion of American public schools that even approach our standard of effectiveness is minuscule" (p. 96). Nor did he claim that his standard was high or comprehensive. To his critics, he responded, "I am not apologetic for the circumscribed and modest character of the standard that I'm talking about. At least for now, I'm prepared to argue that it is a realistic approach to the problem of mass education in the urban environment, and that it is worth a good deal of attention" (p. 103).

From a policy perspective, Edmonds's emphasis on equity can lead to questionable outcomes. To illustrate the problem, examine the simulated data in Table 3–1.

Recall that Edmonds had three measures of effectiveness: (1) a local standard, (2) a national standard, and (3) an equity standard that requires low- and middle-income students to attain mastery at the same rates. Note that school A meets all three of Edmonds's criteria. School B fails the first, but passes the second and third standard. School C passes the first and second standard, but fails the third. By Edmonds's criteria only school A is effective. Yet in both schools B and C, low-income students attained higher test scores than school A. Furthermore, schools B and C both had higher average scores than did school A. These outcomes are the product of Edmonds's equity definition. It requires students from low-income groups to pass basic academic skills tests at the same rates as students from middle-income groups. Despite Edmonds's flawed definition, one should remain concerned about equity of student outcomes based on social class. Presumably it is fundamental to both democratic principle and meritocratic ideology that public education be the institution of choice for overcoming the linkage between the social class of one's parents and life chances.

TABLE 3–1   Student Achievement by School (Scale Range 1 to 100)

	PERCENT OF STUDENTS DEMONSTRATING MASTERY				
Average School	Test Score	Low Income	Middle Income	Local Standard	National Standard
School A	50	50	50	45	50
School B	60	60	60	65	50
School C	75	70	80	65	50

Assume that each school has 500 elementary students, half in each income group.

*Edmonds, R. R. (1986). Characteristics of Effective Schools. In E. Neisser (Ed.), *The Achievement of Minority Children*, pp. 93–104. Hillsdale, NJ: Erlbaum. Reprinted with permission of Lawrence Erlbaum Associates.

MEASURING EFFECTIVENESS

Another difficulty arises, not only with Ron Edmonds's definition of effective schools, but with any definition that seeks to compare schools based on national norms. No common achievement test with national norms is currently required of all schools in the nation. Thus, it would be impossible to determine whether the low-income students in George Washington Elementary School in Milwaukee, Wisconsin, were mastering basic skills in the fifth grade in the same proportion as were the low income students in John Adams Elementary School in Red Bank, New Jersey. Furthermore, there is no agreement among the 50 states to share test data that would permit such comparisons. In addition to these problems, the use of national norms for standardized achievement tests are problematic for at least three reasons: (1) Individual school districts and states require different curriculums, and it is difficult to interpret the results of a nationally normed test against curriculums with varied content and sequence. (2) Districts and states also test different grades and subjects at different times of the year. Meaningful national comparisons would require uniform testing practices. (3) As Dr. Cannell, an educational activist from North Carolina found, virtually all urban school systems in the nation are above the fiftieth percentile on most nationally normed tests (Kretz, 1988). Should we conclude that most urban schools are already effective? This deceptive outcome is due to the fact that norming tests is expensive and local school districts do not want to purchase renormed tests every three years. Consequently, most test manufacturers renorm once every eight years. Old norms that are easier to beat than new norms, teaching to the test, and the current press for increased student achievement encourage school districts to be complacent with old norms. In short, national norms are frequently outdated—which may have more to do with the politics and economics of testing than with what children actually need to know.

The current National Assessment of Educational Progress (NAEP) will report statewide comparisons on student achievement for the first time in 1990, but thus far only 35 states have agreed to participate. However, the NAEP is an unlikely candidate for school level comparisons because the current sampling design does not even permit district level comparisons within states. If states elected to equate their local tests against the NAEP norms, it would then be possible to benchmark the progress of individual schools.

THE POLITICS OF EFFECTIVENESS

Most of the studies associated with research on effective schools did not use Edmonds' definition (Purkey & Smith, 1983; Good & Brophy, 1986). The equity measure essential to Edmonds's definition has been widely ignored in the research studies that do attempt to identify the characteristics of effective schools (Newmann, 1990, p. 141, chap. 5). Not only is Edmonds's equity measure ignored, but other equity measures of school effectiveness are also ignored: for example, whether females show comparable mathematics achievement to that of males. Disinterest in equity outcomes is due only partially to the necessity of conducting research with available data. But adapting research to available data has its consequences: the available data themselves reflect social definitions as to which data are important to collect. Thus, the equity standards included in Edmonds' definition of effectiveness were instantly disadvantaged because of the absence of data to establish the appropriate measure.

One further consequence of opportunistic data analysis has been to shift the research focus from comparable outcomes for low- and high-SES students to higher than expected average achievement. These strategies started with an analysis of outliers—at first with less sophisticated techniques like identifying schools based on the extent to which their average scores exceed the mean—usually in large urban districts. Later, the techniques increased in sophistication and included strategies like estimating multiple-regression residuals to calculate deviations from expected performance.

While quite sophisticated as a statistical technique, the difference-from-the-mean approach did not account for grade-level variations in student achievement, within group low-ability versus high-ability variation, regression toward the mean, and other problems associated with a cross-sectional data analysis of aggregated test scores.[5]

What is of primary importance in this discussion, however, is not the flaws in the data analysis, but the fact that the equity definition of effectiveness promoted by Edmonds was never really accepted by the research community. Rather, a changing political climate and opportunistic data analysis combined to shift the definition of effectiveness to one of performance.

Explicit in Edmonds' perspective was the view that schools could be ineffective because they were unconcerned about providing comparable education to students from low-income families. The new definition left out the racial and class implications of Edmonds's definition and shifted the focus to the managerial components required for effectiveness. The new assumption was that all schools would educate equally if only they had access to the appropriate mix of resources and managerial talent described by effective schools research.

The third stage in the process of shifting the definition of effective schooling occurred when the technical criticisms of the outlier studies grew so strong that the research base for the effective schooling movement was itself at risk (Purkey & Smith, 1983; Good & Brophy, 1986). In this phase of the development of effective schooling, advocates of effective schooling called for a new, context-sensitive definition based on "school improvement" rather than performance.[6] One example of that shift is represented by the effectiveness criterion established by the National School Recognition Program (Sergiovanni, 1987):

1. Improved test scores
2. Improved attendance
3. Increased number of writing and homework assignments, with the amount of homework appropriately adjusted to the age of the student
4. Increased instructional time for mathematics, English, science, history and social science, foreign language, and fine arts
5. Community and parent participation
6. Student participation in extracurricular activities
7. Awards and recognition for student and teachers
8. Quality of support for students with special needs

Four of the foregoing eight indicators emphasize the notion of improvement as a measure of effectiveness. The school improvement approach measures schools in terms of their year-to-year gains on selected indicators, usually including test scores and attendance profiles. While school improvement is a desirable policy outcome, it is not obvious that improvement is better than sustained performance or equity as outcomes by which we define effectiveness. To illustrate, would a school that consistently performs at the ninetieth percentile on nationally normed achievement tests be more or less effective than one that demonstrates consistent improvement over three years from the fiftieth to the eightieth percentile? How much homework is too little or too much? How should quality support for students with special educational needs be defined and measured?

Interestingly, several of the indicators promoted by the National School Recognition Program are only weakly related to school outcomes in the effective school research. For example, even Ron Edmonds, while recognizing the desirability, disputed the necessity of community and parental participation in effective schools. These and other basic definitional issues have yet to be addressed by many proponents of effective schools.

Most recently the school improvement definition has been modified to account for the growing concerns of the business community about the international competitiveness of the American labor force. This new definition is responsive to the business community's concern for performance standards in education. Often called the "value-added" approach, it takes the position that the production function model used in industry to specify inputs and outputs has an analogy to education. In industry, land, labor, and capital are combined in a way that adds value which is embodied in the product. The product, embodying its added value, is sold for a profit. In education, both children and society should profit when schools add educational value above and beyond what individual families could contribute on their own (Mann, 1989, 1991).

The responsiveness of the effective schools movement to this effort to shift the definition to a value added approach remains to be seen. But the pressure from the business community is genuine and informed. Robert Warner, CEO of The Prudential Insurance Company, offered these observations:

> In standardized tests between 1983 and 1986, American high school seniors came in last in biology among students from 13 countries. And a recent survey of teen-agers found that two-thirds had no idea what Chernobyl signified. One young lady thought it was Cher's real name.... By the year 2005, most of our entry-level workers—over half the workforce in New Jersey—will come from public schools in distressed urban districts. These are kids who were born this year [1988] and will be entering our schools in 1993.... If we continue as we are many of those potential workers will be [educationally] unable to fill the jobs that will be available.[7]

David T. Kearns, chairman of the Xerox Corporation, describes the problem as "the making of a national disaster," and Brad M. Butler, former chairman of Procter & Gamble, fears the creation of a third world within our own country (Fiske, 1989).

The point of these corporate critics of the American education system is not that urban school children are uneducated. Rather, they are worried about the quality and level of education. For example, John L. Clendenin, CEO of BellSouth Corporation in Atlanta, lamented that fewer than 1 in 10 of job applicants (all of whom were high school graduates) had the necessary skills to perform entry-level positions at Bellsouth.

A recent Hudson Institute study (Johnston & Packer, 1989) correlated data on job skill requirements with data on students' educational achievement. Only tests of verbal skills were used in the analysis. Nonetheless, the authors found that average young adults, 21 to 25 years old, are reading at a level significantly below that demanded by the average job available in 1984 and are even further below the requirements of jobs expected to be created between 1984 and the year 2000. The researchers established a scale of reading ability of from 1 to 6, where 1 signifies a rudimentary level of reading and a 6 the level required of scientists, lawyers, and engineers. Current reading levels are estimated at 2.6 while the 26 million new jobs available between 1984 and the year 2000 will require an average reading level of 3.6 (Fiske, 1989).

THE PRODUCTION FUNCTION ANALOGY

If effective schools are redefined by the value added to student learning and rely on the production function analogy to define the most efficient means by which such value is added, then some critical reflection on the appropriateness of the production function model is necessary. There are three components to an educational production function that must be correctly specified before conclusions can be drawn about the organizational determinants of effective schools. The first requirement is that all the significant inputs to student learning be identified and measured as accurately as possible. This includes out-of-school and in-school contributions: for example, variations in organizational structure, leadership, and the technology of instructional production be specified as thoroughly as possible. This includes such measures as opportunity to learn, time-on-task, pedagogy, textbooks, and homework.

Second, all relevant background variables such as race, sex, and socioeconomic status should be included. Finally, the achievement gains and other learning goals to be measured require pre- and posttesting at the beginning and end of each academic year so that the value added can be determined. When these conditions are met, we have what is called "a fully specified" production function.

The obstacles to establishing a fully specified model are considerable. Previous effective schools research relied almost exclusively on cross-sectional comparisons of schools to define effective schools and had limited information on out-of-school contributions to learning. These limitations in selecting effective schools greatly increased the probability that a school with higher than average achievement levels are selected because the students in the school are drawn from populations with higher than average ability or live in homes with higher than average out-of-school contributions to their education.[8] Since the largest part of the variance in student achievement (somewhere between 50 and 75 percent) is attributable to factors beyond the schoolhouse doors, the problems of correctly identifying school contributions to learning are extremely difficult. These problems are complicated by the fact that out-of-school measures of family contributions (educational values, tutoring, books, computers, restrictions on television, homework supervision, parental academic aptitude) are all far less accurately measured than are in-school factors. Thus, the gains attributed to school effects may actually be capturing nonspecified out-of-school contributions. One solution to this problem is to conduct a study that attempts to capture more precisely the out-of-school contributions to student learning while simultaneously using a value-added calculation with a classroom level pre- and posttesting of students on desired achievement outcomes.

The use of value added as an outcome measure for defining effective schools raises a number of additional policy problems. For example, consistently high-performing schools may actually show lower average gain scores because high-performing schools tend to top out on nationally norm referenced tests. High-performing schools find it hard to show gains because so little room for improvement is left. Schools at the ninetieth percentile on the Iowa Test of Basic Skills have a much more difficult time improving by 5 percent than do schools at the forty-fifth percentile.

Defining effective schools by their average gains on test scores is problematic not only because of testing problems, but also because they create "ratcheting effects." The ratcheting effect is a well-known problem in game theory where players adjust their performance downward so that only small gains in productivity are reported for the group. Organizational members quickly learn that large gains simply raise expectations for the following year and are very difficult to sustain from year to year.

One might well expect this problem to occur in education because of the organizational problems created by having students in one grade exceed their learning norms when they arrive in the next grade. For example, if all teachers in George Washington Elementary School seek to add as much value as possible, the first grade class of 1990 is likely to know a significant part of the second grade curriculum when it arrives in 1991. The burden then falls on the second-grade teacher to shift the curriculum upward and begin teaching the material typically taught by the third-grade teacher. As the first-grade class of 1990 rises in the system, increasingly dramatic changes in the curriculum will be required. This is not to suggest that such an outcome is undesirable, but to establish the point that a highly routinized and bureaucratic educational system has curricular rigidities that must be overcome if the value added approach is to avoid the ratchet effect. By implication, eliminating curricular rigidity would require public schools to adapt a management style that is highly flexible and contingent. This would place significant additional curricular responsibilities on teachers and principals. Currently, the organizational incentives to restructure schools do not exist. In the absence of such incentives one should not be surprised to find organizational resistance to value added performance monitoring of schools.

As must already be obvious, the inputs of a production function model cannot actually be separated from the definition of a desirable outcome. If we take Edmonds's definition of equity as a desirable outcome, it will affect how we mobilize policy-manipulable resources to attain that goal. Again, if efficiency, or school improvement or the value-added approach is our outcome of choice, we will deploy those resources differently. If we conclude that schools are not economic, but political institutions with multiple constituencies who require multiple outcomes, effective schools policies that seek a single-outcome measure against which all resources are mobilized will continue to meet resistance. As Brian Rowan (1984) has concluded, the definitions and measures of school effectiveness vary so substantially depending upon the underlying theories and values of the evaluator that effectiveness should be determined by multiple measures from numerous interest groups and the interrelationships among the different measures should be the subject of further research (pp. 102–3).

An illustration of this problem has already been cited with respect to the concerns of the business community which has a specific set of concerns about school outcomes. It does not seem reasonable to conclude that schools have done their job if the levels of academic achievement attained by students are too low for the needs of their future employers. This is not to suggest that industrial standards should be the sole determinant of what our students learn in school. We encourage serious structural threats to our society, however, if we fail to supply the minimum needs of industry for human capital. Given both the growing sophistication of the technology we employ to run our society and the increasing mobility of the American labor force, it seems highly reasonable that we should have a national standard for what constitutes a basic elementary and secondary education that adequately prepares students for employment. The American Business Conference and the National Alliance of Business plan to design such a test with the assistance of the Educational Testing Service. They propose to establish 20 test sites by 1991 where recent graduates can go do demonstrate their competence. Those graduates who pass the examination are promised preferential hiring by participating corporations.

It does not follow, however, that because we have multiple—and even conflicting—outcomes demanded of schools, we should be uninterested in measuring them. It is possible and even desirable to measure outcomes from the perspectives of equity, efficiency, improvement, and value added (Rossmiller, 1987). With valid and easily comparable multiple-outcome measures, the public debate on their relative importance, and the trade-offs involved in pursuing one against the other, could proceed, with school districts, states, and nations adopting definitions of effectiveness that suit their policy objectives.

None of this can occur in the absence of meaningful measures of multiple-effectiveness outcomes. Recall that the effective schools movement was originally designed to make the case that children from low-income families could attain mastery of a basic education. Effective schools ipso facto were schools that provided the same basic education to low-income school children that it provided to its children from middle-income families. Absent from that definition has been a comprehensive set of comparative indicators of effectiveness. George Washington Elementary School might be effective in comparison to the other elementary schools in its district, but what if George Washington Elementary School is located in Mississippi and the children in the state as a whole place in the bottom quartile on national normed tests like the Iowa Test of Basic Skills? What does an equal educational opportunity imply in such a context? Does it mean that the children at George Washington Elementary School will go on to high school and compete effectively with their age cohort in terms of quality of life and income? The failure to provide meaningful comparative data on similar elementary schools across the nation or even within a given state, is a problem of staggering significance. If teachers, parents, and administrators cannot estimate with confidence the degree to which their schools are providing an effective education against local, regional, national, and even international comparisons, then the definition of effectiveness will be held hostage to local complacency. One consequence of our reliance upon local standards, as past practice has already demonstrated, is that an effective school in one district can be an at-risk school in another.

Effective schools advocates like Ron Edmonds, witnessing a massive failure to educate poor children, thought the holistic approach to outcome measures unrealistic in the short term. He often argued that if just one effective school could be found in an urban setting that successfully educated low-income youth, its existence defined the only research question of relevance: What is that effective school doing that the rest are not? But he never ruled out the need to improve how we define and measure what it meant to be an effective school.

PRODUCTION FUNCTIONS AND POLICY SIGNIFICANCE

The handful of studies that have undertaken production function analyses have largely ignored the problem of multiple outcomes. Even when narrow measures of student achievement have been used as outcomes, the effect size of school inputs has made only a small contribution to student outcomes. Although such models are frequently statistically significant, they should not be confused with policy significance. For example, Holmes reports the magnitude of school effects in the range of 10 to 30 percent of the variance and closer to 10 percent for developed countries (1989, p. 10). Holmes makes a further point:

> ...even the completely successful implementation of school effectiveness ideas will not transform either schools or society. The more we make schools equally successful the more we transfer responsibility for social distribution to the home. Home cultures are not equal, and indeed are probably becoming increasingly different. (1989, p. 10).

This is an extremely critical point. If the principal causes of unequal school outcomes are due to out-of-school factors such as poverty, poor nutrition, and low levels of parental education, and the variance in such factors is increasing between low- and middle-income children, then promoting effective schooling may be no more than a policy placebo.

The following example illustrates the difference between policy significance and statistical significance even further. The so-called private school advantage reported by Coleman, Kilgore, and Hoffer (1982) found an effect size in increased student achievement of one-half of a standard deviation for lower-SES students in Catholic compared to public schools. This finding had a great potential significance for low-SES students because it is an average effect for all low-SES students enrolled in Catholic schools and requires no policy change other than increasing the availability of private Catholic schools to low-SES students. On the basis of their work, intelligent policy would argue to promote opportunities for low-SES children to attend Catholic schools.

However, if we view the effect size of these educational gains in terms of their impact on student earnings after leaving school, we come to a quite different conclusion. This approach is justified because most of those who argue that student achievement is more important than other outcomes do so because basic numeracy and literacy are now critical for employment. Robert Meyer and David Wise (1979) examined the relationship between high school test scores and wage rates in the first four years after graduation for male youths in the 1972 NCES National Longitudinal Study. They found that a standard deviation increase in the total test score is associated with an estimated wage rate increase over four years of about 3 percent. Translating the private school effect reported by Coleman, Kilgore, and Hoffer into its correlation with increased earnings resulted in a wage difference of about 20 to 40 cents per hour in 1976 dollars (Willms, 1983).

The point of this illustration is that effective schools research utilizing the production function approach suggests that school effects are unlikely to shift educational outcomes significantly if other social outcomes like housing, family size, family education, and employment opportunities are not accessible.

CONCLUSION

Public institutions serve many constituencies. Even when we assume that these constituencies have the welfare of children uppermost in mind, they do not agree on which educational goals deserve priority. How effective schools are defined and measured is no less a political problem than other goals of education. In fact, it may be the most urgent of educational policy goals.

Despite this urgency, policymakers should avoid the reductionism of the basic skills approach because it denies other important goals of schooling that are difficult to measure. For example, one important skill that students learn in school is the ability to work in groups toward common purposes, what we might call cooperative problem solving. Currently, effective schools do not measure the degree to which students learn this skill, nor do they have norm-referenced comparisons. Because such skills are neither measured nor easily comparable across school systems, should they be neglected in the curriculum?

Neither is it clear who the constituency would be for the teaching and learning of educational outcomes like cooperative problem solving.[9] In the absence of a vocal constituency, should teachers who believe such skills are important to the educational well-being of students abandon their commitment to teaching cooperative problem solving in favor of drill sheets to boost students vocabulary scores on achievement tests? As Scott (1977, 1981) observed in his discussion of organizational effectiveness, clients tend to prefer outcome measures, teachers prefer process measures that evaluate them on standards of good practice, and administrators prefer to be evaluated on structural measures of the organization like facilities, teacher credentials, curriculum guides, and safety. However, it is unlikely that parents, teachers, or administrators as a group would advocate for cooperative problem solving as a measure of school effectiveness in the current climate of accountability.

Computer technology now makes it possible to create and monitor multiple outcome measures that account for the relative standards of local communities and the broader perspective of state, national, and global labor force requirements. Some specific policy suggestions that this author believes would strengthen the effective schools movement are

1. Recognize the need for multiple-outcome indicators of school effectiveness that include equity, efficiency, and value-added outcomes.
2. Provide report cards that permit comparisons with local, state, federal, and international norms of student achievement.
3. Provide trend data which show graphically how schools are doing over time.
4. Undertake long-term projects to define student achievement in terms of labor force requirements as well as state and national goals for literacy, citizenship, and social integration.
5. Provide appropriate and different outcome indicators for elementary and secondary schools.

The preceding recommendations would significantly expand the set of measures currently used to derive the organizational inputs and processes that produce these multiple outcomes and go a long way toward resolving the definitional problems of school effectiveness. Yet, as currently defined, they are not likely to alter the meaning of school effectiveness so that it is responsive to the educational demands of the twenty-first century. Perhaps inevitably, the logic of description and analysis leads to meanings and measures different from the logic of invention. What might some of these differences be? Education for citizenship and creative problem solving are certainly two educational goals not measured by the current crop of standardized tests of student achievement. Certainly a school that defines its effectiveness in terms of its students' capacities for citizenship and their skill in creative problem solving can be invented in many ways. Perhaps the means to such inventive ends can be developed only by altering the belief structure of the organization, its capacity to learn, and the strategies it employs to do so. Thus, a sixth recommendation might be added:

6. Expand the current research and development effort to create indicators for higher-order thinking skills, cooperative problem solving, citizenship, and other goals of education deemed important but not currently measured by existing instruments.

In sum, the most common meanings and measures of the effective schools we know may not be those most useful for inventing a new kind of effective school, one that might seek outcomes like autonomous learning and cooperative problem solving. Inside this paradox may lie as yet unformulated strategies. New strategies, however, depend upon the freedom to break away from effective schools as we know them and consider effective schools as they might be. It may be such a strategy that leads to a fundamental restructuring of schools and thus to a redefinition of the relevant variables of analysis.

REFERENCES

BROOKOVER, W. B., & LEZOTTE, L. W. (1977). *Changes in school characteristics coincident with changes in school achievement.* East Lansing, MI: State University, College of Urban Development.

COLEMAN, J. S., ET AL. (1966). *Equality of Educational Opportunity.* Washington, D.C.: U.S. Department of Health, Education, and Welfare.

COLEMAN, J. S., KILGORE, S., & HOFFER, T. (1982). *High School Achievement: Public, Catholic & Private Schools Compared.* New York: Basic Books.

EDMONDS, R. R. (1979). Effective schools for the urban poor. *Educational Leadership, 37,* 15–27.

EDMONDS, R. R. (1983). *Search for effective schools: The identification and analysis of city schools that are instructionally effective for poor children,* Unpublished final report. East Lansing: Michigan State University.

EDMONDS, R. R. (1986). Characteristics of Effective Schools. In E. Neisser (Ed.), *The Achievement of Minority Children,* pp. 93–104. Hillsdale, NJ: Erlbaum.

FISKE, E. (October 5, 1989). Impending U.S. jobs "disaster": Work force unqualified to work. *The New York Times,* p. 10.

GOOD, T. L., & BROPHY, J. E. (1986). School effects. In *handbook of research on teaching,* 3rd ed., pp. 570–602. New York: Macmillan.

HOLMES, M. (1989).   From research to implementation to improvement. In M. Holmes, K. A. Leithwood, & D. F. Musella (Eds.), *Educational policy for effective schools*, pp. 3–30. New York: Teachers College Press.

JENCKS, C. (1972).   *Inequality: A reassessment of the effect of family and schooling in America.* New York: Basic Books.

JOHNSTON, W. B., & PACKER, A. H. (1989).   *Workforce 2000: Work and workers for the 21st century.* Washington, D.C.: Hudson Institute.

KANTER, R. M., & SUMMERS, D. (1987).   Doing well while doing good: Dilemmas of performance measurement in nonprofit organizations and the need for a multiple-constituency approach. In *The nonprofit sector: A research handbook*, pp. 154–66. New Haven, CT: Yale University Press.

KEISLER, S., SIEGEL, J., & MCGUIREM, T. W. (1984).   Social psychological aspects of computer-mediated communication. *American Psychologist, 39*, 1123–34.

KRETZ, D. (1988).   "Arriving in Lake Woebegone: Are standardized tests exaggerating achievement and dictating instruction?" *American Educator, Vol. 12*(2), pp. 8–15, 46–52.

MANN, D. (1989).   Pedagogy and politics: Effective schools and american education politics. In D. Reynolds & B. Creemers (Eds.), *Effective schools in international perspective.* Amsterdam: Swets & Zeitlinger.

MANN, D. (1991).   *Killing school reform.* New York: Teachers College Press.

MEYER, R. H., & WISE, D. A. (1979).   *High school preparation and early labor force experience,* Working paper no. 342. Cambridge, MA: National Bureau of Economic Research.

MOSTLER, F., & MOYNIHAN, D. P. (Eds.).(1972).   *On equality of educational opportunity.* New York: Basic Books.

NATIONAL CENTER FOR EFFECTIVE SCHOOLS RESEARCH AND DEVELOPMENT. (1989).   A conversation between James Comer and Ronald Edmonds. Okemos, MI.

NEWMANN, F. (1990).   Student engagement in academic work: Expanding the perspective on secondary school effectiveness. In J. Bliss, W. Firestone, & C. Richards (Eds.), *Rethinking effective schools: Research and practice*, pp. 58–75. Englewood Cliffs, NJ: Prentice Hall.

OFFICE OF TECHNOLOGY ASSESSMENT, U.S. CONGRESS. (1988).   *Technology and the American economic transition: Choices for the future.* Washington, D.C.: U.S. Government Printing Office.

PURKEY, S. C., & SMITH, M. S. (1983).   Effective schools: A review. *Elementary School Journal, 83*, 427–52.

REDER, S., & SCHWAB, R. G. (September 26–28, 1988).   The communicative economy of the work-group: Multi-channel genres of communication. *Proceedings of the Conference on Computer-Supported Cooperative Work*, Portland, Oregon, pp. 39–51. New York: Association for Computing Machinery.

ROSSMILLER, R. A. (Spring, 1987).   Achieving equity and effectiveness in schooling. *Journal of Education Finance, 12*, 561–77.

ROWAN, B. (1984).   The assessment of school effectiveness. *Reaching for excellence.* San Francisco: Far West Laboratory.

RUTTER, M., MAUGHAM, B., MORTIMORE, P., OUSTON, J., & SMITH, A. (1979).   *Fifteen thousand hours: Secondary schools and their effects on children.* Cambridge, MA: Harvard University Press.

SCOTT, W. R. (1977).   Effectiveness of organizational effectiveness studies. In P. S. Goodman, J. M. Penninger, et al., *New perspectives on organizational effectiveness*. San Francisco: Jossey-Bass.

SCOTT, W. R. (1981).   *Organizations: Rational, natural and open systems*. Englewood Cliffs, NJ: Prentice Hall.

SERGIOVANNI, T. J. (1967).   *The principalship: A reflective practice perspective*. Boston: Allyn & Bacon.

STEEN, D. (September 18–22, 1989).   Teaching mathematics for tomorrow's world. *Educational Leadership, 7*(1).

WEBER, G. (1971).   *Inner city children can be taught to read: Four successful schools*. Washington, D.C.: Council for Basic Education.

WILLMS, D. J. (1983).   Do private schools produce higher levels of academic achievement? New evidence for the tuition tax credit debate. In T. James & H. Levin (Eds.), *Public dollars for private schools*. Philadelphia: Temple University Press.

ENDNOTES

[1]The author wishes to acknowledge the Center for Policy Research in Education, which has funded several studies on school performance accountability systems, and James Bliss, William Firestone, Susan Fuhrman, Dale Mann, and Fred Newmann for many helpful ideas and criticisms of earlier drafts of this article. The author is alone responsible for the arguments presented herein.

[2]However much the school effectiveness movement was dependent upon social science research for its legitimacy, it was never their exclusive terrain. Effective schooling has also been imbued—as the appellation "movement" implies—with a ritual and mythic significance.

[3]I think it is fair to say that Ron Edmonds's definition of effective schooling in 1983, while operationally the most specific, did not differ substantially from his earlier definitions.

[4]This article was published posthumously by Ulric Neisser with the assistance of Lawrence Lezotte. The article is based on a lecture given by Edmonds at a conference at Cornell University in 1982.

[5]For a review of these and other methodological problems with the use of linear regression models and correlational studies, see Good and Brophy (1986).

[6]See the chapters by Bliss, Firestone, and Miles in this text.

[7]Remarks of Robert C. Winters, Woodrow Wilson School, Princeton University, Princeton, NJ, November 18, 1988.

[8]In the production function model, students and out-of-school contributions to student achievement are both considered as inputs. The value added by the school is considered an output. (Most models ignore interaction effects between in-school and out-of-school contributions to student achievement.) Effective (productive) schools are those that attain higher than average output with the same inputs. If a school has higher-quality inputs (e.g., higher-ability students or greater out-of-school contributions), then it is inappropriate to conclude that it is more effective.

[9]As Steen (1989) writes in an article arguing for a rethinking of the mathematics curriculum: "As the workplace shifts to an emphasis on group task performance and problem solving, collaborative learning will become more important." Information technology tools may

increasingly be designed for use by teams rather than individuals working in isolation, and new types of interpersonal skills will be needed for occupational roles in which computer-mediated communication is important (Keisler et al., 1984). In such an economic environment, adults who lack sophisticated experiences in shared machine-enhanced interaction may be at a disadvantage (Reder & Schwab 1988). Students in conventional classroom settings have few opportunities to build skills of cooperation compromise and group decision making. Shifts in teaching must occur so that computer-supported collaborative learning becomes a major type of student interaction.

4

STRATEGIC AND HOLISTIC IMAGES OF EFFECTIVE SCHOOLS

James R. Bliss
Rutgers, The State University of New Jersey
Department of Educational Theory, Policy, and Administration

INTRODUCTION

Generally the term "effective schools" has invoked images of the urban schoolhouse, based on research made popular by the late Ron Edmonds and others. From his earliest writings forward, Edmonds believed that inequalities in education were willful, not inadvertent or based on a lack of technical knowledge (Edmonds, et al., 1973; Edmonds, 1977a, 1977b). Also according to Edmonds, five factors were chiefly responsible for the effectiveness of inner-city schools. These factors included (1) style of leadership, (2) instructional emphasis, (3) school climate, (4) teacher expectations, and (5) emphasis on procedures for monitoring student achievement.

Although Edmonds's correlates of effective schools have proven to be controversial, substantial progress has been made in confirming that effective schools can and do exist (Edmonds, 1981; Lezotte, 1986; Stedman, 1988). Yet the search for effective schools has been far more complicated and uncertain than one might expect (Purkey & Smith, 1983; Murphy et al., 1985; Deal, 1985; Mackenzie, 1986; Good & Brophy, 1986). Despite the growing complexity of research findings, the main line of argument coming from Edmonds and some of the reviewers was that "effective" schools were well understood and capable of being replicated.

The correlates of effective schools have been difficult to verify, but images of effective schools have prompted widespread programmatic initiatives. Apparently, almost half of the nation's schools districts have begun or are planning to implement programs based on effective schools research, according to the U.S. government's

General Accounting Office (Snider, 1989). For an analysis of this inconsistency, see Chapter 2 in this volume by William A. Firestone.

Images of effective schools have provided a source of optimistic and reasonable aims. They have helped to clarify the roles of teachers and principals. They have partially filled the void left by the Coleman Report (1966). They have supported the notion that distinctive style and leverage can be developed. Finally, they continue to stimulate research activity, even though the early surge of empirical research has passed. Specifically, two fairly distinct images of effective schools have materialized. No single research effort has been responsible for these images; rather, an accumulation of primary studies and reviews has produced them.

One image can be described as strategic, because of its emphasis on basic skills, standardized testing, and close supervision of instruction; the other image, as holistic, because of its parallel emphasis on student-centered curricula, varied teaching methods, and teacher autonomy. This chapter will address these images, offer an analysis of how they can interact, and suggest an outline based on effective schools imagery for modeling some of the choices that have potential for bringing about distinctively effective schools. While there is every reason for expecting too much from current knowledge of effective schools (Cuban, 1989), it remains to be seen how far schools can go to counteract the power of socioeconomic determinism.

STRATEGIC AND HOLISTIC IMAGES COMPARED

Curriculum

Much disagreement over the elementary curriculum has focused on how much emphasis should be given to learning skills versus content (Zais, 1976). Some curricular designs have appeared to be content centered and others skill centered. Although certain skills can be learned in first grade, for example, the attempt may only lead to frustration and failure. In settings where emphasis is on content, first graders may be taught something else in first grade and introduced to those difficult skills later on. The problem, of course, is that subsequent curricula may require those very skills as prerequisites.

SKILLS. Central to the strategic image of effective schools has been the emphasis on basic reading and arithmetic skills. Weber (1971), for example, identified eight factors common to "successful" elementary schools. Among these factors were a strong emphasis on reading skills and phonics. The tone of Weber's descriptions of successful schools contributed a lot to the strategic image of effective schools. The strategic image has also emerged from, and can be interpreted as, a reaction to the turbulent political demonstrations and perceived chaos of the 1960s. The time had come to downplay explosive content, get back to the basics. But as Stedman (1987) indicated,

> Many school systems that have adopted the effective schools formula are returning to the pre-1900 notion of a uniform curriculum, using a single set of textbooks and workbooks for a given grade, regardless of individual differences. Such schools have embarked on a "single-minded quest for higher test scores," and, though this is raising some scores, it has severely narrowed the curriculum.

Standardized testing of basic skills has been the most common means of distinguishing "effective" and "ineffective" schools (Brookover, et al., 1973; Brookover &

Schneider, 1975; Brookover et al., 1976; Brookover et al., 1977; Austin, 1978; Wellisch et al., 1978; Brookover & Lezotte, 1979; Stedman, 1987; Stringfield & Teddlie, 1988). Even Weber (1971), in one of the two earliest studies of effective schools in the United States, administered a standardized test of basic skills to identify outlier (unusually effective) schools.

CONTENT. From the outset, academic emphasis has been one of the most uncontroversial characteristics of effective schools (Rutter, 1983). But while some effective schools, perhaps even most of them, have emphasized basic skills, others have stressed content (Froelich et al., 1976). Finley School (P.S. 129 in New York City), for example, where 78 percent of the students were eligible for free lunch (89 percent were African-American and 10 percent were Puerto Rican) boasted an impressive academic record above national norms. And by all accounts, the extent of academic emphasis was impressive (Silberman, 1970).

From all appearances, Finley's success had been achieved through high quality decision making and efforts to help students feel good about themselves and their school. Reading instruction often began with an "experience story," which students and teachers composed each day. According to Silberman, the teacher wrote the story on the board in large letters and then ran off a copy for each child, who pasted it into his or her notebook. Reading involved much more than mastering a set of skills. A typical second-grade student was likely to read anywhere from 50 to 80 books in a single year.

The holistic image of curriculum in effective schools, based on the progressive tradition and reflected somewhat in the current literature on teacher professionalism, has included art, music, and literature. It has also included an emphasis on ethnic identification. Not surprisingly, then, holistic images of the curriculum have raised a multitude of issues including multicultural education, race and role models, and school and urban society. But the holistic image of curriculum in effective schools has been in place all along.

Teaching

Teachers generally focus on certain aspects of teaching and give less emphasis to the others. Edmonds thought that teachers' decisions regarding instruction derive from certain intellectual premises as to the origins of achievement, and teachers trained in a school-effects analysis of the origin of achievement fix professional attention on those within-school staff behaviors about which something can be done. Alternative models of teaching are available to decision makers (Hyman, 1974; Joyce & Weil, 1986). In this section, however, only two kinds of teaching will be considered: direct teaching, aimed at the elaboration of behavior, and indirect teaching, focused on the social elaboration of meaning.

Throughout the literature on effective schools, references have been made to the importance of high teacher expectations. The emphasis on high teacher expectations has been attributed to Rosenthal and Jacobson (1968) and, even farther back, to myths of personal transformation through caring. The concept of high teacher expectations has pervaded the effective schools literature. Yet of greater analytic value, perhaps, has been the distinction between direct and indirect instruction.

DIRECT. Much of direct teaching is based on B. F. Skinner's theory of operant conditioning. Direct teaching, in austere form, involves manipulating students' behavior through reinforcement. The teacher tries to build complex patterns of responses by adjusting provision of rewards, including things as stickers, smiles, and compliments. A variety of reinforcers, positive and negative, can be utilized.

Strategic images of effective schools have generally emphasized direct teaching. Strategic images emphasize classroom management, and the classroom management literature has a distinctly behavioral focus (Brophy, 1983). In addition, studies of time-at-task that have gained impetus from the work of Rosenshine and Furst (1971) and Harnischfeger & Wiley (1976) have pointed to the importance of direct instruction in student engagement. Finally, the strong relationship between perceived expectations and sense of control has been interpreted to mean that direct instruction contributes to self-confidence (Gigliotti & Brookover, 1975).

According to the proponents of direct teaching, the teacher has an important responsibility as classroom leader or decision maker. The leadership role in directive teaching has several facets: to maintain the academic focus of the classroom, to pose the questions and even to remain the center of attention, to use grouping strategies and seat work judiciously in view of the wasted time that accrues when students are left alone, and to use low-level questioning in order to strengthen basic skills.

INDIRECT. Indirect teaching has been described as focusing primarily on improving the general faculties of the individual and particularly the ability to develop on something like one's own terms. The teacher strives to create an accepting climate, and classroom activities are determined as teachers react to the students. Thus, classroom activities may be emergent and responsive to students' needs, interests, and capabilities. The notion of teacher as the one who interprets the curriculum operates fully well here, but indirectly. The teacher's method of work may rely more often upon setting up the conditions for discovery and reacting to students in ways that heighten authentic participation in subject matter.

Holistic images of effective schools have placed more emphasis on indirect teaching. Holistic teaching in effective schools has emphasized projects, differentiated classrooms, activity centers, problem solving, complex planning, and hands-on activities. On balance, holistic images have been relatively weak in the sense that fewer studies seem to support them.

Governance

A number of useful distinctions have been drawn among various approaches to governance taken by the principal. At least two kinds of governance are relevant, instructional leadership and institutional leadership.

INSTRUCTIONAL. Leadership matters because teachers have long functioned in isolation, more so in elementary schools. What goes on in the classroom has always been to a great extent under the teacher's individual control. When demonstrating instructional leadership, the principal works closely with teachers on curricular and teaching issues. Whereas instructional leadership has its focus on the classroom reducing supporting classroom activities, it can also be intrusive and unwelcome.

The strategic image of effective schools has emphasized the importance of the strong instructional leader. The strong instructional leader often has been a content specialist, assertive and uncompromising on pedagogical and curricular issues. The strong instructional leader in certain schools has been the principal. Although most effective schools research has concerned low-SES schools and most principals of effective low-SES schools appear to be strong instructional leaders, evidence has developed that principals of effective middle-SES effective schools may exhibit less or less direct instructional leadership than do low-SES counterparts.

INSTITUTIONAL.   Institutional leadership has been described as system mainte-nance. Since the school's effectiveness may depend on relationships with external environments, institutional leadership helps both to protect the school's academic program from inappropriate outside influence and to secure outside resources. Insti-tutional leadership intrudes less into the classroom than does instructional leadership. Further, institutional leadership, culminating in school-level policies, may contribute much to a productive workplace (Hallinger & Murphy, 1985).

The holistic image of effective schools has *inconsistently* cast the principal in the role of strong instructional leader. The principal, according to this image, may be somewhat withdrawn from the daily problems of instruction, as shown by the sketch of Seymour Gang, the principal of P.S. 192 (Silberman, 1970):

> Seymour Gang does not concern himself with the curriculum or the teaching methods and indeed is hard put to describe just how reading is taught or even what texts are used in his school. In general, instruction in reading is the joint responsibility of the regular classroom teachers and a team of nine reading specialists.

The author goes on to say that Gang's charge to the teachers was simple and blunt: "I don't care what you do as long as the children are reading at the norm." Students apparently expressed a good deal of affection for Gang, even though Silberman's description allowed that his leadership fostered a number of questionable teaching methods.

The distinction, however, between holistic and strategic governance has rested on the notion of teacher autonomy. Institutional leadership clearly has focused on establishing the conditions for teaching without intervening much in teaching itself. Comer and his colleagues (1987–1988) have developed a school governance model as a part of their School Development Program (SDP) model. An essential character-istic of Comer's model has been to move the school from a bureaucratic method of management to a system of democratic participation in which parents play a key role. The governance and management group, as identified, systematically structures and coordinates the various activities to improve the climate of the school. This model has a strong, 20-year track record in urban schools and seems to exemplify the holistic image of school governance.

INTERACTING CORRELATES AND MULTIPLE PATHWAYS

As depicted in the literature, effective schools have occurred through deliberate high-quality choices rather than luck or random activity. To gain perspective on these choices and to understand better how effective schools may occur, alternative path-ways based on current imagery must be considered. If effective schools have happened as the result of deliberate choices, conventional choice may be able to shed at least some light on this process (Pitz & McKillip, 1984).

Briefly, choices are made from known alternatives. Yet the attractiveness of each alternative depends upon previous conditions at the time. As decision makers, building-level administrators and policymakers have been aware in addition that some outcomes are preferable to others. Each alternative, however, may be cloaked in uncertainty. To each pair of alternatives and conditions, there will be a consequence or outcome. If we can describe the value of each outcome, we can summarize this choice problem without difficulty. Descriptively, we can identify the alternatives that have been selected. Should this framework seem obscure at first, a moment's reflection may indicate how completely ordinary such choice problems are.

The decisions made by individuals and groups create different pathways to effective schools. Without a doubt, teachers and principals who set out to develop effective schools have encountered branching alternatives. The challenge of selecting a certain curricular emphasis, whether content or skills, is only the beginning. From these choices of whether to emphasize a direct or indirect teaching style or to emphasize instructional or institutional leadership also may interact.

If effective schools represent deliberate choices on the part of teachers and principals, path models can be developed to represent them. Different sets of correlates have been associated with effective schools. These correlates have indicated crucial choices along the way to greater effectiveness. High-quality choices around the issues of curriculum, teaching, and governance all together are the things that seem to have the effects people are looking for. If so, Edmonds may have been only partially correct when he argued that sufficient knowledge already existed to create more effective schools; knowledge of how correlates interact has been lacking.

Although mixed imagery at first may aggravate some of the confusion regarding what makes a school effective, strategic and holistic elements of education have been combined to produce *programs* that are comprehensive, intensive and responsive (Slavin & Madden, 1989). The resolution of likely inconsistencies will require local policy makers to discard the weight of restrictively uniform practices. In addition, the feasibility of year-around school calendars that allow opportunities for concentrated programmatic self-evaluation must be considered.

What Works in Effective Schools?

SES CONTEXT.   The correlates of effective schools have depended strongly upon SES context, according to several studies. Low-SES effective schools have benefited from moderately authoritarian principals who emphasize routines leading to goal attainment, believe that all students can/will learn, mobilize consensus on school goals, and disagree with superiors (if necessary) around choices of key school routines (Sizemore, 1985). Middle-SES effective schools, by comparison, have benefited from a style of leadership that emphasizes moderated surveillance of teachers (Teddlie, Stringfield, Wimpleberg, & Kirby, 1987). Other contextual differences have been found as well, including differences by ethnic composition of school and degree of urbanization (Brookover et al., 1973).

In general, however, the image of low-SES effective schools has been one centering on the principal as one who operates with watchfulness, protectiveness, and top-down control, compared to his or her middle-SES counterparts. Low-SES effective schools also seem to rely less on public displays of success, more on administrative support for academic initiatives, and more on close supervision guided by academic emphasis. Low-SES effective schools in some cases have placed greater emphasis on social skills and on the notion that schools under the principal's leadership must actively support students in their adjustment to school.

Effective schools research has spread beyond the cities or other low-SES settings, and researchers have been focusing lately on how middle-SES and above schools can overcome the effects of class to achieve higher levels of performance. The logic of extending effective schools research to schools other than low-SES urban schools has been plausible, clearly. Whether policymakers for suburban elementary schools have given thought to the impact of student social class upon scholastic achievement remains unclear.

STRONG LEADERSHIP.   Gross & Herriott (1965), in a study of urban principals, described this kind of leadership as "executive professional leadership" or EPL, "the efforts of an executive to improve the quality of staff performance." EPL was positively related to staff morale, teachers' professional performance, and student learning. Not surprisingly, EPL itself drew strength from collaboration, egalitarianism, supportiveness, along with an overall businesslike approach. Some teachers, however, were less accepting than others of control by the principal over classroom-related issues, while the top-rated 15 activities identified by principals as an important part of the principal's job nearly all concerned instructional leadership.

According to Cuban (1984), the effective schools movement has heightened the level of conflict between administrators and teachers, through its emphasis on strong leadership. Others have found that teachers may prefer strong instructional leaders (Venezky & Winfield, 1979; Brandt, 1987). The results on this question have been mixed, as one would expect. Just as some teachers may find strong instructional leadership difficult to tolerate, some principals may be reluctant to attempt instructional leadership. Teacher autonomy can be of benefit to the principal in these cases when coupled with mechanisms that help to ensure quality.

Absent such mechanisms, the lack of instructional leadership from the principal has been a persistent problem (New York State Department of Education, 1974). In settings that lack both strong collegiality norms and pressure from parents to perform well, the situation may be impossible without the strong instructional leader. Where the leadership has been weak, other avenues of leadership may emerge (California State Department of Education, 1980). Presumably, however, passive choices such as leadership by default work are less attractive than more deliberate forms of leadership.

Edmonds wrote,

> One of our very firm conclusions is that the principal of the school has to be the person to whom the instructional personnel look for instructional leadership. We know that one of the measures of instructional leadership is that the principal has to visit classes, systematically observe, and respond to observations. Therefore, if we discovered that the principal seldom does that, we would respond by assigning a person to work with the principal to teach what he or she might need to know in order to be a sophisticated and consistent evaluator of teacher performance in the classroom.

Adamant support has been lacking, however, to claim that high-quality leadership must be instructional. There are good reasons for this. Teachers differ in training, experience, and maturity. Not all teachers can benefit from close supervision; some, of course, may need more direct help than others. The main effects of strong instructional leadership have been unclear. In low-SES schools, the associations are pronounced, whereas in middle-SES or high-SES schools the associations may be nonexistent.

Teacher autonomy.   Lanier and Sedlak (1989) have presented by implication a different perspective on the concepts of instructional leadership and teacher autonomy. Strategic approaches to schooling may work in the foregoing sense, but also promote rituals of school activity rather than "understanding, intellectual competence, and commitment to the sustenance and continued development of a good society." The question of what works must take into account the general aims of education and the related question of for what does it work. Citing work by Devaney and Sykes, the authors have suggested that students often bring home 1,000 workbook pages and skill sheets completed in reading during one year, although such activities rarely develop higher-order cognitive abilities.

Lanier and Sedlack (1989) also point out that variables like "orientation of children toward reading in school" have greatly improved reading abilities and have brought about the recognition that reading requires constructive activities such as formulating questions and making summaries and predictions, as well as evaluative ones such as analyzing and clarifying points of difficulty. In addition, "activities that helped students to apply and utilize their skills" have fostered "an entirely new view of the writing process." Finally, "changes in control strategies and belief systems" have helped to develop "a fundamentally new understanding of mathematics."

TEACHER KNOWLEDGE.   But, according to these authors, changing the scope, depth, and value of subject matter may be only a part of the solution. There are problems of pedagogical knowledge, knowledge of student development, knowledge of multiple cultures, interdisciplinary knowledge, knowledge of broad educational purposes, and other knowledge required to move beyond the status quo. The contention by these authors and others has been that greater professional knowledge along with opportunities to use it argue for new structures and, importantly, new methods of teacher education.

Test-based curricula require teachers to spend much more time in preparing drills, administering tests, and maintaining records than may be the case with content-based curricula. Test-based curricula can induce great amounts of teacher stress. Indirect teaching, even if it requires the same amount of effort, may call for a different distribution of effort that can result in less teacher stress. Teachers have voiced a need for help in mastering a variety of pedagogical techniques (McCormack-Larkin & Kritek, 1983), and a good deal of attention has been focused recently on the qualities of teacher knowledge (Porter & Brophy, 1988). Yet, the evidence in favor of any one best way to teach has been fairly weak, on par with the knowledge base for effective schools, even though advocates for particular models of teaching have been outspoken.

TIME.   It has been commonly assumed that higher-achieving students are more committed to academic work than are low-achieving students (Brookover et al., 1976). Based on findings from a Follow Through Project in Napa County, California, schools over a four-year period (Stallings & Krasavage, 1986), however, it was reported that fourth graders were engaged approximately 90 percent of the time in both reading and mathematics. Second graders were engaged 11 percent less frequently than were fourth graders in reading and 14 percent less frequently in math. Since there were no differences in achievement gains at different grade levels, these results suggested the possibility of grade by time interaction effects on achievement.

In addition, so-called time-on-task may have a curvilinear effect on learning and may be less important than "success rate" (see Bossert et al., 1982). Student engagement may be a powerful influence on achievement, but its bearing on achievement seems to be anything but straightforward. Insofar as images of effective schools contain simplistic expressions of the need for intensive study, they are clearly misleading and should be revised. However, engagement seems to be a component of academic emphasis that will require practitioners and scholars to further differentiate among pathways to greater effectiveness. Effective schools might create different curricular emphases for different grades.

EXPECTATIONS.   A fair amount of attention has been given to teachers' perceptions and principals' perceptions of students. The teacher's future evaluations/expectations of the student's potential along with teacher "push" have been identified in some of the earliest effective schools work as related to student achievement (Rosenthal & Jacobson, 1968; Brookover et al., 1973). These results strongly supported Robert K. Merton's notion of the self-fulfilling prophesy. Expectation effects are most likely to occur in subject areas that allow the greatest variation in instructional styles (Cooper & Tom, 1984).

Apparently, some instructional behaviors are more likely to produce stronger expectation effects than others. Severe self-fulfilling prophecies rarely occur in classrooms but mild self-fulfilling prophecies and sustaining expectation effects should be matters of serious concern. Teacher expectations are primarily determined by the actual ability and motivation levels of students. To complicate these matters, the classroom composition of aptitude levels can mediate expectation effects (Beckerman & Good, 1981).

RESEARCH IMPLICATIONS

The criticisms of effective schools research have been so widely publicized that only passing reference to them will be made. Problems with this research have been conceptual and methodological (Chapter 13 by Craig E. Richards in this volume), that is, criticisms focusing on the meaning of the concept as well as flaws in sampling, data collection, and analysis. The emphasis in this chapter has been different. From almost the beginning, effective schools research has reflected the practical vision of the movement itself. Nearly the whole effort has been devoted to searching for and identifying best practice. My argument has been that we know too little about effective schools to replicate them, but we do know enough to begin a process of modeling and testing alternative pathways to making schools at least more distinctive.

Few studies of effective schools have been impressive either in their precision or ability to build confidence in the power of effective schools correlates. The lack of precision in effective schools research has been partly a function of the cost of precision. Without detailed controls in place for the average effects of home background, for example, very little else about the main effects or the interactive effects of effective schools correlates (process variables) can be determined.

Imprecision also extends to the psychometric issues in the use of tests and surveys. The effective schools research generally ignores these issues of testing that have surrounded the selection of unusual schools. Weber (1971), for example, constructed and field tested an instrument designed to help identify unusually effective schools. But few psychometric details were given. In addition, few studies have done a thorough job of conceptualizing SES to be sure that examples of effective schools are legitimate.

The need has persisted to conduct studies that are sensitive to the differences among various populations. The diversity of populations has created occasions for wider applications of ESR methodologies even within the cities. The effort to consolidate effective schools findings into lists of presumably independent correlates has been understandable but untimely. Rather than consolidate even further the findings of ESR, which, thus far, has tended to shut down inquiry, scholars must now shift back to exploring context-specific differences even if not particularly strong.

Few studies have been able to overcome the practical problems associated with achieving a strong research design. Perhaps no one has discussed this problem with greater insight than Brookover in several places. Some of these problems include the inappropriateness of experimental designs, the difficulties of obtaining samples of unusually effective schools that serve different mixes of minority and nonminority students in urban settings, and the lack of available instruments to collect data on a wider range of characteristics that may help to distinguish between effective and ineffective schools.

Alternative pathways to effective schools suggest a number of useful strategies for designing and sorting out from dozens to hundreds of different approaches to effective schools. Mortimore & Sammons (1987) have reported 12 key effectiveness factors in a British sample, opening an enormous number of interactive possibilities. The group of pathways described in this chapter is only one of countless groups that could be constructed on the basis of what we already know or suspect about effective schools. At this point, there seem to be two kinds of effective schools, but, if further differentiated, these pathways I have mentioned can lead to many more possibilities. And greater clarification is needed.

Evidence can be found that intraschool differentiation of programming has been misused to help some high achievers rather than working with low achievers (Brookover & Lezotte, 1979). The discussion in this chapter does not imply ability grouping or tracking within schools. Instead, the emphasis has been on creating greater distinctiveness between schools. It rests partly on Brookover's premise that the school social system affects school learning outcomes; members of a school social system become socialized to behave differently in a given school than they would in another school (Brookover et al., 1977).

Although images of effective poverty schools have occupied center stage, those of middle-SES effective schools have emerged as well. What we are learning about middle-SES effective schools is that context differences exist between schools and that differentiated pathways to effectiveness need to be considered. Stringfield & Teddlie (1988) have found that effective low-SES schools differ from effective middle-SES schools. Anticipating somewhat the conclusions reached in this review, middle-SES schools conformed much more to holistic than to strategic imagery.

Middle-SES effective schools expanded curricular offerings beyond the basic skills, deemphasized extrinsic rewards, hired more experienced teachers, and increased teacher responsibility for instructional leadership. Low-SES effective schools conformed closely to strategic imagery as discussed throughout this chapter. Further, the impact of school factors may depend strongly on SES (Schneider & Brookover, 1974).

Here are a few thoughts on studies that might be undertaken:

1. Although curriculum, by most standards, means more than instructional materials, a study of curricular materials in poverty and nonpoverty schools could explore the extent to which curricular focus discriminates among effective schools, regular schools, and ineffective schools.

2. Studies of teacher have rarely attempted to aggregate teaching data to the school. If directness or indirectness of teaching could be made operational, sampled, and described at the school level, variations could be delineated across grades and perhaps across subject matters. New empirical studies of teaching paradigms in actual use would help again to discriminate among effective, regular, and ineffective schools.

3. The principal's activities naturally occur at the level of the school. This research problem would be to investigate not so much leadership style as described in educational administration textbooks, but the principal's focus on instruction compared to institutional leadership: activities that cluster about either instructional versus institutional leadership.

CONCLUSION

The effort to summarize effective schools research into a single formula has been highly effective in spreading the word about effective schools, undergirded by a number of premises and assumptions (Lezotte & Bancroft, 1985). Surely, one of these has been that possibility stimulates action; impossibility blocks it (Mann & Lawrence, 1984). Thus, the search for effective schools continues to be of vital importance. As the search continues, however, two images of effective schools have emerged, one strategic and the other holistic. These images have pointed the way to a more analytic conception of the pathways to effectiveness.

Effective schools research has succeeded fairly well, much to the credit of past reviewers, in creating hopeful images of effective schools for students who live in poverty. Reviews have woven effective schools research into the broad fabric of educational research, so that in almost no other subject has the quantity of reviews comparably exceeded the number of important empirical studies. Yet, whether images of effective schools match the reality has been difficult to determine. For this reason, imagery rather than hard substance has been emphasized in this chapter.

Edmonds (1979a, b) believed that some schools are effective in instruction because they have a tyrannical principal, others because they have a self-generating teacher corps, others because they have good systems of instructional accountability. All these explanations point to the importance high-quality decision making or, essentially, people (Clark, Lotto, & Astuto, 1984) and the potential of interactions among correlates to generate uniqueness (D'Amico, 1982).

The significance of these images, however, extends beyond poverty schools. Since publication of the Coleman Report, practitioners and scholars of education alike have sought reassurances that schools make an important difference, beyond the effects of home background. As Coleman and colleagues (1966) put it,

1. For each group (eight ethnic groups were mentioned), by far the largest part of the variation in student achievement lies within the same schools, and not between schools.

2. Comparison of school-to-school variations in achievement at the beginning of grade 1 with later years indicates that only a small part of it is the result of school factors, in contrast to family background differences between communities.

3. There is indirect evidence that school factors are more important in affecting the achievement of minority group students; among blacks, this appears especially so in the South. This leads to the notion of differential sensitivity to school variations, with the lowest-achieving minority groups showing the highest sensitivity.

Coleman's findings were devastating. Yet, just because between-school differences in student achievement have been small does not preclude that poverty schools can do much better in promoting student achievement. Although effective schools were implicit in the Coleman data, the reality of effective schools has often been obscured by methodological problems in much of the effective schools research. Past reviews have explored these flaws in great detail, flaws including the lack systematic data concerning the selection of sites. Because the effective schools movement rests on a moderate number of studies reaching similar conclusions, the validity of the concept has been supported.

Effective schools research has highlighted the importance of choices that people have always known about: content versus skills, direct teaching versus indirect teaching, instructional leadership versus institutional leadership. The decision-making approach to understanding effective schools draws attention to different combinations of choices. Effective schools in the middle-SES context are perhaps even more mysterious than others. But I can see no good reason why the analysis of effective poverty schools would not inform the study of nonpoverty schools and vice versa.

REFERENCES

AUSTIN, G. R. (1978). *Process evaluation: A comprehensive study of outliers,* ED160644. Baltimore: Maryland State Department of Education, University of Baltimore Center of Educational Research and Development.

AUSTIN, G. R. (1979). Exemplary schools and the search for effectiveness. *Educational Leadership, 37*(1), 10–14.

BECKERMAN, T. M., & GOOD, T. L. (1981). The classroom ratio of high- and low-aptitude students and its effect on achievement. *American Educational Research Journal, 18*(3), 317–27.

BOSSERT, S. T., DWYER, D. C., ROWAN, B., & LEE, G. V. (1982). The instructional management role of the principal. *Educational Administration Quarterly, 18*(3), 34–64.

BRANDT, R. (1987). On leadership and student achievement: A conversation with Richard Andrews. *Educational Leadership, 45*(1), 9–16.

BROOKOVER, W. B., GIGLIOTTI, R. R., HENDERSON, R. D., & SCHNEIDER, J. M. (1973). *Elementary school environment and school achievement,* ED086306. East Lansing, MI: College of Urban Development.

BROOKOVER, W. B., & SCHNEIDER, J. M. (1975). Academic environments and elementary school achievement. *Journal of Research and Development in Education, 9*(1), 82–101.

BROOKOVER, W. B., FLOOD, P. K., & WEISENBAKER, J. M. (1976). *Elementary schools social climate and school achievement,* ED131602. Seventy-first annual meeting of the American Sociological Association, New York, New York.

BROOKOVER, W. B., BEADY, C., FLOOD, P., SCHWEITZER, J., & WEISENBAKER, J. (1977). *Schools can make a difference*, ED145034. East Lansing, MI: College of Urban Development.

BROOKOVER, W. B., & LEZOTTE, L. W. (1979). *Changes in school characteristics coincident with changes in student achievement*, ED181005. East Lansing, MI: Michigan State University, Institute for Research on Teaching.

BROPHY, J. E. (1983). Classroom organization and management. *Elementary School Journal*, *83*(4), 265–85.

CALIFORNIA STATE DEPARTMENT OF EDUCATION (CSDE). (1980). *Report on the special studies of selected ECE schools with increasing and decreasing reading scores: A report to the joint legislative budget committee of the legislature as required by item 283 of the supplemental to the 1977–1978 Budget Act*, ED188106. Sacramento, CA: Office of Project Evaluation and Research.

CLARK, D. L., LOTTO, L. S., & ASTUTO, T. A. (1984). Effective schools and school improvement: A comparative analysis of two lines of inquiry. *Educational Administration Quarterly*, *20*(3), 41–68.

COLEMAN, J. S., CAMPBELL, E., HOBSON, C., MCPARTLAND, J., MOOD, A., WEINFELD, F., & YORK, R. (1966). *Equality of educational opportunity*. Washington, D.C.: U.S. Government Printing Office.

COMER, J. P., HAYNES, N., HAMILTON-LEE, M. (1987–88). School power: A model for improving black student achievement. *Urban League Review*, *11*(1–2), 187–200.

COOPER, H. M., & TOM, D. Y. H. (1984). Teacher expectation research: A review with implications for classroom instruction. *Elementary School Journal*, *85*(1).

CUBAN, L. (1984). Transforming the frog into a prince: Effective schools research, policy and practice at the district level. *Harvard Educational Review*, *54*(2), 129–51.

CUBAN, L. (1989). At-risk students: What teachers and principals can do. *Educational Leadership*, *46*(5), 29–32.

D'AMICO, J. (1982). Each effective school may be one of a kind. *Educational Leadership*, *40*(3), 61–62.

DEAL, T. E. (1985). The symbolism of effective schools. *Elementary School Journal*, *85*(5), 601–18.

EDMONDS, R. R. (1977a). *Developing student competency: Alternative means and attendant problems*, ED155243. Cambridge, MA: Harvard Graduate School of Education Center for Urban Studies.

EDMONDS, R. R. (1977b). *Search for effective schools: The identification and analysis of city schools that are instructionally effective for poor children*, ED142610. Cambridge, MA: Harvard Graduate School of Education Center for Urban Studies.

EDMONDS, R. R. (1979a). Some schools work and more can. *Social Policy*, *9*(5), 28–32.

EDMONDS, R. R. (1979b). Effective schools for the urban poor. *Educational Leadership*, *37*(1), 15–27.

EDMONDS, R. R. (1981). Making public schools effective. *Social Policy*, *12*(2), 56–60.

EDMONDS, R., BILLINGSLY, A., COMER, J., DYER, J. M., HILL, R., MCGETTEE, N., REDDICK, L., TAYLOR, H., & WRIGHT, S. (1973). A black response to C. Jencks' inequality and certain other issues. *Harvard Educational Review*, *43*(1), 76–91.

FROELICH, M., BLITZER, F. K., & GREENBERG, J. W. (1976). Success for disadvantaged children. *Reading Teacher*, *21*(1), 24–37.

GIGLIOTTI, J. J., & BROOKOVER, W. B. (1975). The learning environment: A comparison of high- and low-achieving elementary schools. *Urban Education*, *10*(3), 245–61.

GOOD, T. L., & BROPHY, J. E. (1986).   School effects. In M. C. Wittrock (Ed.), *Handbook of research on teaching*, 3rd. ed. New York: Macmillan.

GROSS, N., & HERRIOTT, R. E. (1965).   *Staff leadership in public schools: A sociological inquiry.* New York: John Wiley.

HALLINGER, P., & MURPHY, J. (1985).   Characteristics of highly effective elementary school reading problems. *Educational Leadership, 42*(5), 39–42.

HARNISCHFEGER, A., & WILEY, D. E. (1976).   The teaching-learning process in elementary schools: A synoptic view. *Curriculum Inquiry, 6*(1), 5–43.

HYMAN, R. T. (1974).   *Ways of teaching.* Philadelphia: J. B. Lippincott.

JOYCE, B. R., & WEIL, M. (1986).   *Models of teaching.* Englewood Cliffs, NJ: Prentice Hall.

LANIER, J. E., & SEDLAK, M. W. (1989).   Teacher efficacy & quality schooling. In T. J. Serviovanni & J. H. Moore (Eds.), *Schooling for tomorrow: Directing reform to issues that count.* Boston: Allyn & Bacon.

LEZOTTE, L. (1986).   *Reflections and future directions.* Paper presented at the Annual Meeting of the American Educational Research Association, ED284047. San Francisco, CA.

LEZOTTE, L., & BANCROFT, B. (1985).   Growing use of the effective schools model for school improvement. *Educational Leadership, 42*(6), 23–27.

MACKENZIE, D. E. (1986).   *Research for school improvement: An appraisal of some recent trends,* ED269345. Salt Lake City, UT: Utah State Office of Education.

MANN, D., & LAWRENCE, J. (1984).   A Delphi analysis of the instructionally effective school. *Social Policy, 15*(2), 49–51.

MCCORMACK-LARKIN, M., & KRITEK, W. J. (1983).   Milwaukee's project rise. *Educational Leadership, 40*(3), 16–21.

MORTIMORE, P., & SAMMONS, P. (1987).   New evidence on effective elementary schools. *Educational Leadership, 45*(1).

MURPHY, J. F., WEIL, M., HALLINGER, P., & MITMAN, A. (1985).   School effectiveness: A conceptual framework. *The Educational Forum, 49*(3), 362–74.

NEW YORK STATE DEPARTMENT OF EDUCATION. (1974).   *School factors influencing reading achievement: A case study of two inner city schools,* ED089211. Albany, NY: Office of Education Performance Review.

PITZ, G. F., & MCKILLIP, J. (1984).   *Decision analysis for program evaluators.* Beverly Hills, CA: Sage Publications.

PORTER, A. C., & BROPHY, J. (1988).   Synthesis of research on good teaching: Insights from the work of the institute for research on teaching. *Educational Leadership, 45*(8), 74–85.

PURKEY, S. C., & SMITH, M. S. (1983).   Effective schools: A review. *Elementary School Journal, 83*(4), 427–51.

ROSENSHINE, B. V., & FURST, N. (1971).   Current and future research on teacher performance criteria. In B. O. Smith (Ed.), *Research on teacher education: A symposium,* pp. 37–71. Englewood Cliffs, NJ: Prentice Hall.

ROSENTHAL, R., & JACOBSON, L. (1968).   *Pygmalion in the classroom: Teacher expectation and pupils' intellectual development.* New York: Holt, Rinehart and Winston.

RUTTER, M. (1983).   School effects on pupil progress: Research findings and policy implications. In L. S. Shulman & G. Sykes (Eds.), *Handbook of teaching and policy.* New York: Longman.

SCHNEIDER, J. M., & BROOKOVER, W. B. (1974). *Academic environments and elementary school achievement.* Paper presented at the annual meeting of the American Educational Research Association.

SILBERMAN, C. E. (1970). *Crisis in the classroom: The remaking of American education.* New York: Random House.

SIZEMORE, B. A. (1985). Pitfalls and promises of effective schools research. *Journal of Negro Education, 54*(3), 269–89.

SLAVIN, R. E., & MADDEN, N. A. (1989). What works for students at risk: A research synthesis. *Educational Leadership, 46*(5), 4–13.

SNIDER, W. (1989). Survey confirms rapid spread of "effective schools." *Education Week, 9*(4), 9.

STALLINGS, J., & KRASAVAGE, E. M. (1986). Program implementation and student achievement in a four-year Madeline Hunter follow-through project. *Elementary School Journal, 87*(2).

STEDMAN, L. (1987). It's time we changed the effective schools formula. *Phi Delta Kappan, 69*(3), 215–24.

STEDMAN, L. (1988). The effective schools formula still needs changing: A reply to Brookover. *Phi Delta Kappan, 69*(6), 439–42.

STRINGFIELD, S., & TEDDLIE, C. (1988). A time to summarize six years and three phases of the Louisiana school effectiveness study. *Educational Leadership, 46*(2), 43–49.

TEDDLIE, C., STRINGFIELD, S., WIMPLEBERG, R., & KIRBY, P. (1987). *Contextual differences in effective schooling in Louisiana,* ED286272. Paper presented at the Annual Meeting of the American Educational Research Association, Washington, D.C.

VENEZKY, R. L., & WINFIELD, L. F. (1979). *Schools that succeed beyond expectations in reading,* ED177484. Washington, D.C.: National Institute of Education.

WEBER, G. (1971). *Inner-city children can be taught to read: Four successful schools.* Washington, D.C.: Council for Basic Education.

WELLISCH, J. B., MacQUEEN, A. H., CARRIERE, R. A., & DUCK, G. A. (1978). School management and organization in successful schools. *Sociology of Education, 51*(3), 211–26.

ZAIS, R. S. (1976). *Curriculum: Principals and foundations.* New York: Harper & Row.

5

STUDENT ENGAGEMENT IN ACADEMIC WORK: EXPANDING THE PERSPECTIVE ON SECONDARY SCHOOL EFFECTIVENESS[1]

Fred M. Newmann
University of Wisconsin-Madison

INTRODUCTION

A host of reports on secondary schools in the past decade has generated a long list of variables which seem to boost high school students' achievement. Drawing on the work of several studies[2] I summarize the main themes as

1. a shared sense of academic purpose among faculty, students, parents, and the community, including schoolwide recognition of student accomplishment and good teaching.

2. a high degree of involvement by parents and community members in school affairs.

3. a sense of caring and community within the school, where staff demonstrate broad commitment to student welfare and students participate in and take some responsibility for school affairs.

4. curriculum that emphasizes academic courses for all (placing most students in an academic track) and requires homework.

5. high expectations by staff that all students can learn.

6. maximum time within lessons devoted to on-task instruction.

7. behavioral order and fair-minded discipline.

8. strong leadership that actively recognizes and works to solve problems within the school.

9. teacher and administrator sense of control and discretion in operating the school and in teaching.

10. staff collegiality in planning, teaching, and evaluation.

These features of "good," "successful," or "effective" secondary schools do not thrive simply on resources inside of schools. They depend considerably upon moral, financial, and administrative support from the surrounding community and from the school district that sponsors and supervises the school.

In spite of reasonably consistent themes across several studies, our knowledge of secondary school effectiveness remains embarrassingly inadequate:

1. The general summary just offered has not been systematically tested. Different studies have focused on different items on the list, and so the potency of the variables seems to vary from study to study. For example, Coleman and Hoffer (1987) find academic curriculum and student discipline to be the key school variables, but for Witte and Walsh (1989) parent involvement is the most salient for high school achievement.

2. Information on achievement gains in high school is either nonexistent or almost meaningless. Very few of the U.S. studies collected longitudinal data. Those that did relied largely on the high school and beyond (HS&B) data which includes student performance only at the end of tenth and the end of twelfth grade. The magnitude of these two-year gains is so small (from 1 to 2 items on different tests ranging from about 20 to 40 items) as to raise serious questions both about the validity of the tests and whether high schools have any important influence on student learning. Not until 1992 will we have national data on student gains over four years in high school.[3]

3. Quantitative studies have identified variables associated with individual student achievement across many schools without trying to identify those variables that discriminate between actual schools that are most versus least effective. This is unfortunate, because qualitative studies have shown the importance of unique patterns of interaction within schools among several of these variables.[4] Rather than assuming that such variables add cumulatively to influence student achievement in all schools in the linear form assumed in multiple regression analysis, it is important to discern how they may relate in ways that distinguish particular types of schools from one another.[5] In short, we have gained knowledge about general influences on student achievement and also about general school *effects* on achievement, independent of student social background, but we know much less about school effectiveness.

4. As stated in previous critiques of the effective schools research, we have not conducted sufficient research on school change to understand how less effective schools can become more effective. A general literature on school improvement and change has, to be sure, articulated a variety of themes or guidelines (e.g., Fullan, Miles, & Taylor, 1980; Huberman & Miles, 1984; Marsh & Bowman, in press; Miles, Louis, Rosenblum, Cipollone, & Farrar, 1986), many of which are consistent with the effective schools themes, but these have not been derived through comparative studies of high schools that demonstrate different degrees of longitudinal progress on student outcome variables.

5. Finally, and most important, criteria for school effectiveness remain unclear, or in dispute, and the equity criterion is often neglected in research studies. Which of the following criteria should be used to determine the effectiveness of a high school? Rates of attendance, dropout, admission to higher education or employment; student

scores on achievement tests; student participation and success in extracurricular activities; scores on attitude surveys that assess self-esteem, racial tolerance, political efficacy, or school climate; reductions in teenage pregnancy, drug abuse, or gang participation.[6] When change is called for, what amount of change constitutes effectiveness? How can national studies establish common criteria and at the same time assess progress toward goals that high schools set for themselves? The lack of agreement on these matters inhibits building a cumulative knowledge base.

The central point of the original studies of elementary school effectiveness (Edmonds & Frederiksen, 1979; Brookover et al., 1979) was to see whether some schools were able to raise the achievement of low-income minority children to middle class levels, and to learn how they did it. None of the secondary school studies, however, have defined effective schools as those which most reduce the achievement gap due to social background nor have they studied how this is accomplished. We know that major differences in achievement between socioeconomic groups continue even in "high-performing" schools, but we do not know how much or how this gap might be reduced by some high schools.[7]

Even when it is agreed that effectiveness should be measured by academic achievement, there is mounting dispute over the ways in which achievement should be assessed. In the United States, for example, the dominant approach is through standardized short-answer and multiple-choice tests. These have been criticized on four main grounds: the construction and scoring of these tests obscures meaningful information on what students know and can do; they do not assess the particular content goals of high school curriculum; the exercises fail to assess depth of understanding, integration of knowledge, and production of discourse; and they recognize only a narrow range of human accomplishment—primarily linguistic and logical competencies to the neglect, for example, of spatial, kinesthetic, aesthetic, and interpersonal competencies. In short, as Archbald and Newmann (1988) have explained, dominant approaches to assessment fail to tap authentic forms of academic achievement. The problems just mentioned will continue to plague research for sometime. Resolving them is expensive, and it will require reaching greater agreement on the educational outcomes of high schools than has emerged to date. In working on these issues, however, we should consider a major shortcoming in the overall model of school effectiveness: the variables are usually presented merely as a list of unrelated processes. They are not tied together into a coherent theory that explains how and why certain student and community characteristics and approaches to instruction, curriculum, and school organization are more likely to produce favorable student outcomes than others.

One way to develop such a theory is to begin with what students and teachers see in common as the central problem of schooling. From the students' point of view it is boredom, and from the teachers' point of view it is students' lack of interest in doing the work required for learning. In what ways, if any, do the "effective schools" variables explain how to get students more interested in schoolwork? To answer this question, one needs a clearer conception of student engagement and a theory about the kinds of activities and environmental conditions likely to generate it.

Effective schools models, as well as broader reform policies such as choice plans, blueprints for restructuring, or new forms of assessment may make implicit assumptions about, but they fail to address directly, the most fundamental challenge that teachers face: the difficulty of engaging adolescents in academic work. Variables in the effective schools' list may be associated with student achievement, but a strong case can be made that their ultimate effectiveness rests in their ability to enhance the critical intervening variable of student engagement.

What is student engagement, why is it so important, and what factors must researchers, practitioners, and policymakers pay more attention to in order to increase it? In addressing these issues, the remainder of the chapter offers a new perspective on the effective schools literature.[8] The effort to develop more explicit theory on student engagement could help to integrate disparate strands in the effective schools literature, but more important, it should offer explicit ideas for teachers about how to design school activities that students take more seriously.

A CONCEPTUAL MODEL OF STUDENT ENGAGEMENT

Definition

Academic work consists of the tasks, usually specified by teachers, that students are asked to undertake in order to master the knowledge, skills, and crafts that serve as the instructional objectives of schooling. The work, which may occur as part of classroom instruction, homework, or exams, can include different types of reading, writing, computing, participating in discussions, and individual and group projects. Student engagement in academic work is defined as the student's psychological investment in learning, understanding, or mastering the knowledge, skills, or crafts that academic work is intended to promote. This definition requires elaboration and clarification on several important points that can otherwise be misinterpreted.

1. Engagement is a psychological investment in learning, comprehending, or mastering knowledge, skills, and crafts, not simply a commitment to complete assigned tasks or to acquire symbols of high performance such as grades or social approval. Students may complete academic work and perform well without being engaged in the mastery of a topic, skill, or craft.

2. As a psychological investment, engagement is not a directly observable characteristic, but a construct used to describe an inner quality of how a student relates to learning activity. The student's investment in any given type of mastery should be viewed on a continuum from less to more, not as a dichotomous state of being either engaged or unengaged. Levels of engagement must be estimated or inferred from indirect indicators such as the amount of participation in academic work (attendance, proportion of tasks completed, amount of time spent on academic work), the intensity of student concentration, the enthusiasm and interest expressed, and the degree of care shown in completing the work. All of these, however, can be misleading indicators of engagement; at times they may represent a student's willingness to comply with school routines, rather than an actual investment in mastering, comprehending or learning knowledge, skills, and crafts.

3. Our definition of academic work is not restricted to tasks commonly pursued in the teaching of traditional school subjects of the liberal arts (e.g., mathematics, sciences, humanities, languages). Instead, academic work is more broadly conceived to include attempts to master any field of expertise which is based upon a tradition of accumulated public knowledge and which, through activities of practitioners and/or researchers, continually strives to create advanced levels of understanding or

performance in the field. In this sense the mastery of subjects as diverse as electronics, child care, modern dance, or cosmetology can involve academic work.

4. Tasks that students complete in order to succeed in school often involve meaningless rituals, mechanistic reproduction of knowledge, and trivial forms of learning that offer little opportunity for students to use their minds well, or to develop in-depth understanding and critical, creative mastery. Such tasks promote inauthentic forms of achievement. In contrast, authentic academic work involves disciplined inquiry; the integration of knowledge, and producing outcomes that are meaningful to self and others beyond merely demonstrating success in school tasks.[9] Ideally, we would like all forms of schoolwork to be authentic, both because we consider such activities to be more defensible philosophically, but also (as explained later) because they are more likely to enhance student engagement. Technically, however, our definition recognizes the reality that students are often asked to complete inauthentic academic work.[10]

5. Engagement implies more than motivation. Academic motivation usually refers to a general desire or disposition to succeed in academic work and in the more specific tasks of school. Conceivably students can be motivated to perform well in a general sense without being engaged in the specific tasks of school. Engagement in specific tasks may either precede or presume general motivation to succeed. By focusing on the extent to which students demonstrate active interest, effort, and concentration in the specific work that teachers design, engagement calls special attention to the social contexts that help to activate underlying motivation and also to conditions that may generate new motivation.[11]

Research has not advanced to the point where we can verify internal levels of student engagement through quantitative modeling of latent and observed variables. Our future empirical work will provide initial correlational analyses. This paper's discussion of the significance of student engagement and our analysis of factors that can be expected to affect levels of engagement will hopefully generate additional research to operationalize the construct more thoroughly.

Significance

As they discuss challenges of teaching, secondary school teachers consistently raise the issue of how to get students to concentrate, to invest more effort and to take academic work more seriously. Why is this problem so pervasive? The persistence of the engagement problem becomes clearer if we consider the relationship of teacher to student in contrast to professional/client relationships in other professions such as law, engineering, finance, management, or, in some cases, medicine. First, other professionals can often help their clients merely by giving advice about what to do, and the client can often follow the advice without major effort or inconvenience. In contrast, the success of a teacher depends largely upon how much special effort the client (student) invests. The need for serious effort on the part of the student has been demonstrated both by practitioners' claims and by analytic and empirical research (Cusick, 1973; Cohen, 1988; Powell et al., 1985; Sedlak et al.). Carroll's (1963) widely cited model of school learning, for example, includes the variable of student perseverance which is consistent with our engagement concept. Empirical studies have shown that variables such as student effort and involvement have effects on student achievement independent of student ability (Grabe, 1982; Grabe & Latta, 1981; Laffey, 1982). If eliciting special student effort is critical to successful teaching, we should give careful attention to the conditions that tend to inspire and inhibit such effort.

While necessary for learning, engagement may not always be seen or felt as a completely positive experience. Actively trying to master new subjects and to solve complex problems may involve anxiety, interpersonal disagreement, frustrating ambiguities, and fatigue. Of course, unengaged students may give only token effort and still succeed in school. That is, they can tune out, complete some of the work with only minimal concentration, and even cheat. But if most of their learning is approached in this manner, it will yield only superficial understanding and short-term retention, unlikely to be applied or transferred beyond a few school tests. The proper cognitive demands of formal education cannot be mastered through passive listening and reading, or through being entertained; they require an engaged student worker.

In other professions the client often recognizes a problem and willingly seeks the help of a professional. The teaching of children, however, is more coercive. Children are told by society that they have a problem (ignorance) that must be solved regardless of whether they feel a need for education. They are subjected to a program of labor which the teacher prescribes and whose benefits are rarely self-evident to the student. These circumstances seem to diminish student investment in mastery of schoolwork.

Other professionals focus on the unique needs of individuals, giving help to one person at a time, but teaching school requires the professional to serve the needs of groups, that is, to treat large numbers of clients (20 to 35 per class) simultaneously. Since individual students vary in the kinds of interaction and activities most likely to generate engagement, teaching large groups magnifies the difficulty of eliciting student effort.

The social roles and developmental dynamics of adolescents also pose roadblocks to their engagement in academic work, as other concerns and activities compete for their attention and energy. Interpersonal issues with parents and peers usually take on added significance as do new forms of sexual relations. Adolescents' expanded opportunities for participation in the adult work force and in extracurricular activities present further alternatives that compete with engagement in academic work.

The significance of student engagement becomes clearer when viewed as an instance of the more general challenge of reducing alienation in modern culture.[12] We can describe relations with other individuals, with objects, with the physical environment, with social institutions, with one's own labor, and even with the supernatural or divine on a scale or continuum. At one extreme, relations can be characterized by detachment, isolation, fragmentation, disconnectedness, estrangement, or powerlessness. These bespeak alienation. At the other extreme, relations have more of a quality of attachment, inclusion, integration, unity, connectedness, empowerment. Alienation literature does not identify a single term to characterize its opposite, but if one term were chosen, engagement seems to capture many of these missing qualities in relations to people, to work, or to the physical environment.

The alienation perspective suggests that when people are stressed, unhappy, unproductive, or embroiled in destructive conflict, there is a good chance that the state of affairs is due to underlying relations of alienation. It further implies that if alienating relations are reduced or minimized, conditions should improve. The assumption, of course, is that relations of alienation diminish our productivity, our peace of mind, and our very dignity as humans. Conversely, relations of engagement enhance quality of life.

The concepts of alienation and engagement can help us to assess quality of life in a variety of contexts, but formal analysis and studies of alienation have concentrated on labor and conditions at the workplace (e.g., Blauner, 1964; Braverman, 1974). Our insistence of the point that success in formal learning requires serious effort by the student suggests that insights about reducing alienation at the workplace may be helpful in discovering how to engage students in academic work.[13]

To summarize, our concern for student engagement in academic work is based (1) on the belief that meaningful, long-lasting, and transferable learning cannot occur without student engagement in the work and (2) on the concern that even if this cannot be conclusively demonstrated, it is socially undesirable for schools to coerce students into alienating forms of work.

Factors That Affect Engagement

Research on how to enhance student engagement in academic work is lacking, but scholarship in psychology, sociology, and studies of schooling suggest the importance of several factors. As indicated in Figure 5–1, we construe engagement in academic work to result largely from three broad factors: students' underlying need for competence, the extent to which they experience legitimate membership in the institution, and the quality of the specific academic tasks they are asked to complete.

FIGURE 5–1.   Factors That Influence Student Engagement in Academic Work

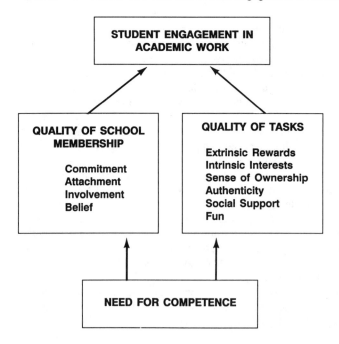

This model is not exhaustive. It does not address a number of factors that may have major influence upon these variables; for example, influences of families and peers on students or influences of the social-political environment on schools or of professional training on teachers. It is important to understand schooling within a broader web of social norms, institutions, and unexamined folkways. Studies by Cusick (1973), McNeil (1986), Metz (1986), Powell and colleagues (1985), and Sedlak and colleagues (1986) offer useful interpretations of how the social context of school life contributes to student disengagement. Here, however, in an effort to discover specific actions that teachers may take to enhance engagement, we have focused most of our attention on qualities of the specific tasks which students are asked to undertake.

NEED FOR COMPETENCE. Most people, especially children, have a powerful need to develop and to express competence. Achieving cognitive understanding and skill mastery—getting it right—are personally rewarding, especially as they enable people to have some impact on the world. When efforts to act competently are met with success, this generates continued investment, and the cycle continues. The need for competence has been recognized as one of the most powerful bases for human action and motivation. Researchers have considered it comparable in significance to sexual energy or to such fundamental needs as autonomy and social affiliation.[14] Mastery of schoolwork offers numerous opportunities for the development of competence, but it can also be expressed through countless other forms such as interpersonal skills; physical development; entrepreneurial projects; or excellence in arts, crafts, and hobbies that schools rarely develop. The question is: What kinds of work must schools design so that students' underlying need for competence will be channeled into academic work?[15] As indicated in Figure 5–1, this depends upon the extent to which students experience full membership in the enterprise of schooling and also upon specific characteristics of the work they do in school.

QUALITY OF SCHOOL MEMBERSHIP. If students are to invest themselves in the forms of mastery required by schools, they must perceive the general enterprise of schooling as legitimate, deserving their committed effort, and honoring them as respected members. Research on students at risk indicates that large numbers of students are so alienated from schools that almost any activities which fall under school sponsorship are suspect (Wehlage et al., 1989; Wheelock, 1986). For many students, school has been a site for failure, rather than success; for arbitrary punishment and ridicule, rather than reason, rewards, and respect; for extinguishing their hope for the future, rather than igniting it; for cultural insult rather than development. For others, the disaffection can seem less damaging; school is a site for meaningless ritual, unrelated to students' serious questions. Thus, before considering the problem of designing specific forms of academic work that engage students, we should stand back and acknowledge the influence of the general social milieu in which the tasks are undertaken.

Building on the work of Merton (1953), Connell (in press) characterizes engagement in social institutions by the model illustrated in Figure 5–2. An individual's bonding to or integration with a social institution involves commitment to both the institution's perceived goals and the means it prescribes for members to pursue the goals. The extremes of engagement and disaffection may be expressed in different patterns. All three forms of engagement (top half of the figure) reflect an acceptance and commitment to the goals of the enterprise. But conformist and innovative patterns differ in their acceptance of the institutionally prescribed means for achieving the goals. The conformist is more engaged with the means than the goals (e.g., students who work hard to please teachers, but care less about mastery of the topics). The innovator accepts goals, but not means, perhaps by refusing to complete homework, but studying hard enough to learn the material. In contrast, the completely engaged or enmeshed pattern finds complete congruence between personal goals and means and those of the institution. At the other end, withdrawal represents rejection of goals and means, with no attempt to appear engaged with any part of the enterprise. A ritualistic response shows passive, superficial cooperation with means, while rejecting goals, and a rebellious pattern shows commitment to apparently different goals and different means (e.g., students who disrupt class in order to humiliate the teacher). Rebellion can include leaving the institution as well. Using this model, it would be easiest to engage "enmeshed" students in specific academic tasks; conformists might show much involvement in the procedures of school, and innovators may tune out of many of the tasks, yet find their own ways of mastering the material. Wehlage et al. (1989) present another perspective on student bonding to schools that builds from the work of Tinto (1987) and others. Bonding or a sense of membership develops through affective, cognitive, and behavioral connections. Schools must demonstrate commitment to the same purposes that students want for themselves. Staff in the school must show sufficient caring and concern for students that students feel a personal attachment to their teachers. A sense of membership cannot develop unless students are involved

FIGURE 5–2.   Patterns of Engagement and Disaffection in Cultural Institutions

ENGAGED AND DISAFFECTED PATTERNS OF ACTION
Self-System Processes

ENGAGEMENT

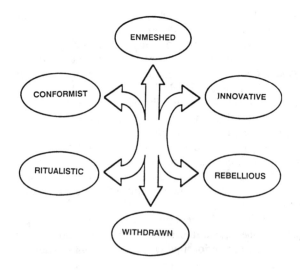

DISAFFECTION

Source: Connell, in press, adapted from Merton, 1953.

in school activities; that is, attend classes, participate in other functions, and complete assigned tasks. Finally, students must believe that the school will in fact help them succeed in learning. For the large proportion of students who "buy into" the schooling process, sense of membership is often taken for granted, but for students at risk, this presents a formidable challenge. How schools might develop the necessary conditions of commitment, attachment, involvement, and belief is beyond the scope of this paper (see Wehlage et al., 1989). Our purpose here is to indicate its importance to student engagement in the more specific work of school. Bonding or membership is a necessary, but not sufficient, condition for student engagement in academic work. In addition, the level of engagement will be affected by the way in which we design specific work tasks.

QUALITY OF TASKS.   Assuming that basic conditions to nurture bonding and sense of membership can be established, how can academic work itself be designed so as to maximize student engagement? The guidelines we identify are extrinsic rewards, intrinsic interest, sense of ownership, authenticity, social support, and fun.

Extrinsic rewards.   Committed effort should increase if mastery of the tasks is accompanied by rewards such as high grades, admission to higher education, attractive jobs, increased income, social approval, and status. What may appear to be powerful extrinsic rewards for some students, however, may have no effect on or actually decrease the engagement of others. Only when students value the rewards, perceive that academic achievement will lead to them, and believe that their own hard work will result in academic achievement, would we expect student engagement to increase.[16] Another problem is that the powerful extrinsic rewards such as jobs and income tend to be distributed for long-term, cumulative effort rather than engagement in specific daily tasks; this makes it is difficult for teachers to offer impressive extrinsic rewards. Nevertheless, many instructional tasks can be designed to produce social approval, official credentials (grades), public displays of impressive accomplishment, and special privileges.

Intrinsic interest.   Regardless of perceived extrinsic rewards, students may invest or withdraw from learning, depending on how interesting they find the material. Interest refers to the fact that some topics and activities are more stimulating, fascinating, and enjoyable to work on than others.[17] Whether some school subjects are generally found to be more interesting than others is an empirical question, but interest will probably be enhanced when tasks permit expression of diverse forms of talent. Schooling concentrates primarily upon abstract verbal and mathematical competence, to the neglect of aesthetic, interpersonal, intrapersonal, kinesthetic, and spatial competencies (Gardner, 1983). Students may be interested in developing competence in several of these dimensions. Limiting school tasks to a narrow range diminishes the opportunity to respond to students' intrinsic interests and to build their competence upon their prior knowledge. What will be interesting probably depends not simply upon the subjects or topics, but largely upon the way the topics are approached by the teacher, the student's prior experience with similar material, and other factors discussed in the paragraphs that follow.

Adult learners also acknowledge (perhaps more so than youth) the value and significance of academic study for reasons other than interest and extrinsic benefit. That is, it can be considered "worthwhile" to understand the logic of mathematics, the process of scientific inquiry, or the foundations of culture, even when these subjects may be less interesting or lead to less impressive extrinsic rewards than other subjects. The belief that mastery of certain topics, skills, or crafts can be not only interesting, but intrinsically valuable or worthwhile will also enhance engagement.

Sense of ownership.   Engagement with and internalization of knowledge depend to a large degree on the opportunities students have to "own" the work. Rather than toiling always under predetermined routines to master skills and knowledge dictated arbitrarily from school authorities, students need some influence on the conception, execution, and evaluation of the work itself.[18] At a minimum this entails flexibility over the pace and procedures of learning, opportunity for students to ask questions and to study topics they consider important, and students' constructing and producing knowledge in their own language rather than merely reproducing the language of others. There are, of course, important limits on the extent to which students can control the learning of academic subjects. Certain facts, definitions, concepts, algorithms, and processes of verification must be assimilated according to predetermined standards of the fields of knowledge to be taught. But even for this kind of learning, students' sense of ownership can be enhanced if learning tasks offer some autonomy in the way students study and apply the material.

Authenticity.   Students often explain their disengagement by calling schoolwork irrelevant, that is, unrelated to issues, competencies, or concerns of the "real" world. Why devote effort to the mastery of knowledge that seems necessary to success only in school, but in no other aspects of life? We use the term "authenticity" to suggest qualities that render work real, meaningful, useful, and valuable not simply in order to succeed in school, but to achieve important human purposes beyond school as well. Extrinsic rewards, intrinsic interest, and ownership may contribute to the authenticity of tasks, but other features are also important.

The most important general feature of authentic work is that it has value and meaning beyond the instructional context. To the extent that the messages students speak and write, the products they make, and the performances they complete (music, dance, sports) make an impact on others and upon students themselves beyond certifying students' level of competence or compliance, these activities gain in authenticity. Writing to persuade a friend or to publicize one's views in a letter to the editor is more authentic than is writing only to show a teacher that one is capable of organizing a coherent paragraph. Studying the habits of animals or fish when one is also responsible for their care is more authentic than is learning about their behavior from texts.[19]

Authenticity may be enhanced when feedback on the results of one's efforts is prompt and nonmystified. Some activities such as music, sports, or mechanical repair provide almost instant and clear evidence of success or failure. One need not wait for a teacher's response to learn whether you got a hit in baseball, whether the sweater you knitted fits, or whether you remembered your lines in the play. In contrast, after completing abstract academic tasks, the feedback students receive is often much delayed and difficult to comprehend (What did I do wrong in this homework assignment and why was it wrong?).

Authenticity is also enhanced when the conditions of work allow for flexible use of time and cooperation. These two characteristics are seen as critical for competent performance in adult workplaces, but generally they are denied to students in school. Adults often rely on collaboration with others to accomplish difficult tasks, but students are usually required to learn and to prove their competence without help from peers. Adult work is usually scheduled flexibly to correspond to the demands of the job, but students must learn within standard time frames such as five 50-minute periods per week.

Social support. Students are surrounded by individuals and institutions that send messages of support and disapproval for engagement in different kinds of work. These messages affect both the extrinsic rewards and intrinsic interests and values that, in turn, influence engagement. Beyond these messages, however, other forms of social support are critical to student engagement.

Learning involves risk taking: making mistakes and trying again. Unless one can trust teachers and peers to offer support for the hard work of making and correcting mistakes while trying to assimilate new material, the learning process can be too punishing to try. Especially in a society as competitive as ours, the social disrespect that often accompanies failure can suppress engagement in academic work and divert the basic need for competence to alternative, psychologically more comfortable activities.

If students are to build the confidence and the willingness to invest themselves, their participation in academic tasks must be accompanied by social support from teachers and peers.[20] Support must not, however, be contingent on student success in daily learning tasks; it is needed most as security to *fail* in the short run so that success in the long run becomes more likely. In addition to support from teachers, cooperative learning among peers also offers forms of social support to counteract alienating aspects of competitive learning.[21]

Academic success must not be the sole criterion for social support. There is more to life than academic achievement. Students' moral worth and dignity must be affirmed through other avenues as well, such as nonacademic contact between staff and students—in athletics, music, outings, and personal advising. This sense of caring is critical both for student investment in the specific tasks of learning and also for developing the more general sense of attachment to and membership in the school.

Fun. By emphasizing qualities that help to generate serious effort and concentration on academic tasks, we must not overlook the importance of fun, play, and humor. Learning can be hard work, but to sustain engagement, the tasks should also provide opportunities for lighthearted interaction, for playlike and imaginative activity. Fun reduces the distress of the intense pressure to succeed that some students may feel and the boredom of unchallenging, but perhaps necessary, routines. When it is unfeasible to arrange in advance for fun in specific academic tasks, it can be planned for other times during a lesson or the school day, and this should enhance student sense of bonding or membership in the school as a whole.

In summary, we have indicated a number of guidelines for the design of academic work that should maximize student engagement. Ideally, plans for student assignments, projects, and classroom discourse should indicate how they will provide extrinsic rewards, cultivate intrinsic interests, permit a sense of student ownership, maximize authenticity, ensure social support, and have some fun.[22] This may be a lot to ask of every activity, but if student engagement is to be taken seriously, criteria such as these should play a prominent role in the design of instruction.

CONCLUSION

Dominant concerns in the educational reform movement and in effective schools research have neglected one of the problems most critical to the improvement of high schools: how to engage students in academic work. Engagement is defined as the student's psychological investment in mastering the knowledge, skills, and crafts that academic work is intended to produce. The significance of this problem is illustrated through the relationship of professional to client in teaching versus other professions, the unique social-psychological characteristics in adolescents' roles, and the more general problem of alienation in modern culture. A conceptual model is presented to identify factors which schools and teachers might effect to enhance student engagement in academic work.

Based on the assumption that all humans share a fundamental need to develop competence, the model indicates that educators can enhance student engagement in academic work by attention to two general factors: building a sense of student membership in the school at large and designing academic tasks to maximize extrinsic rewards, intrinsic interests, sense of ownership, authenticity, social support, and fun. Studies at the National Center on Effective Secondary Schools will offer further analyses and findings on the relevance of these and other variables to secondary school effectiveness.

REFERENCES

AMES, C. (1984).   Competitive, cooperative, and individualistic goal structures: A cognitive-motivational analysis. In R. Ames & C. Ames (Eds.), *Research on motivation in education. Vol. 1, Student motivation.* Orlando, FL: Academic Press.

ARCHBALD, D. A., & NEWMANN, F. M. (1988).   *Beyond standardized testing: Assessing authentic academic achievement in the secondary school.* Reston, VA: National Association of Secondary School Principals.

BISHOP, J. H. (1989).   Why the apathy in American high schools? *Educational Researcher, 18*(1), 6–10.

BLAUNER, R. (1964).   *Alienation and freedom: The factory worker and his industry.* Chicago: University of Chicago Press.

BRAVERMAN, H. (1974).   *Labor and monopoly capital.* New York: Monthly Review Press.

BROOKOVER, W. B., BEADY, C., FLOOD, P., & SCHWEITZER, J. (1979).   *School systems and student achievement: Schools make a difference.* New York: Praeger.

BROPHY, J. (1987).   Synthesis of research on strategies for motivating students to learn. *Educational leadership, 45*(2), 40–48.

BRYK, A. S., & DRISCOLL, M. E. (1988).   *The high school as community: Contextual influences, and consequences for students and teachers.* Madison, WI: National Center on Effective Secondary Schools.

BRYK, A. S., LEE, V., & SMITH, J. B. (1989).   *High school organization and its effects on teachers and students: An interpretative summary of the research.* Paper prepared for Invitational Conference at the Robert M. LaFollette Institute of Public Affairs, University of Wisconsin-Madison.

CARROLL, J. B. (1963).   A model of school learning. *Teachers College Record, 64,* 723–733.

CHUBB, J. E. (Winter 1988).   Why the current wave of school reform will fail. *The Public Interest, 90*, 28–49.

CHUBB, J. E., & MOE, T. M. (December 1988).   Politics, markets, and the organization of schools. *American Political Science Review, 82*(4), 1065–87.

COHEN, D. K. (1988).   *Teaching practice: plus ca change....* East Lansing, MI: National Center for Research on Teacher Education.

COLEMAN, J. S., & HOFFER, T. (1987).   *Public and private high schools: The impact of communities.* New York: Basic Books.

COLEMAN, J. S., HOFFER, T., & KILGORE, S. (1982).   *High school achievement: Public, Catholic, and private schools compared.* New York: Basic Books.

CONNELL, J. P. (November 1990).   Context, self and action: A motivational analysis of self-system processes across the life-span. In D. Cicchetti (Ed.), *The self in transition: Infancy to childhood.* Chicago: University of Chicago Press.

CORCORAN, T. B. (1985).   Effective secondary schools. In R. Kyle (Ed.), *Reaching for excellence: Effective schools source book.* Washington, D.C.: National Institute of Education.

CORCORAN, T. B., & WILSON, B. L. (October 1986).   *The search for successful secondary schools: The first three years of the secondary school recognition program.* Philadelphia: Research for Better Schools.

CSIKSZENTMIHALYI, M., & LARSON, R. (1984).   *Being adolescent: Conflict and growth in the teenage years.* New York: Basic Books.

CUSICK, P. A. (1973).   *Inside high school: The students' world.* New York: Holt, Rinehart and Winston.

DECHARMS, R. (1984).   Motivation enhancement in educational settings. In R. Ames & C. Ames (Eds.), *Research on motivation in education.* Vol. 1: *Student motivation.* Orlando, FL: Academic Press.

DECI, E. L. (1975).   *Intrinsic motivation.* New York: Plenum Press.

DECI, E. L., & RYAN, R. M. (1985).   *Intrinsic motivation and self-determination in human behavior.* New York: Plenum Press.

DWECK, C. S. (1986).   Motivational processes affecting learning. *American Psychologist, 41*(10), 1040–48.

EDMONDS, R. R., & FREDERIKSEN, J. R. (1979).   *Search for effective schools: The identification and analysis of city schools that are instructionally effective for poor children,* ED 170396. MA: ERIC Document Reproduction Service.

EKSTROM, R. B., GOERTZ, M. E., & ROCK, D. A. (1988).   *Education and American youth: The impact of the high school experience.* Philadelphia: Falmer Press.

ERICKSON, F. A. (1987).   Transformation and school success: The politics and culture of educational achievement. *Anthropology and Education Quarterly, 18*(3), 335–56.

FULLAN, M., MILES, M. B., & TAYLOR, G. (Spring 1980).   Organization development in schools: The state of the art. *Review of Educational Research, 50*(1), 121–83.

GARDNER, H. (1983).   *Frames of mind: The theory of multiple intelligences.* New York: Basic Books.

GRABE, M. (1982).   Effort strategies in a mastery instructional system: The quantification of effort and the impact of effort on achievement. *Contemporary Educational Psychology, 7*, 327–33.

GRABE, M., & LATTA, R. M. (1981).   Cumulative achievement in a mastery instructional system: The impact of differences in resultant achievement motivation and persistence. *American Educational Research Journal, 18*(1), 7–13.

HACKMAN, J. R. (1986).   The psychology of self-management in organizations. In M. S. Pallak & R. O. Perloff (Eds.), *Psychology and work: Productivity, change, and employment.* Washington, D.C.: American Psychological Association.

HAERTEL, E. H., JAMES, T., & LEVIN, H. M. (Eds.). (1987).   *Comparing public and private schools.* Vol. 2, *School achievement.* Philadelphia: Falmer Press.

HUBERMAN, A. M., & MILES, M. B. (1984).   *Innovation up close: How school improvement works.* New York: Plenum Press.

LAFFEY, J. M. (1982).   The assessment of involvement with school work among urban high school students. *Journal of Educational Psychology, 74*,1, 62–71.

LIGHTFOOT, S. L. (1983).   *The good high school: Portraits of character and culture.* New York: Basic Books.

MAEHR, M. L. (1984).   Meaning and motivation: Toward a theory of personal investment. In R. E. Ames & C. Ames (Eds.), *Research on motivation in education.* Vol. 1, *Student motivation,* (pp. 115–44). Orlando, FL: Academic Press.

MARSH, D. D., & BOWMAN, G. A. (1989).   State-initiated top-down versus bottom-up reform. *Educational Policy.* Vol. 3, No. 3, 195–216.

MARSHALL, H. H. (1988).   Work or learning: Implications of classroom metaphors. *Educational Researcher, 17*(9), 9–16.

MCNEIL, L. M. (1986).   *Contradictions of control: School structure and school knowledge.* New York: Routledge & Kegan Paul.

MERTON, R. (1953).   *Social theory and social structure.* London: Free Press of Glendale.

METZ, M. H. (1986).   *Different by design.* New York: Routledge & Kegan Paul.

MILES, M. B., LOUIS, K. S., ROSENBLUM, S., CIPOLLONE, A., & FARRAR, E. (November 1986).   *Improving the urban high school: A preliminary report. Lessons for managing implementation.* Boston: University of Massachusetts, Center for Survey Research.

MOOS, R. H. (1986).   Work as a human context. In M. S. Pallak & R. O. Perloff (Eds.), *Psychology and work: Productivity, change, and employment.* Washington, D.C.: American Psychological Association.

NEWMANN, F. M. (1981).   Reducing alienation in high schools: Implications of theory. *Harvard Educational Review, 51*(4), 546–64.

NEWMANN, F. M., & AARCHBALD, D. A. (in press).   The nature of authentic academic achievement. In H. Berlak (Ed.), *Assessing achievement: Toward the development of a new science of educational testing.* Albany, NY: SUNY Press.

OGBU, J. U. (1974).   *The next generation: An ethnography of an urban neighborhood.* New York: Academic Press.

PENG, S. (1987).   Effective high schools: What are their attributes? In J. J. Lane and H. J. Walbergh (Eds.), *Effective school leadership.* Berkeley, CA: McCutchan.

POWELL, A. G., FARRAR, E., & COHEN, D. (1985).   *The shopping mall high school: Winners and losers in the educational marketplace.* Boston: Houghton Mifflin.

PURKEY, S. C., & SMITH, M. S. (1983).   Effective schools: A review. *The Elementary School Journal, 83*(4), 427–52.

RESNICK, L. B. (1987).   Learning in school and out. *Educational Researcher, 16*(9), 13–20.

REYNOLDS, D. (Ed.). (1985).   *Studying school effectiveness.* Philadelphia: Falmer Press.

ROSENHOLTZ, S. J. (1989). *Teachers' workplace: The social organization of schools.* New York: Longman.

RUTTER, M., MAUGHAN, B., MORTIMORE, P., & OUSTON, J. (1979). *Fifteen thousand hours: Secondary schools and their effects on children.* Cambridge, MA: Harvard University Press.

SEDLAK, M. W., WHEELER, C. W., PULLIN, D. C., & CUSICK, P. A. (1986). *Selling students short: Classroom bargains and academic reform in the American high school.* New York: Teachers College Press.

SMITH, M. B. (1968). Competence and socialization. In J. A. Clausen (Ed.), *Socialization and Society.* Boston: Little, Brown.

STIPEK, D. (1986). Children's motivation to learn. In T. M. Tomlinson and H. J. Walberg (Eds.), *Academic work and educational excellence.* Berkeley, CA: McCutchan.

TINTO, V. (1987). *Leaving college: Rethinking the causes and cures of student attrition.* Chicago: University of Chicago Press.

WEHLAGE, G. G., RUTTER, R. A., SMITH, G. A., LESKO, N., & FERNANDEZ, R. R. (1989). *Reducing the risk: Schools as communities of support.* Philadelphia: Falmer Press.

WHEELOCK, A. (1986). *The way out: Student exclusion practices in Boston middle schools.* Boston: Massachusetts Advocacy Center.

WHITE, R. W. (1959). Motivation reconsidered: The concept of competence. *Psychological Review, 66,* 297–333.

WITTE, J. F., & WALSH, D. J. (1989). *A systematic test of the effective schools model,* unpublished manuscript. University of Wisconsin-Madison.

ENDNOTES

[1]This paper was prepared at the National Center on Effective Secondary Schools, supported by the U.S. Department of Education, Office of Educational Research and Improvement (Grant No. G-00869007-89) and by the Wisconsin Center for Education Research, School of Education, University of Wisconsin-Madison. The opinions expressed in this publication are those of the author and do not necessarily reflect the views of the supporting agencies.

[2]Bryk and Driscoll (1988); Bryk, Lee, and Smith (1989); Chubb (1988); Coleman and Hoffer (1987); Coleman, Hoffer, and Kilgore (1982); Corcoran (1985); Corcoran and Wilson (1986); Ekstrom, Goertz, and Rock (1988); Haertel, James, and Levin (1987); Lightfoot (1983); Metz (1986); Peng (1987); Purkey and Smith (1983); Rutter, Maughan, Mortimore, and Ouston (1979); Wehlage, Rutter, Smith, Lesko, and Fernandez (1989); Witte and Walsh (1989).

[3]Since 1980 important progress has been made in establishing national databases on U.S. high schools, their students and staffs, through the HS&B and NELS 88 projects of the National Center on Education Statistics and surveys conducted by the National Assessment of Educational Progress and the College Board.

[4]As Witte and Walsh (1989) point out, variables within the general list tend to correlate so highly with one another that it becomes difficult to isolate contributions of individual variables.

[5]Design limitations such as small numbers of schools (e.g., 12 schools in Rutter et al., 1979) or small numbers of students per school (36 students in the HS&B database) may have inhibited high-quality studies of school effectiveness at the secondary level.

[6]The collection of papers in Reynolds (1985) indicates the diversity in outcomes that may be accepted as evidence of school effectiveness.

[7]Coleman and Hoffer (1987) found that Catholic schools are generally more successful in this regard than public schools.

[8]A new perspective on effective schools should also give more attention to the issues of community and autonomy. It is difficult to build commitment to clear, shared goals in high schools that suffer from fragmentation (Newmann, 1981; Powell, Farrar, and Cohen, 1985). Writing from quite different perspectives, Bryk and Driscoll (1988), Coleman and Hoffer (1987), Rosenholtz (1989), and Wehlage et al. (1989) suggest that community building within the school may be one of the most critical tasks facing high schools today. Initial literature on effective schools also paid little attention to the school's relations within the broader network of district, state, and national policy. More recent research has clarified the enormous impact of education policy and agencies beyond the school, but also the importance of institutional autonomy to high productivity (Chubb, 1988; Chubb and Moe, 1988). Further research is needed, however, on the arenas in which school autonomy is most critical (e.g., staffing, curriculum, student discipline policy) and how these may be balanced with external control in those areas in which agencies beyond the school are entrusted to enforce the public interest (e.g., in equity, racial integration, comparable assessment standards).

[9]The concept of authentic academic achievement was recently proposed in Archbald and Newmann (1988) and refined in Newmann and Archbald (in press).

[10]The prevalence of inauthentic academic work in schools is due in part to our limited visions of curriculum and teaching, to organizational constraints that limit opportunities to make learning more "real," and to the fact that some kinds of learning may inevitably require forms of repeated practice, memorization, and other forms of labor that seem inauthentic.

[11]Syntheses of research on motivating students to learn (Brophy, 1987; Stipek, 1986) distinguish between motivation to perform and motivation to learn. Discussions of the latter include factors that we see as critical to engagement.

[12]Newmann's (1981) study of the implications of philosophical, psychological, and sociological literature on alienation for high school reform offers a more detailed analysis of this topic.

[13]Marshall (1988) observes that using the metaphor of work to describe learning can have unfortunate implications for how teachers relate to students and how students regard the process of learning. This is because the properties of adult work settings often involve lack of worker autonomy and labor for the profit of others, rather than self-improvement and other conditions that may inhibit meaningful learning. Our use of the term "academic work" is not meant to suggest that schools should replicate dominant conditions of adult labor, but instead to emphasize the point that meaningful learning requires serious effort by the learner and further that the design of the work tasks themselves must aim toward enhancing engagement in mastery, rather than simply securing compliance in task completion. We would agree with Marshall that the characteristics of academic work that engages students would differ from characteristics in the typical work and recreational settings she discusses.

[14]See the original research on "effectance" by White (1959) the synthesis on competence by Smith (1968), DeCharms's discussion of agency (1984), and Connell's (1990) analysis of motivation.

[15]Dweck (1986) explained how students' social cognitions about their competence affect motivation to learn. Stipek (1986) described how particular classroom activities can affect these cognitions positively and negatively and thereby affect engagement. Stipek's review of motivation research also supports our conclusions below related to intrinsic interests and student sense of ownership over the work.

[16]Bishop (1989), for example, claims that job placement and salary levels offer few extrinsic rewards for academic engagement, because they are not tied to students' achievement

levels in high school. He also argues that an economic system that provides only a competitive reward structure (a zero-sum game where winners emerge only by creating losers) offers no incentive for students in the bottom half to become academically engaged. Ogbu (1974) also showed how students' perceptions of future economic opportunity affects engagement in school.

[17]See Deci (1975) and Maehr (1984) for syntheses of research on intrinsic motivation.

[18]The need for a sense of control over one's work has been established in the literature on alienation (Blauner, 1964; Braverman, 1974), motivation (DeCharms, 1984; Deci & Ryan, 1985; Connell, in press), and self-management at the workplace (Hackman, 1986).

[19]Resnick's (1987) analysis of learning in school versus more practical problem solving out of school reflects a similar conception of authenticity.

[20]Students from minority cultures or low status groups face special threats to self-esteem from the dominant culture. Social support through culturally responsive pedagogy is necessary to transform student opposition into engagement (Erickson, 1987).

[21]Moos's (1986) summary of literature on workplace conditions indicates that social acceptance and cohesion produces higher worker morale and less stress. See also Ames (1984) on the motivational aspects of competitive, individualistic, and cooperative reward structures and Wehlage et al. (1989) for an extended treatment of the importance of social support through school membership.

[22]The factors are consistent with conditions that define a flow experience according to Csikzentmihalyi and Larson (1984). In these experiences a person concentrates on mastering a specific challenge which has usually been voluntarily chosen. The challenge demands extending one's skills to new levels of complexity, but not so far as to generate extreme anxiety. To meet the challenge one must abide by certain "rules" of interaction or discipline, and the process entails concrete feedback on the degree of success.

6

EFFECTIVE SCHOOLS FROM A BRITISH PERSPECTIVE: RESEARCH AND PRACTICE

Peter Mortimore
University of Lancaster, England

INTRODUCTION

The search for *effective* schools has long been a regular activity for those members of the British public who live in areas of the country where the local school boards (local educational authorities) have permitted choice and for those parents who have chosen to pay for their children to attend private (curiously, more commonly called "public") schools. Perhaps surprisingly, this conviction was not shared by those academic researchers who have queried the possible influence of the school as a social institution. However, for the last 20 years a number of British educational researchers have been questioning whether, despite the well-known arguments to the contrary, similar schools can exert differential effects on students.

In order to understand the issues concerning British schools, it is necessary to comprehend the social context in which schools operate. Recently, the British context has been modified as a result of a major government intervention. This intervention, in the form of a new act of Parliament (The Education Reform Act, 1988), has sought to change a number of critical aspects of educational practice. Essentially, it has sought to provide *all* parents with a choice of school and removed the right of school boards to restrict entry, except when the school is full to the capacity of its physical limits. The act has also introduced the necessity for all, except the smallest, schools to have delegated authority over their total budgets (site-based management). It has thus given authority to the principal (head teacher) and the governing body (a group of trustees made up of parents, teachers, and those representing the community and school board) of the school to determine the nature and number of courses offered in the school, the size of the establishment of teachers and other posts, and given them numerous other powers and responsibilities. At the same time the act has removed some of the responsibilities traditionally held by the school through the establishment of a national curriculum and an associated series of assessments to be undertaken by all students in their second, sixth, ninth, and eleventh years of schooling.

A further section of the act—with as yet unknown significance for those interested in effective schools—enables schools to "opt out" of the jurisdiction of the local school board. At the time of writing, a small number of schools, after proposals from their governing bodies and positive ballots from parents, have opted out. Such schools now receive a comparable level of funding direct from the national government and are not subject, in any way, to their former school board.

As might be expected, such radical changes have evoked powerful responses from British educationists. Before the act was passed, these frequently took the form of organized opposition. Since the act's incorporation into the law of the land, it has been accepted with varying degrees of enthusiasm. (See McLure, 1988; Simon, 1988.) Principals, teachers, and school board officials—both superintendents and consultants (the British terms are education officers and inspectors/advisors)—have been given the tasks of implementing the changes made necessary by the act.

This is the educational context in Britain today. In order, however, for American readers to understand the value of British studies of school effectiveness, it may be helpful to sketch out some of the key features of the British system and to highlight the main differences from the systems found in most of the states. Accordingly, the remaining sections of this chapter will consist of a brief section describing some of the key features of the British system. (For the sake of brevity, the British system described will be that as operated in England and Wales. Comparative educationists will know that this is different to those operated in Scotland and Northern Ireland.) This will be followed by the exposition of, and answers to, three questions:

What are the methods and findings of British research on effective schools?
What have been the main findings from this research?
What has been the reaction of practitioners to this research?

KEY FEATURES OF THE BRITISH SYSTEM

As with any educational system, the British pattern of provision is rooted in complex historical and cultural developments. Some recent changes—brought about by the Educational Reform Act of 1988—have already been described. The following is a list of those features which have little or no counterpart in the systems operating in different parts of the United States.

Governance

The basic system of organization derives from an education act which became law in 1944. Powers and responsibilities are divided between a number of different partners: the secretary of state for education and science, 109 elected local education authorities (like large school boards but elected on a party-political basis as part of general local government arrangements), and individual schools.

The secretary of state has general powers to oversee the system and specific powers on particular aspects of it. Local education authorities are responsible for providing schools and services, employing teachers, formulating policies, and ensuring the quality of the education on offer. In recent years, however, their authority has been reduced considerably by the extra powers taken by the secretary of state.

Individual schools are led by a head teacher (the principal—customarily a curriculum leader and former practitioner rather than an administrator) and are overseen by a governing body. Head teachers are now appointed by governing bodies after national advertisement. The superintendent (chief education officer) of the school board has the right to offer advice but not to veto appointments. Contracts are normally permanent but, very recently, the first time-limited contracts have been agreed. Unlike the United States, it is not possible for head teachers to be moved between posts between the school board. Some head teachers choose to apply for different posts, but this will involve competing with other candidates for advertised positions.

Finance

The education service is financed from a variety of sources. National government contributes approximately 50 percent, mainly through nonearmarked payments. The remainder is raised by the local authorities through a form of property tax known as "Rates." (This is due to be replaced by a poll tax to be known as the community charge). Traditionally, the amount of money raised by local authorities was limited only by how much local citizens were prepared to pay but, in recent years, high-spending local authorities have been limited by "clawback" penalties and by "rate capping."

Despite these regulatory mechanisms, revenue spending on education varies considerably from one authority to another. The latest figures show that the highest spending authority had a unit cost of $2,233 for each elementary student and of $3,588 for each secondary one. These figures contrast with $1,193 and $1,752 for the lowest authority.

Supervision

Britain has a long tradition of inspection with the first of "Her Majesty's Inspectors" being appointed 150 years ago. Currently, there are nearly 500 of these in post, drawn from successful careers in education and, increasingly, with business and commercial experience.

H. M. inspectors report to the secretary of state and inform him or her of the state of education in schools. Formal inspections are used to gather information, as are informal visits. A formal inspection will be carried out by a team of as many as 10 or 12 inspectors visiting the school over several weeks. Reports on formal inspections are published and, frequently, commented upon by national and local press. In addition to formal inspections, H. M. inspectors visit schools informally and offer advice to heads and teachers. They also organize a series of in-service training courses.

In addition to H. M. inspectors, all local authorities employ their own inspectors or, as they are sometimes called, advisors. They are involved in the advising on the selection of teachers, developmental projects, and in-service training. While they do not have the same status as H. M. inspectors, they have, in the past, enjoyed considerable influence over schools through access to special funds and, in some cases, patronage over senior appointments. It remains to be seen whether, in the light of increasing site management and reduced funds at the school district level, this influence will decline.

In a number of authorities, some individual schools are also involved in self-evaluation exercises: monitoring their own progress and reporting back to governors. There are also six, government-funded pilot schemes on teacher appraisal currently being undertaken. A national scheme is likely to be introduced within the next couple of years.

Structure and Scale of the Service

There are approximately 6.8 million students in English schools taught by just over 401,500 teachers. The average student-teacher ratio is 22:1 for elementary schools and 15.4:1 for secondary schools.

The usual form of provision is for elementary schools to take students from age 5 to age 11 and for high schools to take them from 11 to either age 16—when 50 percent leave school—or age 18. There are two common variations, however. A system divided into three, rather than two, with middle schools catering for students of 9 to 13 years and a different system—also divided into three—with students who remain in education at age 16, transferring into colleges for the remaining two years.

The concept of "grade" is not used in Britain in the same way as in the United States. Almost all students move up each year with peers who are of a similar age. The only standard exception to this system is where elementary schools—either for philosophical reasons or because of small numbers—group students of two or three different year groups together.

Over the last ten years schools have been subject to considerable demographic change. In some parts of the country, enrollments have declined by up to 40 percent. Many authorities have sought to close schools and rationalize provision. The procedures for closure, however, are slow and cumbersome and, in each case, a final decision rests with the secretary of state.

Curriculum and Assessment

Until the advent of the national curriculum (noted earlier), the curriculum taught in each school was the prerogative of the principal and the teachers. This meant that there were considerable variations between elementary schools in what was taught to students. At secondary level, the existence of a formal system of "public examinations" meant there was much greater standardization.

The public examinations system has dominated secondary education for over 100 years. It has considerable advantages for educational researchers looking for standardized assessments but, in other ways, acts as a constraint on innovation. The General Certificate of Secondary Education (GCSE) is a single-subject examination taken after five years secondary study (at the end of grade 10). Students usually take seven or eight subjects. The top three grades are accepted as a sign of sufficient achievement for further study. A commonly used benchmark is the acquisition of high grades in five subjects. This, however, is achieved by only about 25 percent of the student body.

The Advanced Level General Certificate of Education (A-level) is also a single-subject examination. It is usually taken in two or three subjects by 18-year-olds (grade 12) after two years specialist study. Admittance to prestigious universities will depend on the achievement of three high grades in this highly competitive examination.

There are also many other examinations that British students can take. Some are variations of the academic exams but most involve at least some vocational content. For instance the Business and Technician Education Council (BTEC) courses (as the name implies) include examinations in a number of vocational skills. Likewise, the Certificate of Prevocational Education (CPVE), which strives to equip young people with basic skills and personal and social competences for the world of work, includes examinations as part of its assessment repertoire. In general, courses like these depend less on the traditional final examination than on a range of assessment techniques, some of which involve the student in carefully structured self-appraisal.

There are plans to rationalize all vocational education qualifications into a single unified framework. Recently, a new initiative in assessment—the production of records of achievement—based on involvement of students in self-assessment and recording techniques has been adopted within schools. Unlike traditional examinations the emphasis of records of achievement has been on success rather than failure.

These then are some of the main features of British education where there are likely to be major differences with systems common in the United States. There are, of course, many other topical issues debated in British schools. Some of these, such as race inequality, the role of special education, and issues concerning gender, mirror similar debates in the American systems.

WHAT ARE THE METHODS AND FINDINGS OF BRITISH RESEARCH ON EFFECTIVE SCHOOLS?

Over the last 20 or so years, a considerable number of British studies have addressed, directly or indirectly, questions concerning the effectiveness of individual schools. The following description of British studies is not meant to be an exhaustive account but rather an illustrative summary of this work. (For a fuller list, see Rutter, 1983, or Reid et al., 1987.)

Power and colleagues (1967) were some of the earliest researchers to investigate school effects. In a crude attempt to control for intelligence, the research team excluded schools taking the most academic pupils yet still found substantial differences between schools in the delinquency rates of students. Differences between schools remained stable over a six-year period. Furthermore, they were shown to be relatively independent of the catchment area in which the schools were sited, although the absence of data collected before the students entered secondary schools remains a methodological weakness. Unfortunately, due to disagreement with one of the teachers' unions over early publication of results, this study was never completed. Its chief benefit, therefore, was in the way it opened up the research questions to subsequent researchers.

Unlike Power, Brimer et al. (1978) chose to focus on the academic achievement of students. Although the research team was able to collect information on the prior achievement of only a small subsample of their 2,650 student subjects (drawn from 44 schools), it was able to use measures of parents' occupation and educational levels to control for differences in home background. In a study of public examination results the team found substantial differences between schools especially in subjects like science and mathematics which, unlike reading, are not generally taught or even "coached" in the home.

Both delinquency and academic achievement, together with attendance and student behavior, were included in the measures adopted by the high school study with which I was involved (Rutter et al., 1979). This study was based on only a small sample of inner-city schools but used a wide range of data collection methods in order to address the question of whether—since allowance had been made for variations in student intake—there were differences in effectiveness between individual schools. The controls for intake factors adopted by this study, such as the use of socioeconomic background, students' prior test scores, attendance records from elementary school, and behavior questionnaires completed by elementary school teachers, were more comprehensive than were those adopted by previous British research. The study, thus, was important in that it developed a feasible methodology to evaluate the effectiveness of schools. Nevertheless, it was still criticized for "the paucity of intake measures."

Using a small sample of schools in a totally different environment, Reynolds (1982) examined the impact of schools on attendance, attainment, and delinquency in a Welsh mining community over six years. Reynolds did not have intake data on individual students, but the team collected systematic evidence about the catchments of the schools that showed that they had roughly comparable intakes. Major variations in rates of attainment, delinquency, and attendance were found, as was a difference in student unemployment rates four months after leaving school. These differences remained relatively stable over a period of six years.

Although these British studies, carried out prior to the 1980s, attracted methodological criticisms, their impact on researchers stimulated the development of a number of methodological and statistical developments which enabled the question of school effectiveness to be addressed in a much more sophisticated way (Aitkin et al., 1981; Gray, 1981; Goldstein, 1984, 1987).

Gray, McPherson, and Raffe (1983) used a sample of Scottish schools and sought to examine the effect of the varied histories of the schools—with their different forms of organization—on student achievement. Their main source of data was a survey of over 20,000 former students from nearly all Scottish schools. Social class measures were collected and other sources of information were drawn upon in order to address the question of school effects. Their general finding was that given schools achieved more or less well than predictions based on social class suggested. However, they also found that schools varied according to the criteria (academic achievement, truancy, satisfaction, punishment) adopted.

The study by Willms and Cuttance (1985) consisted of a secondary analysis of data from the 1977 Scottish School Leavers Survey. Using a subsample of 15 secondary schools, the researchers adopted multilevel modeling techniques to examine differences in academic attainment (English and arithmetic) while controlling for student intake variations. Their measures included verbal reasoning quotients, fathers' occupation, number of siblings, and mothers' education.

In choosing to study elementary schools, my own research team (Mortimore et al., 1988) moved outside the seeming British tradition of studying secondary schools. We followed a cohort of nearly 2,000 students through four years of schooling from age 7 to age 11. Measures of progress included reading, mathematics, writing, attendance, behavior, and attitude to schooling. Data were also collected on speaking skills and on the students' attitudes to themselves as learners. Very full data were collected on the students' backgrounds including their language and ethnic group, the occupations of their parents, whether they received welfare benefit (free school meals), family size, health record, and kindergarten and early school experience. In addition, prior attainment in reading, mathematics and writing, and a behavior rating were also collected for each student. Methods of analysis recognized the three levels of data (school, class, and individual student) by the use of multilevel modeling techniques. (For a further description of this work, see Mortimore et al., 1988.)

Tizard and colleagues (1988) studied 33 elementary schools, focusing on the first two years of compulsory schooling. Although their sample was not random but was deliberately constructed to contain higher proportions of students from minority ethnic groups, the study was able to investigate the effects of schooling on student achievement. Again very careful attention was given to the collection of information on home background of students. In addition to measures such as those collected by Mortimore and colleagues (1988), Tizard and her colleagues collected data on the educational activities of the students' mothers. Other data included teachers' judgments about students, the curriculum coverage of schools in the sample, and students' views of academic achievement, "naughtiness" at school, and other related areas. Methods of analysis—which recognized the different levels of data—included the use of structural equation modeling.

Designed to study the impact of race on students' achievement, the work of Smith and Tomlinson (1989) also addressed the question of school differences in high school students' achievement. Their data included detailed information about the ethnic background of students, their religion, the employment status, and the socioeconomic group of parents and their educational backgrounds, as well as records of student progress. Their sample was made up of 20 multiethnic secondary schools in four school districts. They used a variety of instruments to collect data, including attainment tests, student questionnaires, and parental surveys. In their analysis the researchers made use of methods of variance component analysis which took account of the multilevels of the data (schools and students).

Using data collected by the Inner London Education Authority, Nuttall and colleagues (1989) studied the examination performance of over 31,000 16-year-old students drawn from 140 schools over three years. Intake measures included a verbal reasoning score, ethnic group, sex, and a measure of family income based on the right to free school meals. The research team found large average differences between the performance of different ethnic groups. It also found that school performance varied along several dimensions with some schools having more powerful effects on some groups of students. Finally, taking advantage of the very large size of its sample, it found evidence of a lack of stability of effects over time.

As noted earlier, this list is just a sample of the studies relating to school effectiveness that have been carried out by British researchers. More comprehensive listings are available elsewhere.

WHAT HAVE BEEN THE MAIN FINDINGS FROM BRITISH RESEARCH?

The 20 years of research effort have resulted in general agreement on a number of related issues.

Importance of Intake Measures

The British studies have demonstrated how necessary it is to take account of differences in student intake when attempting to study the efficacy of individual schools. No matter the age of the students—Mortimore and colleagues (1988) studied schools receiving students of 7 years of age; Rutter and colleagues' (1979) sample schools received students aged 11—the variation on a range of dimensions is likely to be considerable. Mortimore and colleagues (1988) found significant differences in parental occupations, level of income, family size, fluency in the English language, and experience of nursery education as well as in attainment in reading, writing, and mathematics and in behavior. To have attempted to have assessed the effectiveness of their schools without taking such differences into account would have been futile.

Differences between Schools When Student intake Has Been Taken into Account

British studies have found evidence of differential school effectiveness. School effects are themselves open to a number of different definitions (see Rutter, 1983, for a discussion of this issue), but, broadly speaking, those studies have supported the argument that—even when differences in intake have been taken into account—some schools are more likely than others to lead to good student outcomes. As has been noted earlier, a variety of outcomes—attendance, behavior and attitudes as well as measures of academic attainment—have been investigated.

The finding of school differences applies to both elementary and high schooling. Although it is difficult to compare the size of the impact of one study with that of another, school influence is important for individual students in both phases of schooling. Performance in elementary schooling may influence the perception of a student's capability in secondary schooling; performance in secondary schooling is related to success or failure in life after school. (For a discussion of school effects on subsequent working life, see Gray et al., 1980.)

Differences between Groups of Students

Five of the British studies examined, directly, the question of whether particular groups of students stood to gain more or less from effective schools. The findings are divided. Three studies (Gray et al., 1983; Cuttance, 1985; and Nuttall et al., 1989) show that some schools are more effective with some groups of students then with others. One study (Smith & Tomlinson, 1989) found the opposite: that the differences between groups of students were insignificant in comparison to the differences between schools. The findings of the ILEA study of elementary schools (Mortimore et al., 1988) were less clear cut: in general it was found that schools that had positive effects for one group were likely to have such effects for others. In their sample of 50 schools, they found no case where students with parents from manual occupations performed markedly better than those from nonmanual groups. What they did find was that students from manual groups in the most effective schools outperformed those from nonmanual groups in the least effective ones. However, they also found that there was some variability in effects. So, for example, some schools had positive effects in promoting reading progress for girls but not for boys, and vice versa. This finding, therefore, remains to be resolved.

The Need for More Sophisticated Analysis and Better Theory

Between 1967 and 1990, the British studies cited here have become increasingly more sophisticated. By collecting fuller measures about students and about schools, by recognizing the nature of the different levels of data—such as school, class, and individual student—and by employing more powerful analytical techniques with which to analyze these data, British researchers have increased their understanding of how schools operate and of how they are likely to influence their students.

Further improvements are needed, and Cuttance (1985), for example, drew attention to a series of methodological and statistical improvements that, in his view, needed to be incorporated into later studies. Some of these, such as the use of multilevel modeling, have been adopted by British researchers, as the last section of this chapter illustrates.

More recently an American researcher, Raudenbush (1989), has argued for further modifications, building on longitudinal techniques and the use of multilevel models, in order to capture the "dynamic" quality of school life. Similarly, Dutch researchers Bosker and Scheerens (1989) have argued that not only should future research designs become more sophisticated (especially with regard to criterion choice, effect size, and stability of effects) but that there has to be further development of theory.

The question of theory has also been addressed by Scheerens and Creemers (1989). In their view school effectiveness has to be conceptualized to take account of contingency theory, organizational commitment, mastery learning, and (again) the multilevel nature of school data. Their model recognizes the context in which schools operate, uses background information and school-level input to make sense of class-room level activity, and examines student output measures that are, themselves, affected by contextual influences. British empirical work stands to gain considerably from these ideas. The refinement of methodology and the development of theory, and—more important—the fruitful combination of the two, should foster a second generation of better school effectiveness studies.

Factors Related to School Effectiveness Controlling for Student Background

Like many U.S. studies, British work indicates that a number of factors are associated with school effectiveness.

LEADERSHIP. The research shows that having a principal who is purposeful but neither too authoritarian nor too democratic, who is able to "share" ownership of the school with colleagues is important. The quality of leadership, however, also includes the ability to delegate to a deputy without feeling threatened and to involve the members of the faculty in the management of the school.

MANAGEMENT OF STUDENTS. Organizing schools so that students are involved and can be rewarded for their efforts is important. Studies also show that having a form of behavioral control that is neither too weak nor too harsh is likely to be most effective.

Ensuring that sessions are structured and work centered and include teaching that is intellectually challenging is a major task for school administrators.

MANAGEMENT OF TEACHERS. Involving teachers in the corporate life of the school and pursuing consistency in their approach to students is likely to make the school a less stressful place for both parties.

Encouraging teachers to be good models of punctuality, politeness, and consideration is also important, as is ensuring that classrooms have positive psychological climates in which students are encouraged to communicate with their teachers.

Providing a broad, balanced curriculum which recognizes the academic role of schooling but values students with special educational needs is a difficult, but crucial, task for administrators. Having a limited focus within sessions in the elementary school, so that students generally work in common curriculum areas and teachers can support their learning without being "pulled in different directions" is also difficult, but appears to be conducive to effective learning.

STUDENT CARE. Treating students with dignity and encouraging them to participate in the organization of the school gives a positive signal, as does using rewards rather than punishment to change behavior. Involving parents in the life of the school and treating education as a partnership between parents and school is likely to increase the confidence of the community in the efficacy of the school. Keeping systematic records of students' progress is crucially important if the curriculum is to have any coherence for individuals.

SCHOOL ENVIRONMENT. Ensuring that the environment is made as attractive and stimulating as possible, taking trouble over classroom displays, and removing graffiti are relatively simple tasks, but they may have a profound effect on the attitudes of students attending the school.

SCHOOL CLIMATE. Endeavoring to achieve a consensus on the values and aims of the school as a whole needs to be a fundamental aim of the principal.

Expressing a general attitude that is positive toward learning and positive about young people will be a clear signal of what the school stands for and where its priorities lie.

Establishing clear rules and guidelines for student behavior and maintaining high expectations for all students are ways in which the goals and values of the institution are translated into daily life. Such actions appear to be highly influential in creating more effective schools.

These have been some of the factors identified by the British studies. The picture, however, is far from uniform: some factors have been identified by most researchers, others have been noted by only a minority and require follow-up to clarify their importance. What is interesting, however, is the identification of a pool of related factors that, in a number of studies, have been associated with greater effectiveness. These various factors have been culled from studies of effective schools. They are not necessarily the only factors—or even the best ones—to be sought by a principal striving to turn a noneffective school into a more effective one. But they provide a corpus from which she or he might begin to move forward.

WHAT HAS BEEN THE REACTION OF PRACTITIONERS TO THIS RESEARCH?

British teachers do not have a strong tradition of continuing academic study after graduation. Traditionally, initial training, perhaps supplemented by a few short courses, was deemed to be sufficient for a lifetime's service. This tradition is changing, however, and, increasingly, British principals, teachers, and central administrators have sought continuing education through the pursuit of masters' degrees, diplomas, and other courses. The awareness of research findings and the reading of educational articles and books are clearly related to this change.

School effectiveness has become a topic of interest to practitioners. It is not possible, in the absence of any reliable data, to estimate what proportion of educators will have read accounts or summaries of the research but, over the last ten or so years, it has become a popular topic for professional training days and has been featured on the programs of many conferences. (For the time being, however, it is likely to be eclipsed by the need for practitioners to study the details of the government's current reform program.)

Despite, however, the emerging interest by practitioners and the fulsome treatment of the topic in the educational press, the impact of the research on practice, in many ways, has been disappointing. While many of the concepts—and the language of school effectiveness—have been adopted (the term "ethos" is used widely to describe the atmosphere of the school and "whole school" programs are now common), the number of schools working directly on school improvement programs has been very limited. In comparison with the situation in the United States and Canada this has been disappointing.

There is probably a multitude of reasons for the lack of systematic attempts to improve schools but four stand out as important. These are

The lack of suitable instruments.
The differing traditions of British inspectors/advisors.
The negative impact of well-publicized disagreements between researchers.
The conservative effect of examinations on secondary school innovations.

The Lack of Suitable Instruments

Unlike the United States or Canada, there has not been a tradition of generating instruments either by researchers or by publishers. Furthermore, the absence of any formal structures for the dissemination or development of research findings—such as found in the system of regional laboratories—has meant that there has been little support for such work. Two examples of such studies are reported by Phillips and colleagues (1985) and Ouston and Maughan (1988). Without the instruments, an individual school faces a major task before it can even begin to estimate its current effectiveness. It is, perhaps, hardly surprising that few get beyond this point to the introduction of change and the subsequent evaluation of its impact.

The Differing Traditions of Inspectors/Advisors

One strength of the British system has been the existence of a pool of successful educators able to evaluate performance, to help in-service training, and to advise practitioners of new developments. This undoubted strength, however, may also be partly responsible for the lack of research-based programs of improvement. Because many inspectors/advisors have not been trained in research skills, they may have opted for alternative approaches. Undoubtedly there have been exceptions, such as the research-based scheme of self-evaluation pioneered by the London inspectorate, but in the main this has not been the case.

Furthermore, there is no counterpart in England to the structure of regional educational laboratories. The functions of dissemination of research findings and the consequent developmental programs that are carried out in the United States by these institutions are sadly lacking. There are no national discussion networks other than through the allocation of an earmarked grant to school boards by government. Up to now, school improvement—based on the school effectiveness research—has not been one of the areas selected for government earmarked funding.

The Negative Impact of Well-Publicized Disagreements between Researchers

The British tradition for academic debate is well known. This tradition, however, has led to a number of often bitter attacks on educational researchers. These attacks have been well publicized by the educational media and have probably had the effect of reducing public confidence in the validity of research findings. This is a difficult issue: a healthy skepticism in results is no bad thing in itself. The problem comes if, as a result of these debates, a majority of practitioners lose confidence in the value of any research.

Three particular debates are worth noting in connection with this point: first, the debate that followed the publication of *Teaching Styles and Pupil Progress* (Bennett, 1976) and led to the eventual reanalysis of much of the data (Aitkin & Bennett, 1980); second, the publication of *Examination Results in Selective and Non-selective Schools* (Steedman, 1983); and, finally, the methodological debates that followed publication of *Fifteen Thousand Hours*. See, for instance Acton (1980), Rutter and colleagues (1980), Goldstein (1980), and Tizard and colleagues (1980).

Although, strictly only the last of these debates was concerned with a study of school effectiveness, the impact of such debates on publications arising out of educational research has been considerable. This is a difficult point to deal with, for if the criticisms of the research are so serious that the findings are shown incontrovertibly to be invalid then, clearly, it is important that practitioners are made aware of this fact. If, however, the criticisms are less clear cut, of interest primarily to other researchers, or peripheral to the main issues, then the publicity surrounding the debates is highly undesirable.

The Conservative Effects of an Examinations Systems on High School Innovations

As noted earlier, the existence of "public examinations" set and—in general—marked outside the school has acted as a regulator on much of the life of high schools. While this influence has tended to keep schools in line in choice of a curriculum, it has also acted as a barrier to innovation.

Given the interest of students, parents, and the general public in examination results, and the lack of availability of many other indicators of performance, principals and teachers have tended to use these annual results as barometers of the success of the school. However, as educationists will readily appreciate, these examination results are highly sensitive to variations in socioeconomic status and racial and gender differences among candidates. Thus schools with advantaged students tend—other things being equal—to obtain better results than those with less advantaged ones. (This, of course, is the reason for the development of research techniques which can estimate the effectiveness of schools while taking account of such student differences.)

Underperforming schools—in terms of examination results—have frequently set about innovatory changes. Where those have been successful, however, their effect has sometimes been masked by the robustness of the relationship between intake and examination success. In such cases the "real-world" feedback of the examination results tends to wipe out the more positive indications from the innovatory program. This situation has inhibited the widespread adoption of school change.

U.S./U.K. DIFFERENCES. This chapter has provided information on the methods and major findings of British research on effective schools. Additional information has been presented to help American readers to understand the British system and, especially, the way the current school reforms are being implemented.

In a number of ways the British and the American systems of education are fairly similar. At the macro level, students in both systems are grouped in dedicated institutions staffed by adults trained in instruction. Both students and teachers are constrained by a curriculum which deals both with subject knowledge and with attitudinal and value contents. The aims of the institutions are to foster the quality of learning, yet, in both countries, success for some has to be set against the failure and dropout of others.

In other ways, there are considerable differences between the two countries. For instance, while researchers have pursued studies of school effectiveness in both countries, programs of school improvement have been neglected in Britain. Certainly the contrast with the situation in many states, where there are well-defined traditions for intervention studies, is marked.

In Britain there is a tendency to "blame the individual" and to see the role of the school as peripheral to the success of the student (Reynolds, 1988). The contrast to the "American Dream" view of individual potential—and its implications for the school she or he attends—is striking. Furthermore, the systems of assessment in the two countries are imbued with these cultural values. Thus, in Britain the formal public examinations are constructed to have high failure rates. Even though there have been recent changes in the organization of the examinations, the reality in Britain is that three out of four students do not reach a level of generally accepted academic success. In these circumstances it is perhaps not surprising that one out of every two students opts to drop out of full-time education at the age of 16. In contrast, as readers will know, "average" students in America leave school feeling successful and the school dropout rate is far lower than in Britain. Despite the criticisms of American schooling and the need for such interventions as Project Equality (Redman, 1982) in order to ensure that college students are sufficiently prepared for advanced study, the system appears to be more efficient in that a far higher proportion of each age group enters higher education (approximately 60 percent compared to approximately 14 percent) in the United States than in the United Kingdom.

These are some of the possible reasons why the results of research studies of school effectiveness have not been utilized more in England in the generation of school improvement interventions. It now remains to be seen if the reforms inaugurated by the government—and backed with the force of legislation—will be successful. The existence of a body of research evidence may well prove useful to this endeavor. Provided that the grave technical difficulties of new types of assessment and methods of reporting achievement scores (so that these take account of school differences in student intake) can be overcome, it may aid the reforms to deliver the hoped for improvements.

CONCLUSION

My personal view is that some of the reforms, such as the national curriculum and local site-based management, have a reasonable probability of assisting schools to become more effective. Others such as the open enrollment with no concern for equity—or the facility to opt out of the jurisdiction of the local school board, while they may—in the short term—aid individual schools, will prove ultimately to be inimical to the effective education of our community.

R E F E R E N C E S

ACTON, T. (1980). Educational criteria of success: Some problems in the work of Rutter, Maughan, Mortimore and Ouston. *Educational Research, 22,* 163–69.

AITKIN, M., ANDERSON, D., & HINDE, J. (1981). Statistical Modelling of Data on Teaching Styles. *Journal of the Royal Statistical Society, 144*(4), 491–61.

AITKIN, M., BENNETT, S. N., & HESKETH, J. (1981). Teaching style and pupil progress. *British Journal of Educational Psychology,* 51, 170–86.

BENNETT, N. (1976). *Teaching styles and pupil progress.* London: Open Books.

BOSKER, R. J., & SCHEERENS, J. (1989). Issues in the interpretation of the results of school effectiveness research. *International Journal of Educational Research, 13*(7).

BRIMER, A., MADAUS, G., CHAPMAN, B., KELLAGHAN, T., & WOOD, R. (1978). *Sources of difference in school achievement.* Slough, England: National Foundation for Educational Research (NFER).

CUTTANCE, P. (1985). Methodological issues in the statistical analysis of data on the effectiveness of schooling. *British Educational Research Journal, 11*(2).

GOLDSTEIN, H. (1980). Fifteen thousand hours: A review of the statistical procedures. *Journal of Child Psychology and Psychiatry, 21*(4), 363–66.

GOLDSTEIN, H. (1984). The methodology of school comparisons. *Oxford Review of Education, 10*(1), 69–74.

GOLDSTEIN, H. (1987). *Multilevel models in educational and social research.* London: Charles Griffin.

GRAY, G., SMITH, A., & RUTTER, M. (1980). School attendance and the first year of employment. In L. Hersov & I. Berg (Eds.), *Out of school: Modern perspectives on truancy and school refusal.* Chichester, England: John Wiley.

GRAY, J. (1981). Towards effective schools: Problems and progress in British research. *British Educational Research Journal, 7*(1), 59–69.

GRAY, J., MCPHERSON, A. & RAFFE, D. (1983). *Reconstructions of secondary education: Theory, myth and practice since the war.* London: Routledge and Kegan Paul.

MAUGHAN, B., OUSTON, J., PICKLES, A., & RUTTER, M. (in press). Can schools change? Number I outcomes in six London secondary schools. *School Effectiveness and School Improvement, 1*(3).

MCLURE, S. (1988). *Education reformed.* Sevenoaks, England: Hodder and Stoughton.

MORTIMORE, P., SAMMONS, P., STOLL, L., LEWIS, D. & ECOB, R. (1988). *School matters: The junior years.* Berkeley, CA: University of California Press.

NUTTALL, D. L., GOLDSTEIN, H., PROSSER, R., & RASBASH, J. (1989). Differential school effectiveness. *International Journal of Educational Research, 13*(7).

PHILLIPS, D., DAVIE, R., & CALLELY, E. (1985). Pathways to institutional development in secondary schools. In D. Reynolds (ed.), *Studying school effectiveness*. Lewes, England: Falmer Press.

POWER, M., ALDERSON, M., PHILLIPSON, C., SCHOENBERG, E. & MORRIS, J. (1967). Delinquent schools? *New Society, 10*, 542–42.

RAUDENBUSH, S. W. (1989). The analysis of longitudinal, multilevel data. *International Journal of Educational Research, 13*(7), 721–39.

REDMAN, T. (1982). Preparation for college: A natural approach. *Journal of Development and Remedial Education, 5*, 3–5.

REID, K., HOPKINS, D. & MOLLY, P. (1987). *Towards the effective school*. Oxford: Basil Blackwell.

REYNOLDS, D. (1982). The search for effective schools. *School organisation, 2*(3), 215–37.

REYNOLDS, D. (1988). *Research on school and organisational effectiveness: The end or the beginning?* Paper presented at the BEMAS Third Research Conference on Educational Management and Administration, Cardiff, April.

RUTTER, M. (1983). School effects on pupil progress: Research findings and policy implications. *Child Development, 54*(1), 1–29.

RUTTER, M., MAUGHAN, B., MORTIMORE, P. & OUSTON, J. (1979). *Fifteen thousand hours: Secondary schools and their effects on children*. London: Open Books/Harvard University Press.

RUTTER, M., MAUGHAN, B., MORTIMORE, P., & OUSTON, J. (1980). Educational criterion of success, reply to Acton. *Educational Research, 22*(3), 170–74.

SCHEERENS, J., & CREEMERS, B. (1989). Conceptualising school effectiveness. *International Journal of Educational Research, 13*(7), 691–704.

SIMON, B. (1988). *Bending the rules*. London, England: Lawrence and Wishart.

SMITH, D., & TOMLINSON, S. (1989). *The school effect: A study of multi-racial comprehensives*. London: Policy Studies Institute.

STEEDMAN, J. (1983). *Examination results in selective and non-selective schools*. London: National Children's Bureau.

TIZARD, B., BLATCHFORD, P., BURKE, J., FARQUHAR, C., & PLEWIS, I. (1988). *Young children at school in the inner city*. Hove, England: Erlbaum.

TIZARD, B., BURGESS, T., FRANCIS, H., GOLDSTEIN, H., YOUNG, M., HEWISON, J., & PLEWIS, I. (1980). Fifteen thousand hours: A discussion. *Bedford Way Papers 1*. London: University of London Institute of Education.

WILLMS, J., & CUTTANCE, P. (1985). School effects in Scottish secondary schools. *British Journal of the Sociology of Education, 6*(3), 289–306.

7

TOWARD EFFECTIVE URBAN HIGH SCHOOLS: THE IMPORTANCE OF PLANNING AND COPING[1]

Karen Seashore Louis
University of Minnesota
and
The National Center for Effective Secondary Schools, University of Wisconsin

Matthew B. Miles
Center for Policy Research, New York

INTRODUCTION: THE CHALLENGE

Powell et al. (1985) recently argued that U.S. high schools are organized as "shopping malls" rather than serious educational institutions. Urban high schools are metaphorically more like the shopping intersections that dot our inner cities than the chrome and glass versions of suburbia. Run down and overpriced, they are accused of presenting a limited selection of low-quality goods for their customers. Students— often poor, minority, and immigrant—are shortchanged out of any pretense at equal educational opportunity.

The deterioration of urban education is attributed in editorials to many causes, from changing demographic patterns and reduced public support to political corruption, rigid and old-fashioned administration, and poor-quality or burned-out teachers. Simplistic, popular solutions (such as raising requirements for course work or graduation) may have regressive effects on the performance of low-achieving or at-risk students.

Even so, the prospects for urban school improvement are promising. Education is, at least temporarily, high on the agenda. Many states are enacting massive reform efforts that not only require improved performance, but offer support as well (Anderson & Odden, 1988).

Research on effective schools not only provides clear images of excellence, but moves us past the stage of good intentions: there is a set of tools in the form of "effective schools programs" being implemented in an increasing number of elementary and secondary schools (Farrar et al., 1984; Miles & Kaufman, 1985; U.S. General Accounting Office, 1989).

Really changing high schools is a largely uncharted enterprise, however. There's some doubt that approaches that work in elementary schools will work when transferred to the more complicated and turbulent environment of high schools. Thus, we have "images of excellence" for high schools (Lightfoot, 1983), but we lack information about how ordinary high schools actually move through the process of improvement to become excellent.

We know that schools moving toward improvement face many problems along the way: previous studies of *successful* school innovation efforts report many major and minor implementation crises (Louis et al., 1981; Huberman & Miles, 1984). The literature on planned change suggests that some of these are avoidable, through improved program design, change management skills, and support and training for affected staff (Hall & Hord, 1987; Crandall et al., 1986).

Other problems, however, cannot be "managed," but are a consequence of the way in which schools are organized (Weick, 1976) and the school's vulnerability to changing environmental pressures (Pfeffer & Salancik, 1978). The basic argument of this chapter is that creating more effective schools requires a significant change in patterns of *leadership* and *management* at the school level. While this change may focus most dramatically on the principal, it will also have implications for the roles that other administrators, specialists, and teachers play in the school.

The terms "leadership" and "management" are both complementary and distinctive: Leaders set the course for the organization; managers make sure the course is followed. Leaders make strategic plans; managers design operational systems for carrying out the plans. Leaders stimulate and inspire; managers use their interpersonal influence and authority to translate that energy into productive work. Egan's (1988) description of what good managers do in industry almost sounds as if it were drawn from the research on effective schools. His "management task cycle" involves six steps: setting goals, developing clear work programs, facilitating the execution of work programs, providing feedback, making and monitoring adjustments, and rewarding performance. And his five-step leadership task cycle helps us see how it differs from management: creating visions of how things could be done better, turning visions into workable agendas, communicating agendas so as to generate excitement and commitment in others, creating a climate of problem solving and learning around the agendas, and persisting until the agendas are accomplished.

As Sergiovanni and colleagues (1987) indicate, there is a continuum of demands: good school leaders must understand and be able to cope with the *regularities* and inevitable small crises of daily life, make *situational adjustments* (for example, adapting to new state curriculum requirements), and deal with *change* (addressing a significant challenge, such as revitalizing a "burned-out" staff, or integrating new students and teachers after a school closing).

THE STUDY

The issues just sketched led us to an investigation of the process of designing and implementing major "effective schools" programs in urban high schools. We initiated two data-collection efforts. The first was a survey of 178 urban high school principals involved in change efforts based on the effective schools research.[2]

In the second, we carried out five case studies based on approximately ten days of interviewing and observation in each school during the 1985–86 school year, with a brief follow-up visit in the winter of 1988. The schools were located in diverse cities from a deteriorating neighborhood in New York City to the semiurban sprawl just outside of Los Angeles. They were selected according to several criteria, namely, (1) very poor student performance in the recent past, (2) implementation of a substantial, all-school change program since 1981 based on effective schools principles, (3) reports from more than one knowledgeable informant that indicated considerable progress in their efforts to improve, and (4) the presence of a principal who was not notably charismatic.[3]

Basically, we wanted to develop well-supported generalizations about the process of implementing effective schools programs in urban high schools, and to understand the reasons for success. Previous quantitative studies, such as Purkey, Rutter, and Newmann (1987) describe what urban high schools are doing in comprehensive improvement, but lack data about the process and results of change. Case studies such as Lightfoot's (1983) provide "rich, thick" descriptions, but are not representative of typical schools. In this research, case study data were the primary data source, and survey data were examined largely to determine the robustness of our case study conclusions. In this paper we draw primarily on the case study data, but note that in every instance where comparable topics were treated in the survey, the two sources confirmed each other.[4]

Table 7–1 shows characteristics of the five case study schools. Basically, we selected them not as "excellent" schools, but as typical, racially mixed urban high schools that seemed to be on a trajectory of improvement, using effective schools methods (typically, as part of a "braid" of multiple improvement efforts). All the schools had used diagnostic data collection, were generally acquainted with "effective schools" and often "effective teaching" principles, used task forces to propose solutions to identified problems, had cross-role steering groups, and so on. We included a Southwest city to be sure we had both older/newer cities, in contracting/expanding economies. For a sense of the change projects that were carried out in each school, see Table 7–2 as well.

Two of these schools—Alameda and Agassiz—we judged to have made successful and sustained progress toward major renewal and change in the teaching and learning conditions of the school (compare Prior and Subsequent Outcomes columns). Two others—Burroughs and Bartholdi—moved more slowly and fitfully toward change. Finally, in one—Chester—there was little evidence that the school's staff were able to create an environment for change. In comparing the A-, B-, and C-level cases, we are able to develop some generalizations about the factors that help to explain their differential success—generalizations which, as we have noted, are confirmed in the survey.

This chapter focuses on two major change domains in leadership and management of the change process. The first is a leadership capacity: effective use of evolutionary planning. The second is a management skill: the ability to cope with the inevitable problems that face any major effort to change a school.

EVOLUTIONARY PLANNING

More than a few educational researchers believe planning makes little contribution to serious school improvement. *Real improvement* depends more on implementation, or what happens after a reform actually gets put to the test in classrooms (Berman &

TABLE 7-1. Case Study Sites and Improvement Programs

SCHOOL	LOCATION	GRADES	SIZE	POPULATION	PRIOR OUTCOMES	IMPROVEMENT PROGRAMS	SUBSEQUENT OUTCOMES (1988)
Agassiz	Boston, residential neighborhood	9–12	750	70% black 25% bilingual 31% special needs	1981: 9th gr. math 18th percentile; reading 20th. 50% dropouts. 73% attendance. Low staff morale.	Business-school collaboration (Boston Compact); school-based planning, evolving since 1982. ES principles focal.	34th percentile math; reading 35th. Attendance 83%. Subprogram dropouts 11%, others 22%. Strong positive climate.
Alameda	Los Angeles, urban sprawl	9–12	2,100	35% Hispanic 23% other minority 30% limited English	1978: math 21st percentile; reading 16th. Attendance 72%. Gang violence.	State school improvement program (SIP), plus heavy staff development; since 1979.	Math 78th percentile, reading 63rd. Attendance 89%. Stable school, academic emphasis.
Bartholdi	New York, deteriorated poor neighborhood	9–12	2,100	70% Hispanic 29% black 12% special needs	1984: 18% annual dropouts; attendance 68%. 59% failing grades. Math test failure 11th gr. 33%; reading 44%.	Comprehensive dropout prevention program; since 1985. [Effective schools work (SIP, HISIP) since 1983.]	8% annual dropouts; attendance 74%. Suspensions reduced from 250 to 154. Modest test and grades improvement.
Burroughs	Cleveland, working-class/ poor neighborhood	7–9	600	66% black 25% whites bussed in	1981: attendance, 85%. 27% below norms on reading, 7th gr. Teacher absenteeism 15%. 241 suspensions.	Middle schools planning, program (MGAP 1981); then local effective schools. program (1981) and team teaching.	Attendance 90%. 1986: 13% below norms on 7th gr. reading. Teacher absenteeism 5%. 341 suspensions 1988: Reading 7th gr. 21% below norms.
Chester	New Jersey, working-class neighborhood	10–12	2,300	78% black 12% Hispanic 13% special needs	1985: attendance, 85%. Seniors' math and reading @ 10.5 One-third need remediation.	State comprehensive programmatic planning, plus effective teaching program, since 1985. [School-based planning and effective schools work (PDK) 1981–83].	1987: dropouts 26% (increase), 33% of students need remediation. Writing scores up slightly; reading and math down. Staff morale worse. Attendance 85%.

McLaughlin, 1974; Berman, 1981; Louis, Rosenblum, & Molitor, 1981); some studies suggest that "top-down, technological" planning should give way to a more fluid model, in which "a thousand flowers bloom" (Clark, McKibbin, & Malkas, 1980).

But planning is not as easily dismissed as these critiques imply. The real issue is what kind of planning model is used. The traditional *rational or semirational* model (Allison, 1971) emphasized the development of long-range master plans based on demographic and economic projections, and short term goals set by each unit in the organization. More recently, there has been advocacy of *strategic planning,* emphasizing external adaptation, setting medium-range goals (two to three years), doing assessment and evaluation through the judgment of the leaders rather than precise statistical models, and focusing on the broad participation of members (Steiner, 1979; Tichy, 1983; McCune, 1986). Finally, some argue that we should embrace *incremental models,* which imply a day-to-day reliance on the judgments of many people at all levels in the organization (Lindblom, 1959; Weick, 1976; March & Olsen, 1986).

From our cases and survey data, we came to believe that an eclectic, *evolutionary planning* perspective was most successful. Given the moderate chaos both inside and outside big-city schools, no specific plan can last for very long, and thus the guiding metaphor is that of a journey—where the itinerary, and sometimes even the destination, shifts because of what happens along the way. Such planning is not, however, passive or opportunistic. Instead, the organization cycles back and forth among efforts to gain normative consensus about what it may become, to plan strategies for getting there, and to carry out decentralized experimentation that harnesses the creativity of all members to the change efforts (Pava, 1986).

The case studies suggest that a number of specific actions are needed to make evolutionary planning work in tired urban high schools. These include a principal-initiated core team, action before planning, and the use of change themes rather than specific goals.

The Principal and the Core Team

Here we make three main points. First, initial mass participation in planning is not necessarily effective; second, principals need to work with an empowered core team of planners; third, active principal sponsorship remains critical.

EARLY MASS PLANNING IN DOUBT.   Planning experts frequently advocate the use of a broadly based, representative planning team (Lotto, Clark, & Carroll, 1980), guiding a broadly based process in which most school members have the opportunity to contribute, and a clearly defined planning period focusing on the development of specific goals and action steps.

But a broadly based planning process does not always work well. The initial approach to planning in our Chester site looked like this:

> A district-wide steering group of 87 people was appointed to develop a plan...task forces...met as often as twice a month to develop ideas. However, commitment of energy was low, and actual planning documents were usually prepared by the central office staff. The high school's chronic mistrust of the district office increased when the superintendent chose a major component of the program before the participatory planning process was completed: There was widespread agreement...that "downtown is ramming this down our throats." Low morale at the school level made it difficult to sustain involvement in school-based planning.

Chester was full of teachers who were interested in change, but a long list of recently failed innovations in the school made them skeptical about committing to the district's planning effort. They also saw how decoupled district office planning and their own planning were, reinforcing their sense of powerlessness and lack of interest.

Thus, broad participation can increase alienation by increasing the profound conviction of many urban teachers that they are manipulated by administrators who do not understand the circumstances of their work.

AN EMPOWERED CORE GROUP.   But there are alternatives. In three of our schools—Agassiz, Burroughs, and Bartholdi—the strategy was to find a small, energetic core group whose planning began small—even invisibly. An example from Agassiz illustrates this:

> Principal Cohen turned toward the "old team" that had hung on in the school through the bad years, in part because of strong interpersonal loyalties. As one administrator said "During our darkest hours we gravitated toward collegial networking. We had a hard basis of caring and respect to see us through. We could share our goals, support each other."

In Burroughs, as principal Storm began to plan, she turned toward faculty volunteers:

> Storm told her faculty about [the program], and "eight people stepped forward who were really willing to put forth more it. I felt that was enough support to go ahead." ...during the early months, [the program] consisted largely of that committee...meetings scheduled after school hours...were attended by few faculty.

Miss Storm was reflective about the reason why she chose to run fast with a few players:

> The number one thing is to build a support base. You can't think you have a fantastic dream and expect people to accept it. You have to have gradual movement; you have to build support....You have to know your staff, who are the good teachers, who are interested in working with children and parents, who are committed and non-punitive." And when she had identified those staff, she gave them major responsibilities as well as rewards....

Such empowerment of a core team led the way to broader engagement of the whole faculty, typically on "sensitive" issues of teaching and learning often avoided in urban school reform efforts (Louis & Miles, 1990).

In Alameda, the principal hoped for a school that was largely run by teachers, and these efforts were successful.

Agassiz, located in a more bureaucratic district committed to hierarchical control procedures, did not make such a complete transition. Nevertheless, the control structure of the school became more decentralized, and department heads and teachers talked about their accountability for improvement. In Burroughs, the active cadre of involved teachers became increasingly confident of their ability to manage the program as implementation proceeded.

The cross-role steering group at Bartholdi felt increasingly confident in dealing with instructional issues which used to be "the domain of the A.P.'s."

In Chester, though the engagement of teachers in curriculum alignment work bore some fruit, the imposition of classroom scanning led department chairs to walk away quietly from the effort, and teachers followed suit.

Here too our survey data are confirmatory. Only 38 percent of schools where teacher commitment was low had active, successful efforts at coping with problems; high-commitment schools were twice as likely to be effective (78 percent).

PRINCIPAL SPONSORSHIP.   However, principals by no means abdicated their leadership roles. Although we were intellectually biased against the "charismatic leader" model, and had selected our five cases in order to examine the role of "ordinary principals," in our three most successful schools the principal was nevertheless quite central in early planning. In two initially less successful schools, principals played a less dynamic and central role:

> Chester's principal Hayes took little active initiative in planning for or coordinating the school renewal program, nor did she actively invite other school administrators to take charge. She was unenthusiastic about the superintendent's part of the programs, and did little to deal with staff resistance to it.

In Bartholdi, the principal also initially limited his investment in the district's change program:

> Principal Martinez, in his first year as a principal, was struggling with the need to learn a variety of new skills. He delegated responsibility for the program to another administrator, who proved unequal to it. When Martinez later restaffed the position with a respected associate principal, the project began to take off. In both schools, however, there were noticeable results of limited administrative involvement in planning. The change programs, initially "outside" ones, were seen as irrelevant to solving pressing local problems. And there was no mandate for anyone to resolve conflicting views or supply coordination.

In contrast, the principals of Agassiz, Burroughs, and Alameda gave active sponsorship to their change programs—all of which also originated outside the school. Teachers—even the skeptics—knew that the school's leaders cared about the program, and actively engaged teachers in planning that would make it fit the school's agenda and needs.

Survey data confirm the case findings. For example, in schools where the principal had high influence over initial planning, 55 percent reported effective problem coping later on. In schools with lower-influence principals, the good coping figure was only 35 percent. As we will show below, good coping is a sine qua non of success.

Action Before Planning

Planning theory proposes distinct stages in a change effort, with early planning (or mobilization) coming before actual implementation or activity. But the opposite occurred in Agassiz and Burroughs: first there was action, and then detailed planning. In Agassiz, for example,

> Principal Cohen...realized that if [the program were to succeed] he would need to deliver to the skeptics. One of his...battles was with the district's physical plant staff over budgets for repairs. The central office proposed replacing the heating plant, wiring and pipes, but Cohen reasoned that these would hardly boost the morale of the staff and students. After a hard fight the school received all of the internal cosmetic repairs. Cohen utilized the victory to its fullest advantage, holding a special dedication ceremony in the newly redecorated auditorium.

Many other programs and activities were initiated during Cohen's first year—a new magnet program, junior ROTC, a special program for teenage parents, and various efforts to reduce truancy. All began without the benefit of any formal schoolwide planning at all. Although Cohen was verbally committed to participatory planning, the second year of the program also involved more action than planning.

At Burroughs a similar process unfolded. The school received a small planning grant and spent the summer looking at reading programs and locating possible consultants. In the fall

> ...project planning continued, but Miss Storm and the [program] committee also began to implement some of their ideas...seven workshops [were conducted] during the year on reading in the content areas. And Miss Storm organized a 7th grade team of teachers and arranged their teaching schedules so that they could meet together to coordinate their curricular units and discuss problem students....Planning and implementation were all of one piece during the first year at Burroughs.

Even at Alameda, where the state program formed the basis for the school's project, changes were initiated in the project with limited or no planning. When a new principal came to the school

> ...her first step was to work on campus climate and to restore pride to the school....Rules were tightened, the schedule was changed to stagger arrival and departure...temporary out-transfer of violators, the elimination of in-school suspension, and implementation of Saturday work days...the students were back in class remarkably quickly.

In each of these cases, major activities, including restructuring and the initiation of significant (and sometimes costly) new programs, took place without committee meetings, and with no written plan supporting that action.

Was this bad administration? An error in judgment on the part of the principals and cooperating teachers? Our cases suggest not, and there is theoretical evidence from other settings to support this assertion.

ACTION CREATES ENERGY.   Some researchers agree that starting an innovation program that centers on curriculum and instruction is the best way to get teachers interested and involved (Crandall, Eiseman, & Louis, 1986). In these depressed schools, however, the teachers' collective sense of efficacy was exceptionally low. In both Agassiz and Alameda, the attack on morale and energy emphasized giving the whole school a sense of "being a winner": new facilities, improved climate, and more order. Successful action mobilized faculty energy.

Other research suggests that where doing comes before planning it takes the organization longer to produce results, but that there is more collective commitment than when classical plan-then-do models are used (Miles & Randolph, 1981).[5]

ACTION CREATES LEARNING.   Real increases in achievement, retention, or other outcomes are usually preceded by a profound transformation in a school. People in the organization need to learn how to act in different ways to produce the desired results. Old patterns need to be changed, new ones learned. The greater the anticipated behavioral change, the more learning must occur and the more difficult the process. And the development of a consensus in the school that a new way of doing things is "right" cannot occur until the new behaviors have been tried and tested (Miles & Louis,

1987). Thus, planning cannot be carried out very effectively until people already find themselves in a "learning mode."

Schön (1987) argues that effective professional learning occurs not through logical analysis (plan-then-do), or random accumulation of data (trial-and-error) but through reflection-in-action, a more intuitive way of analyzing and dealing with our own behavioral issues.

In passing, the case studies indicate that formal "data collection" and feedback typically played a less central part in furthering planning than the theorists tell us. In fact, data collection followed by inaction led first to energy, then to much despair in Chester and cynicism in Bartholdi. The issue seems to be connecting planners' understanding through largely informal data to action in the service of a shared vision.

Setting Goals—or Finding Themes?

Strategic planning manuals advocate developing a strong statement of mission prior to program planning (McCune, 1986). All courses of action should be assessed against their potential for achieving that mission. The mission statement should reflect the broad objectives of the system and connect with explicit, concrete change goals.

GOALS FOR CHANGE.   Planning behavior did not fit this image well in any of our schools. They were not, however, operating under a "goal-free" or ad hoc approach to planning. The main differences among the schools lay in the scope of the goals and program. The contrasts among Bartholdi, Burroughs, and Agassiz are instructive.

Bartholdi began the program with narrow goals. The main focus was on chronically absent students. The claim to be improving Bartholdi as an overall system was not supported with schoolwide activities, nor did most staff view the program as anything other than a dropout program.

Burroughs came close to designing their effort around a mission, due to the principal's unswerving commitment to the middle school concept. In her mind, the program centered on changing the teacher's role in student guidance and grouping, but middle school objectives were mixed in with the language of effective schools research, which was the basis for funding support. Other themes, such as reading improvement, were not explicitly linked to either the middle school or effective schools thrusts, but were added because of teacher interest.

In Agassiz, goals were broad and poorly specified. The initial planning document conformed to the district's program, and covered reducing truancy, increasing achievement and graduation rates, and other critical student outcomes. There were also unrecorded objectives known only to the headmaster and close colleagues, which were later seen schoolwide: improving social services, curriculum reform, and changes in planning and supervision in the school. Unstated goals provided more drive for the school than did the official program goals.

Our conclusion fits with other studies of implementation (Farrar, DeSanctis, & Cohen, 1980) and goes against the thrust of the planning literature: narrow and specific goals do little to create an environment for school reform. In schools with broader or vaguer goals, the multiplicity of moving parts and the overarching nature of the reform movement permits lots of positive action to generate support for reform.[6]

MISSION—OR THEMES?   In fact, the more successful of our schools had no a priori mission statements. Instead, multiple improvement efforts coalesced around a set of themes only after activity had begun. The themes, more and more visible to all staff members, became linked, and gradually reflected an image of what the school could become, thus serving to energize and motivate staff.

Themes in the more successful schools were typically interim change goals which helped to organize and direct energy. They were more general than specific program activities (such as implementing an in-school suspension program), but certainly not "end-state" goals (such as "reduce dropout rate"). A "theme" is an answer to the implicit question: "What are we trying to do to improve things right now...what are we working toward?" Rather than being deduced from an explicit examination of values and goals, themes were arrived at intuitively, by looking at what needed to be done in the name of reform. And they shifted over time. Table 7–2 shows the explicit themes from each of our sites, arranged in rough chronological order as they emerged.

In our more successful sites, the themes often began coalescing around something like a vision. In Agassiz, for example, themes reflected a maturation of the improvement effort: initial themes focused on superficial improvements in facilities and school climate, then moved to programs to serve the needs of the "whole child," incorporating social service, self-esteem, school-to-work experience, and dropout intervention. As staff became more accustomed to the program, and as the principal became versed in planning theories, there was an increasingly shared vision of schoolwide decentralized planning and accountability. Each alteration in the themes involved more and more staff.

Similarly, many of the themes at Alameda clustered around the slogan, "We are a school for students, and a university for teachers." At both Alameda and Agassiz, most staff could tell a coherent, post hoc "story" of how various activities and improvement themes fit together into a reasonable (if slightly untidy) whole. In effect, the evolution of themes was an effort to create and recreate value consensus and a collective understanding of the organization. Both the decentralization vision at Agassiz and the "university for teachers" one at Alameda had, like all good visions, a great deal of shared feeling behind them, unlike many abstract mission statements (cf. Block, 1987).

In Chester, on the other hand, the themes began with the need to implement two externally imposed change programs. The mandated curriculum alignment work proved to have usefulness and meaning, but subsequent change themes were driven by state testing and remediation requirements, the district remediation program, and the incredible demands posed by a mandated reorganization. None of the themes really added up to a vision or story, and most were reactive rather than "owned." Perhaps that's a main reason for the failure of Chester's renewal program: even though many teachers were initially positive about some specific activities and goals, they were not able to contribute to the emerging themes. Although it is often easy to attract interest with a good program or new idea (Louis & Dentler, 1988), if much effort is demanded, there is also a need for coherence, internalization, and belief.

The "theme" approach was closely linked with a "start small and experiment" approach that proved successful. It let schools take advantage of unanticipated opportunities that might have been viewed as distractions if a master plan were being followed. Agassiz learned by happenstance about summer programs linking students to area colleges, which became a main thrust in their efforts to increase college application rates.

Starting with small and diverse efforts also helped program components to be locally (and invisibly) tested. Evidence of their value, fit, and impact could be produced without the high risk of public scrutiny. Such strategies address the problem of technical uncertainty facing schools (Perrow, 1979; Cohen, 1989) and deal with the motivation problems uncertainty generates (Brunsson, 1985).

TABLE 7–2. Improvement Themes in the Five Sites[*]

AGASSIZ:
Fix what looks bad cosmetically
Get attendance working better
Get discipline under control
Get specific success in small programs (ROTC, health services, parenting)
Build staff and student energy
Empower administrators and staff (coordinator jobs, etc.)
Provide social services for students
Get good goal-setting and planning going at the department level
Build community involvement, raise image of school through publicity
Expand cluster program
Develop new curriculum

ALAMEDA:
Empower staff, mobilize faculty
Get innovative projects, new courses, going
Clean up environment, fix graffiti
Bring order, better discipline
Go beyond just caring to effective teaching
Do goal setting and strategy planning with entire staff
Get good staff development on teaching content and skills
Model improved supervision/teaching
Build internal cadre of staff development managers
Get staff ownership of change
Build culture of communication and sharing
Empower students
Decentralize decisions
Push for steady curriculum change and development

BARTHOLDI:
Improve attendance
Get social services to students
Get student jobs
Link to public sector organization
Get at-risk students into the program
Improve organizational functions: attendance, security
Make the pieces work, coordinate new and old programs
Develop new programs (both at-risk and across whole school)

BURROUGHS:
Build staff planning group, empowered cadre
Emphasize student skills and attitude development
Mobilize faculty interest in improvement
Improve reading in the content areas
Improve faculty's ability to work with young adolescents
Initiate and support teaming
Develop faculty knowledge about testing
Improve math in the content areas
Change toward a middle school structure (team teaching, attention to student problems)
Improve student motivation
Do faculty advisory groups (improve self-esteem and motivation)
Add new courses

CHESTER:
Implement the MES program pieces (attendance, computers, career resource room, etc.)
Specify curriculum objectives in quarterly lesson plans; align curriculum with testing;
   improve remediation
Implement student incentives/awards
Deal with state requirements (testing, remediation)
Plan to reorganize
Carry out reorganization

[*]Louis, K. S., & Miles, M. B. (1990). *Improving the urban high school: What works and why.* New York: Teachers College Press. Reprinted with permission of the author.

PROBLEMS AND COPING

Next we turn to a major management task: coping with problems as change efforts proceed. Major school improvement efforts, no matter how well planned, encounter a wide range of problems at all stages. Some of these are small and easy—so routine in fact, that they may not even be perceived as problems. Others are more severe, demanding acknowledgment and action.

Any change program represents not only a demand on energy, but a potential threat to existing routines. Change also heightens uncertainty, so that normal responses to problems are not made, or don't seem to work. Finally, the more substantial the change effort, the more likely it is to be complex and to incorporate potentially conflicting parts. It is not surprising that the typical principal in the survey mentioned three or four major problems, and several less severe ones (Louis & Miles, 1990). School improvement is problem rich.

Problems in the case study schools seemed to arise from three general sources: the change program, the people involved, and the organizational setting. They clustered as follows and are arranged roughly from most to least tractable.

Program Problems

PROCESS.   A wide range of problems occurred, from poor coordination (who would provide guidance services to which student groups at Bartholdi) to delays, conflicts (opposition to team teaching at Burroughs), and sheer lack of planning (last-minute frenzy in locating Bartholdi students eligible for awards, when the ceremony had been scheduled for weeks).

CONTENT.   The time-on-task program at Chester ran into severe resistance from high school faculty who said it had no applicability to their daily work; the dropout improvement efforts at Bartholdi ran into a "Catch 22": success with dropouts would make attendance figures worse, and vice versa.

People Problems

TARGET POPULATION.   Implementation at Bartholdi was hindered when the "hard-to-reach" group of near-dropouts proved, in fact, to be hard to reach. Similar problems were encountered in trying to involve parents at Burroughs.

LACK OF SKILLS.   Teachers and administrators lacked the know-how that the change effort required. The Bartholdi cabinet apparently had no idea of how effective group decisions could be reached; the Agassiz leaders knew they were naive in planning processes; the Burroughs teachers had no experience in team teaching.

ATTITUDES AND SENTIMENTS.   Problems with people's feelings ranged from direct resistance and skepticism to lack of hope—"We always start things, we never finish them." Philosophical disagreements arose in some contexts, like the arguments of Burroughs staff with the principal's middle school concepts.

Context Problems

COMPETING EXTERNAL DEMANDS.   Pressures from outside the school required time and energy that should have been devoted to program implementation. For example, at Agassiz, these included a new district-originated curriculum, pressure to raise scores on the state achievement test, and a rash of district-sponsored tests.

Normal crises.   Unexpected events ranged from a heart attack of the key vice principal at Chester, to the unanticipated decision to close the only successful vocational education program at Agassiz.

Powerlessness.   Lack of control over budget, staffing, and key district policies produced problems. In Bartholdi, for example, the principal had no say at all over who would be assigned to teach in his school and described some recent arrivals as "practically bag ladies."[7]

Physical plant.   A typical problem occurred in Bartholdi, where there was simply no office space for nine new counselors funded by the change program.

Resources.   People frequently complained about lack of time to carry out the program, along with feelings of overload. Lack of funds was less frequently mentioned in the case schools.[8]

MINDING THE STORE.   As this list suggests, there is a major change-management need: coordinating or orchestrating the evolution of the program. Any change effort that is more than trivial, or which involves many parts of the school, becomes a set of management issues. None of the decisions may be monumental. But a cumulative backlog of unmade decisions—poor orchestration and coordination—can lead to serious logjams. In Chester and Bartholdi, this did not seem to be appreciated:

> In Chester, the principal was supposedly coordinating the multiple strands of [the programs], but often did not know the status of particular aspects when asked. Furthermore, only one of the sub-programs involved had a coordinator built into the budget.
> In Bartholdi, the desk of the supposed coordinator was usually buried in unsorted paper. Between teaching, meetings outside the school, and work with students, he had almost no time to keep the strands of the overall program together. People complained repeatedly that they did not know what was going on.

In both these schools, weak coordination became a sort of megaproblem that made the other "normal problems" of change much worse.

In our more successful schools, on the other hand, active coordination and orchestration was frequent and taken for granted:

> At Agassiz, the principal met often and repeatedly with a "kitchen cabinet" that included a 25% time Development Officer and two outside resource people to assess where the change effort was going. Most specific sub-programs had appointed managers as well.

We estimate that the sheer amount of time devoted to coordination varies directly with implementation success. Agassiz and Alameda spent at least ten times as much time on coordination as Chester, and perhaps five times as much as Burroughs and Bartholdi.

In addition, in the successful schools, the coordinator role(s) were seen as legitimate by the rest of the faculty. In contrast,

The coordinator at Bartholdi worried that his work would be seen by the assistant principals in the cabinet (where one visitor felt like "a flounder in a shark tank") as infringing on their prerogatives.

Problem Finding

In the more successful schools, deliberate scanning for problems was used on a regular basis. Daily informal base-touching ("management by walking around") and open, regular discussion of problems in meetings were routine and typical, and problems were seen as natural occurrences:

> Faced with teacher skepticism, the planning team at Agassiz did not classify it as resistance....Instead, one member said, "They need to know that people working with them identify with their problems...and know what can be done about them. They need to know they're not alone with the problems they face."

In less successful sites, problems remained invisible and undiscussed until they manifested themselves as overwhelming crises or occasions for blame and defensiveness.

Coping with Problems

Not all problems get solved equally well, even where there is effort to coordinate and orchestrate. The variation in solution quality depends largely on coping efforts—the pattern of behavior that appears when a problem is noticed or defined.

COPING FRAMES. Coping efforts appeared to correspond to a general frame or set of basic assumption that lie behind the pattern. Three general frames that emerged are consistent with the change literature: technical coping, political coping, and cultural coping (House, 1981; Tichy, 1981; Miles & Louis, 1987). Examples of all three frames can be drawn from Agassiz:

> *Technical coping:* [An] effort is made to ensure that each problem has a solution perking...the key external support personnel feel that it is their role to come up with support for technical solutions. For example, the problem of staff morale was approached through a training program, "Investments in Excellence," that focuses on problems of burnout and low efficacy.
>
> *Political coping:* The principal recognized very early that his standing in the school would depend on his willingness to challenge [the central office] and back his staff. He forestalled the elimination of a key voc. ed. program, fought for cosmetic improvements in the building, and negotiated for extra time to hire a more talented new bilingual department chair than was found in the original pool of applicants.
>
> *Cultural coping:* The principal publicizes school successes heavily, keeps a notebook of press clippings, found money for a lavish Christmas dance and a pancake breakfast to bring staff and parents together, and put pressure on kids to show up with at least one relative for "back to school night"; the staff was deeply affected by the evidence that parents cared.

As these examples show, many coping activities exhibit characteristics of more than one frame. For instance, a change in the schedule so that the English department could meet had distinct technical benefits, but its visibility symbolized the seriousness of the principal's commitment.

COPING STYLES AND STRATEGY.   Some problems can be solved simply. Other issues are less tractable, and require *deep coping*. In our schools, examples of non-trivial problems included key change leaders leaving the school; a new state mandate that distracted staff from the school's own programs; a serious student discipline problem that undermined a campaign to increase positive community involvement; and, after a review, staff's rejecting a major component of the program that did not "fit" the school.

The tendency of solid change managers is to search constantly for, acknowledge, and confront serious problems when they first appear and to act rapidly to make major adjustments to solve them. Less effective change managers use only *shallow coping* techniques that are more appropriate for small or transient problems. For example, in response to an urgent need to have teachers in a specific program activity meet and plan, the shallow coper may postpone making a decision ("we'll deal with that in next year's schedule") or avoid a structural solution in favor of exhortation (urge the teachers to meet after school voluntarily). The deep coper, on the other hand, might rearrange the school's schedule or negotiate with the district to provide a stipend for weekend work.

Coping also involves enormous *persistence and tenacity*. Good copers choose targets for long-term action, and stick to them. If lack of school control over personnel assignments affects the change program, they will attack this problem from every possible angle over a period of months (or even years). If staff need new skills, but many don't yet perceive this, the good coper will recognize the need for a long time line, modeling of the desired behaviors, training, or technical assistance—and will muster all possible resources to address the problem.

Altogether we found 23 distinct coping strategies used by the five schools. Table 7–3 shows a list of these strategies, arranged in an order from most shallow to most deep, and clustered into 9 coping styles.

TABLE 7–3.   Coping Styles and Strategies[*]

STYLE	TYPICAL STRATEGIES
Do nothing	No coping (either by omission or deliberately).
Temporize	Delaying, postponing, rescheduling.
Do it the usual way	Firefighting, giving problem to existing group or role, following through, applying a routine.
Ease off	Simplifying, aiming for less.
Do it harder	Pressuring, supporting, exhorting adding energy, providing rewards or incentives.
Build personal capacity	Training, coaching, giving supervisory feedback, teaching new concepts.
Build system capacity	Creating new groups for coordination, vision building, doing "rolling planning," providing assistance.
Restaff	Recruiting and hiring large numbers of new staff, to change the mix of attitudes, skills, and knowledge.
Redesign the system	Empowering of new roles or groups; changing procedures, time use, tasks, responsibilities; reorganizing.

[*]Louis, K. S., & Miles, M. B. (1990). *Improving the urban high school: What works and why.* New York: Teachers College Press. Reprinted with permission of the author.

The cases show a clear and strong relationship between coping depth and implementation effectiveness; good implementation was in turn closely associated with positive program effects on students, teachers, and general organizational functioning. Most of the instances of "shallow" coping (none at all, temporizing, using "normal routines") appear in the two less successful sites, Chester and Bartholdi. Coping at this level did not seem to lead to implementation success. Deeper managing and coping strategies (improving capacities of persons and the system, restaffing, and role/organizational redesign) were used mostly by more successful sites, and were notably absent in Chester. Burroughs and Bartholdi employed a few "deep" strategies, but fewer than those at Alameda and Agassiz.

HOW GOOD COPING WORKS.   A further look at the cases also suggests two additional principles: *assertiveness* and *problem appropriateness*. Our more successful sites were proactive about coping. They never failed to act, and they very rarely postponed action—doing this only when a holding action was required. At Agassiz, even holding actions became strong programmatic improvement efforts:

> Agassiz's principal deliberately postponed attention to the difficult problem of teacher resistance to program changes until he could, in effect, buy credibility through serious attention to school order and safety, through a strong discipline-guidance activity coordinated by the three assistant principals.

A careful look at the linkage between the type of problem (more to less tractable) and coping style also suggests that more successful sites keyed the depth of their coping to the difficulty of the problem. In metaphorical terms, they did not carry out major surgery when a Band-Aid was needed. The survey data are strongly confirmatory: 76 percent of schools that did wide-range, problem-appropriate coping reported above-average changes in the school organization (improved communication, problem solving, departmental collaboration). For schools with narrower coping styles, only 35 percent reported organizational impact. Wide-range coping also had a moderate effect on teachers' morale, teaching methods, and skills; on student achievement, attitudes, and behavior; and on local institutionalization of the program. (Interestingly, problem-appropriate coping in individuals follows a similar pattern, according to Roth and Cohen, 1986. They divided coping into "approach" and "avoidance" categories and, in reviewing studies found that healthy individuals tended to use "avoidance" strategies such as denial or postponement when they seemed appropriate, but were also capable of strong "approach"-oriented strategies when the problem required it.)

We should also note that the more successful sites were likely to use a mix of technical, political, and cultural interventions (as we saw at Agassiz) while less successful ones were characteristically more focused on technical interventions, with occasional forays into the political. In fact, successful use of cultural strategies was largely limited to Agassiz and Alameda—although attempted at Burroughs, they never reached the staff as a whole. And at Chester

> ...though cultural norms ("don't rock the boat") and beliefs ("we are not good finishers") were a major barrier, it was rare to see any cultural coping at all. The only one tried (putting program goals on a school banner) had almost no impact.

WHAT LEADS TO BETTER COPING?   Better coping is more likely when certain preconditions have been worked out. First, *coherent, shared themes and vision* about the plan for improvement seem to increase confidence in making active coping decisions. In the survey, 67 percent of schools with high goal consensus had good coping; only 21 percent of low goal-consensus schools coped well.

Vision provided change managers with an ability to sense at an earlier point when things were "going wrong" and seemed to create the conditions needed for more open discussion about the need for coping. A negative example comes from Chester:

> The program had been mandated from the central office, and was not discussed or "owned" by the faculty or even the administrators. Thus shallow coping (delaying, avoiding) was frequent—as a method of successfully avoiding the pains of implementation.

Awareness and effort were also important. Good coping rests on routines for personal and organizational learning (Abbey-Livingston & Kelleher, 1988; Lowy et al., 1986; Hedberg, 1981), such as empowerment of key groups, good information flow to managers, and encouragement of self-reflective action. In actively coping schools, such as Agassiz, Alameda, and Burroughs, the principal and others were very self-conscious about thinking and learning from the consequences of their coping. Reflectiveness was aided in these three schools by the presence of a core group with whom the principal felt very free to discuss implementation dilemmas.

Assistance was important in several of the schools—usually in the form of a helper outside the schools, who could provide open feedback on success and problems. In Agassiz, this came from the school's business partner, who was deeply interested in improving management skills in the school; in Bartholdi, improvement occurred in part because of the advisory services of a retired principal; in Alameda, the principal and the superintendent were close, and of like minds with regard to the school's vision.

The survey data were very strong here: 87 percent of schools with high levels of external assistance were good copers; only 35 percent of low-assistance schools coped well.

Finally, deep coping itself—as a way of mobilizing further good coping through *durable structures*—was important. Some of the early deep-coping activities, such as setting up new coordinating roles (Alameda), redesigning the school schedule to permit work on change (Agassiz), or initiating grade-level teams (Bartholdi)—appeared in turn to mobilize a wider range of coping efforts because they *involved more people* in the coping arena. Thus, human resources available to cope were expanded beyond the principal's office.

THE ENDURING EFFECTS OF PLANNING AND COPING

This analysis has spun out several arguments. First, we have said that it is not necessary to abandon schoolwide planning just because the real world of educational decision-making is messy and nonrational. Instead, schools wishing to make major shifts in their operations and effectiveness must recognize that they are embarking on a long journey during which their goals and activities—and the nature of the school itself—will evolve. Major reforms are not planned and then implemented, in blueprint-to-building style.

We've argued that evolutionary planning departs from most other descriptions of planning in three significant ways:

- The first premise of evolutionary planning is *act—then plan.*
- The second premise is to *pay less attention to "mission" and more to inspirational themes* to guide the change process.
- The third premise is that evolutionary change requires *reflection on the relationship between action and improvement,* including the careful effort to renew staff commitment to both.

These characteristics of leadership in planning turn out, when we look at coping, to have multiple effects. The notion that action creates learning that induces more and better action is reflected in the finding that deep coping creates the conditions for improved future coping; attention to inspirational themes promotes a vision that increases sensitivity to specific problems that need to be dealt with; reflectiveness is a precondition for organizational learning from action—whether plans are being made for future directions, or decisions are contemplated about how to deal with unanticipated or recurrent problems. If evolutionary planning is mainly a strategic, leadership function, then coping is its tactical, managerial counterpart.

But the reader may still be left with a "so what" feeling. Do planning and coping really make a difference in most schools, or are these case studies unusual? This chapter has emphasized the processes of planning and coping, but if we briefly summarize our survey data, we find an answer to this final question. Multiple regression analysis, a statistical technique that permits examination of the influence of a wide variety of different factors that may affect whether or not schools actually become more effective, was used. No matter what we looked at—the initial emphasis of the program, the employment history of teachers, the socioeconomic characteristics of students in the schools, the implementation problems that the schools encountered, or the pressures and support from the district office and state—good planning and coping contributed significantly to the movement of schools toward improved student achievement (see Louis & Miles, 1990).[9]

CONCLUSION

Our analysis confirms that there are no simple blueprints for changing urban high schools. But it can be done, and we know how it works. In both the five case study schools and the larger survey sample, we can identify clear leadership and management approaches—including concrete action suggestions—that will make success much more likely in the enormous, urgent task of urban school reform.

R E F E R E N C E S

ABBEY-LIVINGSTON, D., & KELLEHER, D. (1988). *Managing for learning in organizations: The fundamentals.* Toronto: Ministry of Tourism and Information.

ALLISON, G. (1971). *The essence of decision: Explaining the Cuban missile crisis.* Boston: Little, Brown.

ANDERSON, B., & ODDEN, A. (1988). State initiatives can foster school improvement. *Phi Delta Kappan, 67,* 578–81.

BERMAN, P. (1981). Educational change: An implementation paradigm. In R. Lehming & M. Kane (Eds.), *Improving schools: Using what we know.* Beverly Hills, CA: Sage.

BERMAN, P., & MCLAUGHLIN, M. (1974). *Federal programs supporting educational change.* Vol. I. *A model of educational change.* Santa Monica, CA: Rand.

BLOCK, P. (1987). *The empowered manager.* San Francisco: Jossey-Bass.

BRUNSSON, N. (1985). *The irrational organization.* New York: John Wiley.

CLARK, D., MCKIBBIN, S., & MALKAS, M. (1980). *New perspectives on planning in educational organizations.* San Francisco: Far West Laboratory.

COHEN, D. (1989). Plus ça change, (unpublished paper). East Lansing: Center for the Study of Teaching, Michigan State University.

CRANDALL, D., EISEMAN, J., & LOUIS, K. S. (1986). Strategic planning issues that bear on the success of school improvement efforts. *Educational Administration Quarterly, 22,* 21–53.

EGAN, G. (1988). Change agent skills: Assessing and designing excellence. San Diego: University Associates.

FARRAR, E., DESANCTIS, J., & COHEN, D. (1980). Views from below: Implementation research in education. *Teachers College Record, 82,* 77–100.

FARRAR, E., NEUFELD, B., & MILES, M. B. (1984). Effective schools programs in high schools: Social promotion or movement by merit? *Phi Delta Kappan, 65*(10), 701–706.

HALL, G., & HORD, S. (1987). *Change in schools: Facilitating the process.* Albany, NY: SUNY Press.

HEDBERG, B. (1981). How organizations learn and unlearn. In P. Nystrom & W. Starbuck (Eds.), *Handbook of organizational design,* Vol. 1, pp. 3–27. Oxford: Oxford University Press.

HOUSE, E. (1981). Three perspectives on innovation. In R. Lehming & M. Kane (Eds.), *Improving schools: Using what we know,* pp. 17–41. Beverly Hills, CA: Sage.

HUBERMAN, M., & MILES, M. (1984). *Innovation up close.* New York: Plenum Press.

IACOCCA, L., & NOVAK, W. (1984). *Iacocca: An autobiography.* New York: Bantam Books.

KANTER, R. M. (1983). *The change masters.* New York: Simon & Schuster.

LIGHTFOOT, S. (1983). *The good high school.* New York: Basic Books.

LINDBLOM, C. (1959). The science of muddling through. *Public Administration Review, 19,* 79–88.

LOTTO, L., CLARK, D., & CARROLL, M. (1980). Understanding planning in educational organizations: Generative concepts and key variables. In D. Clark, S. McKibbin, & M. Malkas (Eds.), *New perspectives on planning in educational organizations,* p. 20. San Francisco: Far West Laboratory.

LOUIS, K. S., & DENTLER, R. A. (1988). Knowledge use and school improvement. *Curriculum Inquiry, 18,* 33–62.

LOUIS, K. S., & MILES, M. B. (1990). *Improving the urban high school: What works and why.* New York: Teachers College Press.

LOUIS, K. S., ROSENBLUM, S., & MOLITOR, J. (1981). *Strategies for knowledge use and school improvement.* Washington, D.C.: National Institute of Education.

LOWY, A., KELLEHER, D., & FINESTONE, P. (June 1986). Management learning: Beyond program design. *Training and Development Journal*, pp. 34–37.

MARCH, J., & OLSEN, J. (1986). Garbage can models of decision making in organizations. In J. March & R. Weissinger-Babylon (Eds.), *Ambiguity and command: Organizational perspective on military decision-making*. Marshfield, MA: Pitman.

McCUNE, S. D. (1986). *Guide to strategic planning for educators*. Alexandria, VA: Association for Supervision and Curriculum Development.

MILES, M. B., & KAUFMAN, T. (1985). A directory of programs promoting effective practices at the classroom and building levels. In R. M. J. Kyle (Ed.), *Reaching for excellence: An effective schools sourcebook*. Washington, D.C.: U.S. Government Printing Office.

MILES, M. B., & HUBERMAN, M. (1984). *Qualitative data analysis: A sourcebook of new methods*. Newbury Park, CA: Sage.

MILES, M. B., & LOUIS, K. S. (1987). Research on institutionalization: A reflective review. In M. Miles, M. Ekholm, & R. Vandenberghe (Eds.), *Lasting school improvement: Exploring the processes of institutionalization*. Leuven, Belgium: Acco.

MILES, R., & RANDOLPH, W. A. (1981). Influence of organizational learning styles on early development. In J. R. Kimberly & R. H. Miles (Eds.), *The organizational life cycle*, pp. 44–82. San Francisco: Jossey-Bass.

PAVA, C. (1986). New strategies for systems change: Reclaiming non-synoptic methods. *Human Relations, 39*, 615–33.

PERROW, C. (1970). *Organizational analysis: A sociological view*. Monterey: Brooks/Cole.

PFEFFER, J., & SALANCIK, G. (1978). *The external control of organizations: A resource dependence theory*. New York: Harper.

POWELL, A., COHEN, D., & FARRAR, E. (1985). *The shopping mall high school*. New York: Houghton Mifflin.

PURKEY, S. C., RUTTER, R. A., & NEWMANN, F. M. (1987). U.S. high school improvement programs: A profile from the high school and beyond supplemental survey. *Metropolitan Education, 3*, 51–91.

ROTH, S., & COHEN, L. J. (1986). Approach, avoidance and coping with stress. *American Psychologist, 41*, 813–19.

SCHÖN, D. (1987). *Educating the reflective practitioner*. San Francisco: Jossey-Bass.

SERGIOVANNI, T. J., BURLINGAME, M., COOMBS, F., & THURSTON, P. (1987). *Educational governance and administration*, 2nd ed. Englewood Cliffs, NJ: Prentice Hall.

STEINER, G. (1979). *Strategic planning: What every manager must know*. New York: The Free Press.

TICHY, N. M. (1981). *Managing strategic change*. New York: John Wiley.

U. S. GENERAL ACCOUNTING OFFICE. (1989). *Effective schools programs: Their extent and characteristics*. Report GAO/HRD-89-132BR. Gaithersburg, MD: GAO.

WEICK, K. (1976). Educational organizations as loosely coupled systems. *Administrative Science Quarterly, 21*(1), 1–19.

ENDNOTES

[1]Authorship of this chapter was shared equally, and the order of our names was determined by the flip of a coin. We would like to thank our colleagues Anthony Cipollone, the late Eleanore Farrar, and Sheila Rosenblum who prepared some of the case studies on which

this chapter is based. Our research was funded, in part, by the Regional Laboratory for Educational Improvement of the Northeast and Islands, the Far West Laboratory for Educational Research and Development, the Conrad Hilton Foundation, the Fund for New Jersey, the Boston Foundation, the North Central Regional Educational Laboratory, and the U. S. Office of Educational Research and Improvement through the National Center for Effective Secondary Schools at the University of Wisconsin. The conclusions and opinions expressed in this chapter are the sole responsibility of the authors, and do not necessarily reflect the views of the supporting agencies.

[2]The survey, carried out in 1985, aimed at reaching all nonspecialized high schools in cities of over 75,000 that had been implementing an effective schools-derived program beginning between 1981 and 1984, with some visible signs of improvement. A sample of 279, drawn from nominations by foundation, association, and effective schools program developers, was reduced to 178 using the foregoing criteria. A 27-page interview guide was administered by phone to the principal or equivalently knowledgeable administrator. The data set of 130 variables was analyzed using simple frequencies, cross-tabulations, and regression analysis.

[3]We used the last criterion to rule out reform that succeeded mainly because of a single individual's personality.

[4]A more complete description of the data-collection strategies, and an integration of the two data sources, are found in Louis and Miles (1990).

[5]A note of caution: This works only if the do-then-plan action takes place at the school level and a core group of faculty are already supportive of change. In Chester, district action and training on Instructional Program Leadership preceded planning at the school level, and this was viewed as a threat. Action in the district office does not necessarily produce learning in the school.

[6]The need for specific goals is probably greater when the "innovation" is a single program. But if broad reform of the school is needed, it may be more appropriate to think of "targets of change"—classroom teaching, department functioning, whole-school climate— rather than "goals." A look at change efforts in business suggests that urban high schools are not unique in this respect. See Kanter (1983) and Iacocca and Novak (1984). Having broad goals need not necessarily conflict with the traditional effective schools focus on student outcomes. See Table 7–2 for examples of goal focus in the case study schools that illustrate this.

[7]Note that even in this very bureaucratic and centralized district, principals in other schools were exercising creative insubordination by hiring teachers through advertisements in *The New York Times* rather than through the central personnel office.

[8]The case study schools had higher levels of dollar resources allocated to the change effort than most schools in the survey.

[9]Multiple least squares linear regression, using the SAS analysis package.

8

ASSISTING CHANGE FROM WITHOUT: THE TECHNICAL ASSISTANCE FUNCTION

Susan Loucks-Horsley
The Regional Laboratory for Educational Improvement of the Northeast and Islands

Susan Mundry
The NETWORK, Inc.
Andover, Massachusetts

INTRODUCTION

Designing and implementing an effective schools program tailored to a particular school or district setting is a complex and challenging task, one that few educators have the knowledge, expertise, and time to undertake on their own. In one way, mounting an effective schools program is like building a house. One can hire a contractor to oversee and manage the plumbing, electricity, and painting, and so forth, or one can "self-contract" and handle all components oneself. Having someone from outside the school assist with program development and implementation is much like having a contractor. Knowing what it takes to implement an effective schools program and sharing responsibility for success, the external assister can help schools make more informed decisions about how to improve and who can best help them do so at various stages.

External assistance combines a great many functions—including training, evaluation, information provision, coordination, coaching, consultation— that are critical to the success of effective schools programs as well as other improvement efforts. This chapter first introduces the concept of external assistance. It then introduces three models for providing assistance and isolates key commonalities to help educators better choose external assisters for their own programs.

THE CONTRIBUTIONS OF EXTERNAL ASSISTANCE

Rosenblum (1981) defines technical assistance as

> ...a process of providing the best available information, guidance, and help, in an appropriate time and manner, in order to increase the effectiveness of local educational practice. It involves an in-person relationship between a helper and a help-needing system or individual. The helper, usually external to the local system, provides assistance to the client in addressing some current needs or priorities. (p. 1)

Twenty years ago the term "technical assistance" was rarely used in educational circles. Yet in the past ten years, it has become an increasingly well-known and desirable aspect of development and improvement activity at all levels of education. Hundreds of entries on the topic can be found in the professional literature, many federal programs now include funds for technical assistance to grantees, state and regional agency personnel are providing technical assistance, and many district improvement programs build in technical assistance for program implementation.

While the term and its operations are relatively new, its origins and contemporary connections lie deep in older disciplines, among them human services, organizational development, agricultural extension, and continuing education. Yet there remains little consensus about what technical assistance is, how it should be done, and what specific impact it has, because for each instance in which it is used, it is designed to address different conditions and purposes (Crandall & Williams, 1981).

While technical assistance has increased, many educational settings are still untouched by it. Historically, schools have had a limited number of options for help in their efforts to improve. These included journal articles and other descriptions of research and new strategies and approaches, training through university courses or special programs such as summer institutes which targeted individual educators rather than schools, and ad hoc consultation. The inadequacy of each of these approaches is amply supported in the research. Research reported by Crandall and Loucks (1983), Emrick and Peterson (1980), and Stearns and Norwood (1977) indicates that schools and the people within them do not change their practices as a result of print materials—even those that are very explicit about the behaviors, procedures, and structures needed to succeed. In-person assistance is required for change to occur.

Evaluations of the National Science Foundations summer institutes in the 1960s and 1970s point out the inadequacy of training educators outside their school settings. Even the most skillful teachers have difficulty implementing new practices without follow-up help at home and the support of school administrators who make appropriate structural changes and have appropriate expectations.

Ad hoc consultation has its drawbacks as well (Clifford & Trohanis, 1980). If choosing experts either because they are accessible or because they come recommended by others in similar situations, schools who contract with consultants to share their expertise and experience are often disappointed in the results. This is typically because (1) the expert's skills sometimes do not match the specific needs of the school, and they are all he or she is able to deliver; (2) the time frame is usually limited, for example, a one- to two-day visit or workshop, during which it is impossible to understand sufficiently the context and work on an adequate course of action; and (3) consultants lack the long-term commitment required for meaningful change to occur (Clifford & Trohanis, 1980). This explains why some research on program implementation finds outside assistance of limited value: ad hoc consultants rarely share responsibility for the success of the effort (Berman & McLaughlin, 1978).

The kind of changes called for to foster effective schools, and school improvement in general, require more intensive and extensive assistance for schools than materials, training, or consultants alone can supply. In their introduction to a recent book on external support for schools in developed countries around the world, Louis and Loucks-Horsley (1989) noted that external support to schools can help them address the factors demonstrated by research to contribute to successful improvement. Some of these factors, critical as well to effective schools programs, are

> *The Requirement of Sustained Time and Attention.* Change is a process that takes time and considerable attention if it is to succeed. Yet the primary business of schools is to deliver services to students on an ongoing basis, a demanding task that requires the full attention of staff. External assistance can help school people engage with the activities required to design and implement an effective schools program, often serving as a catalyst, providing a focus for their attention to other than the ongoing running of the school.

> *The Centrality and Quality of the Innovation.* Improvement is likely to occur when it is focused on core educational activities such as curriculum, instruction, and the learning environment of the school—the core of effective schools programs. Innovation in these activities can be fostered through the use of experts with specialized knowledge as well as the ability to work with teachers in an ongoing way to develop and incorporate new practices that fit their students and their communities.

> *The Scope and Complexity of the Innovation.* Improvement efforts succeed more frequently when they require significant changes by individuals and when a critical mass of individuals from a school is involved. Both are requirements of effective schools programs. Helping a school staff and community—with their many different skills, interests, and motivations—to design and develop an effective schools program can be aided by a neutral third party with loyalty to none of the special interests represented.

> *Administrator Advocacy.* All the research points to the importance of commitment and support from district-level administrators and active involvement and direction from those at the building level. Yet these individuals are often not equipped to facilitate the kinds of activities and create the kinds of environments where effective schools programs can occur and be sustained. Assistance in developing necessary skills and structures, while supporting the efforts of administrators on a continuing basis, can substantially improve the chances of success.

With these kinds of needs suggested, it is clear that technical assistance for effective schools is not a sporadic, episodic activity. Good technical assistance shares responsibility with the school for the success of its effort. A recent definition captures the complexity:

> Technical assistance [is] an ongoing, interactive, intensely personal process, built on a trusting and open system of communication, that is able to provide access to the best up-to-date information, adapted to the needs of the client. T[echnical assistance] is sensitive to the client's institutional history, the current state of affairs, and the level of understanding of the issues at hand. T[echnical assistance] includes discrete activities...but those discrete activities are never provided alone. They must occur in the context of an exploration and clarification of the needs of the client: preparatory activities to...adjust the process to be appropriate to the stages of concern and of development of

the client with regard to the specific activity, facilitation during the activity, attention to transition of the client back to their setting, follow-up conversations to insure usefulness and adaption to client needs, and thought as to the next steps. It is an objective-oriented problem solving approach. (Watkins, 1989, pp. 2–3)

Individuals who provide technical assistance to effective schools programs can fruitfully play a number of different roles, and these are described at length in the literature on educational field agents (Butler & Paisley, 1977; Crandall, 1977; Havelock, 1969). Crandall (1977) describes the external assister as a "specialized generalist," someone who must have specialized skills to play the various roles, but be able to apply them to nearly any situation. He discusses both prerequisite attributes and technical skills needed by assisters. He believes that it is far more difficult, and perhaps impossible, to train assisters in the nontechnical areas and that selecting individuals who have the prerequisite attributes is far more efficient if it can be done. Prerequisite attributes include

> *Cognitive habits and abilities* such as the ability to abstract and conceptualize basic elements of a problem, provide original ideas and fresh perspectives, and resist premature closure while proceeding to closure when appropriate.
>
> *Intrapersonal competencies* such as proactivity, maturity, and systematic reflectivity (using past experience to influence and inform the nature of subsequent experience).
>
> *Work-related characteristics* such as taking initiative and being dependable and productive.
>
> *Personal qualities* such as being able to express himself or herself openly and directly, being self-directed, and having a sense of and concern for justice.

Technical skill clusters are problem solving, communication, resource utilization, planning, process helping, implementation, content/subject matter knowledge, evaluation and documentation, and survival (Crandall, 1977).

Miles, Saxl, and Lieberman (1988) note that empirical research on the skills of effective assisters is relatively thin. Their study of assisters for three New York City effective schools programs has begun to provide an empirical base to the literature on successful change agents. On the basis of interviews, observations, and additional measures, they identified 18 skills, including trust/rapport building, confrontation, confidence building, diagnosing organizations, and managing/controlling.

While an external assister's skills play an important role in determining the effectiveness of the assistance, the process the assister uses also greatly influences outcomes. The process of providing technical assistance to a client in an effective schools program involves several critical elements which may be weighted or emphasized differently, depending on the setting and the overall strategy or strategies employed. Six critical elements involved in technical assistance are

- Understanding and awareness of context
- Building support
- Establishing goals and plans
- Allocating materials and resources
- Problem solving
- Installing the change permanently or transferring responsibility (institutionalization)

The following discussion describes the common features and the issues that may ensue at various points of the process. Then, three different strategies or models of technical assistance are presented and compared.

It is important to note that the success of technical assistance depends on a high degree of commitment from both the external assister and the changing organization. Particularly within the context of effective schools, hit-and-run or one-shot assistance will rarely bring about sustained changes or lasting school improvement. Effective technical assistance requires an up-front commitment to support the process for some time and to implement change to its fullest intent (Huberman & Miles, 1984; Carlson, 1987; Fuhrman, Clune, & Elmore, 1988).

Understanding and Awareness of Context

Schools operate in a context of confused priorities, buffeted by political forces and community crosscurrents (Crandall, Eisman, & Louis, 1986). Given this, understanding the context of a school takes on critical importance. School improvement does not happen in a vacuum but rather is a human dynamic that results when people within an organization improve their practices, systems, and structures. The external assister effectively helps organizations to change by assisting the individuals within those organizations to change. External assisters determine what is presently happening within the organization; they learn about the people, policies, processes, and practices that make up the present context of the system. The challenge to the external assister engaging an organization in planning is to understand fully what is happening both in the classrooms and organizationally.

What activities are needed to understand the context of the change? Effective schools research indicates that school improvement efforts should start with a data-collection effort (Maryland State Department of Education, 1983). The external assister may conduct a formal assessment of the organization; identify and talk to key individuals representing several constituencies; observe classrooms, parent groups, and staff meetings; and convene focus groups to examine the present state of the organization. These activities provide information about how the school is organized for such things as collaborative planning, staff development, parent involvement, student assessment and monitoring of progress, leadership, roles for staff, and so on.

As schools begin to explore practices that could improve their effectiveness, staff members need to understand what the new practices are and how the practices will affect them (Hord et al., 1987). For this reason, it is critically important for the technical assister to provide information and opportunities for staff to ask questions about the new practices. Often this is done through awareness sessions and materials that clearly and succinctly describe the proposed changes, the steps to making the changes, how staff will be supported, a time line for implementation, and how the program will be assessed.

Building Support

Carving out clear roles for staff and others (e.g., parents) is a critical element of effective schools programs. The external assister's role is to orchestrate the dissemination of information and the convening of groups to help define roles for staff and others and to build the needed support for the changes the school will undergo. Collegial activities such as committees help to build the commitment needed to sustain new efforts (Clark & McCarthy, 1983; Fuhrman, Clune, & Elmore, 1988). The external assister helps to manage this process by making sure that most people are involved in some way and by assessing when people are ready to move into deeper involvement, and when they need new or different information. To help sustain the changes, the external assister often trains an on-site person called a "local facilitator" to take over this role (Cox, 1983).

Once knowledgeable about the proposed changes and what they will look like in action, school personnel are more likely to make informed decisions about what must change within the school and how to make the necessary changes.

Establishing Goals and Plans

A critical part of the strategy for building support for change within an organization is goal setting or visioning. Goal setting is often tied to an assessment process; external assistors help schools administer instruments such as the Connecticut School Effectiveness Survey (Villanova et al., n.d.) or the New York state survey (Fitzgerald, n.d.) to pinpoint where interventions for improvement are needed. In planning for an effective school, the vision is far from open ended. The effective schools research provides a framework made up of the correlates of effective schools. Local contextual issues are also considered. The external assister helps school personnel and others in the school community to build their knowledge of the effective schools research in order to provide a basis for establishing goals and plans for improvement.

Allocating Materials and Resources

If schools are to achieve effectiveness, it is critical to move beyond goal setting to action. Unfortunately, great plans are often never implemented and the external assisters' function is over once the plan is developed. Effective outcomes will not be present until schools implement their planned changes (Bambur & Andrews, 1988).

One major pitfall cited by teachers and administrators who try to implement new programs is that they are not given the materials and resources they need. The effective external assister identifies the resources needed initially and helps the school to plan for replenishing any consumable materials.

Problem Solving

As people use a new practice or implement a plan they often encounter problems unaddressed in the training program or planning process, think of new or different ways to do things, and question whether they are implementing the new program effectively. Unaddressed questions or unsolved problems usually result in a lapse of use of the new practices. Initially, resolution of problems may be initiated by the external assister; as the users become more and more comfortable with the practice, someone from the organization making the change assumes responsibility for organizing to solve the problems.

Installing the Change Permanently

The most important step in any change intervention—planning for institutionalization—is often neglected. Much is known about the factors that contribute to institutionalization (e.g., administrative commitment, assistance, and mandates) as well as the factors that threaten institutionalization (e.g., stability of leadership and environmental turbulence) (Miles, 1983). External assisters play a critical role when they act to enhance the contributing factors and decrease the threatening ones.

The technical assister can help to plan for institutionalization from the very beginning by engaging clients in activities that affect institutionalization such as establishing policies, identifying funding, replenishing materials, planning for the transfer of responsibility from the external assister to internal staff, and providing refresher training and training for new staff.

THREE ASSISTANCE MODELS

Different models of technical assistance for effective schools programs put varying degrees of emphasis on each of the six elements just described. Now we compare three distinctive school improvement models—a planning and capacity-building model, a training and follow-up assistance model, and an adoption assistance model—to illustrate further alternative external assisters' roles in promoting effective schools.

Planning and Capacity-Building Model

Discussed in the work of Ronald Edmonds, Lawrence Lezotte, Wilbur Brookover, and others, the planning and capacity-building model is most frequently used to promote effective schools. For example, in a recent Council of Chief State School Officers report, 21 of 37 states reported using planning and capacity building as a comprehensive model of school effectiveness (CCSSO, 1988).

As the name suggests, this model emphasizes planning. Its purpose is not only to plan changes in school organization, classroom practice, and other processes within the education organization, but also to train and enable individuals within the organization to continue to improve and to institutionalize improvements. The external assister's role over time diminishes as individuals in the organization take a greater and greater role in managing the school improvement process.

The external assister operating within this model serves as a facilitator of change and linker to a knowledge base. The external assister must fully understand the components of an effective school and know what they look like in action. What, for example, is strong instructional leadership and what form works best in the context of a particular school? What mechanisms have successfully built support in schools implementing an effective schools model? The external assister focuses primarily on determining what the situation is within the school or educational institution and making recommendations and developing plans for necessary changes. The role also includes helping the organization to build support for changes that will be made. This includes developing systems to enable support at both the administrative and grass-roots levels and developing staff's content expertise in the area of effective schools research.

In the school effectiveness model disseminated by Lezotte and his associates, a building planning committee—with teacher, administrator, and often parent and student representatives—is formed and empowered to plan changes in the school (Sudlow, 1985). The commitment as well as the broad range of views represented on the building planning committee helps expand support for changes. Administrators introduce the reform movement to all staff and provide opportunities to discuss expectations and proposed changes. Everyone in the school takes responsibility for becoming effective. Some people serve on a committee, others gather information, all attend training and learn about effective schools. Use of school planning teams is a common component of the planning and capacity-building model. In a recent survey of our nation's schools, 89 percent of school districts with effective schools programs used school teams; 66 percent used school teams and written plans (U.S. General Accounting Office, 1989).

In effective planning and capacity-building models, goal setting is tied to an assessment process. After survey data are collected to pinpoint where improvements are needed, the external assister helps school personnel to interpret those data to identify where they are on the "effectiveness map." Further the assister helps the staff to plan what they need to do to create a more effective school.

To increase their meaning and usefulness, goals are written in measurable terms and the activities that will be implemented to meet the goals are specified. Clear time lines are established. Progress is tracked and reported regularly so the support for the change continues to build and goals are adjusted as needed. The external assister helps key individuals such as a planning committee to manage this process, continually feeding new information and new goals into the process.

To transfer responsibility for action to the organization itself, the external assister and school personnel identify someone internally who will continue to orchestrate the process, to assign resources such as release time, budgets, and consultants to back up the plan. The external assister convenes groups to discuss progress and incorporates the information into plans for next steps. By continuing the external assistance role through several cycles of implementation and phasing out gradually, priorities are more likely to stay on track, and internal capacity to sustain the changes will develop.

Training and Follow-up Assistance Model

Another model of technical assistance widely used to bring about effective schools is the training and follow-up assistance model. For example, almost 20 states provide staff training as part of a state school effectiveness program (U.S. General Accounting Office, 1989). This model has been studied extensively (Joyce & Showers, 1988; Crandall & Associates, 1982; Emrick & Peterson, 1980). Its purpose is to change a particular practice in the school, classroom, or school community. Programs such as Teacher Expectations/Student Achievement (TESA), Learning Styles, Cooperative Learning Methods, and the like are classroom-focused innovations that address the research on effective instruction. Organizationally focused programs addressing discipline, student and teacher leadership development, site-based management, and so on, also help schools become more effective. Many of them employ a training and follow-up assistance model for implementation.

The training and follow-up assistance model typically focuses on the implementation of single innovations, for example, more time-on-task in the classroom or shared decision making. In the context of effective schools, it is best used as part of the bigger picture. That is, a school involved in a reform initiative may implement a training and follow-up assistance model to change many different practices within the school, all aimed at developing different components of the effective school.

This model emphasizes training, but rather than offering one-shot instruction, uses a staged series of staff development activities including awareness sessions, demonstrations, hands-on training, problem-solving sessions, provision of materials, creation of support mechanisms, and evaluation. In the most successful programs, hands-on training is provided so that participants experience the innovation. Participants see the practice in action, learn the content behind it, try it themselves, receive a critique of their use of the practice, and later, discuss and solve common problems associated with its use. The training program is carried out over an extended period of time. Depending on the innovation, the time frame can often be from 2 to 20 days. Several external assisters may be involved over the entire course of the assistance.

A common failing of some applications of the training and follow-up assistance model is to rely heavily on the initial training and provide little if any follow-up assistance and support. Where schools have limited resources, they may start a process that includes training and support, but funding gets cut off. Experience and research show this results in little sustained improvement. External assisters working in this model should establish clear expectations for the amount of time and commitment needed to produce the desired changes.

Operating on the principle that external assisters cannot be everywhere at once, effective training and follow-up assistance models establish a local support system for the change. While the support system may come from more than one person, a common approach is to identify a building-based individual who serves as troubleshooter, coach, advocate, and expert. The external assister helps these local facilitators by setting up problem-solving meetings and training them as trainers and to act as change agents in the school or district. The external assister works with the local facilitators until they feel comfortable assuming their new roles. The external assister then maintains contact with local facilitators to assess progress and determine when additional intervention may be needed. The local facilitator plays a critical role in coordinating and integrating the new practice into the schools' larger plan for improvement.

Having a system for collecting information continuously enables educators to monitor the use and effectiveness of a new program. In a training and follow-up assistance model external assisters provide instruments and evaluation help to monitor progress with the program. Further, evaluation data are used to plan follow-up meetings and agendas for new training programs as well as to decide whether the schools should continue with the project.

Adoption Assistance Model

As more and more programs for school effectiveness were developed throughout the 1980s, people began to ask if school effectiveness programs that worked in one context could be disseminated en masse to other schools to achieve the same or similar results.

This question led to a new model for helping schools become more effective. This adoption assistance model has not been studied as extensively as the other two, but knowledge does come from craft knowledge and action research (Mundry, 1986; Roody, 1989). The model has two layers. First, state departments of education or other entities identify schools that exhibit the correlates of effective schools. Staff of these schools are then helped to "package" what made them effective and trained to help bring what they learned to other schools.

The second layer of assistance occurs when staff from the model schools are paired with schools that wish to adopt the model school's approach. This school-to-school dissemination process has been used nationally through the National Diffusion Network's National Network of Successful Schools and within several states, including New Jersey and Florida, to support school improvement. It is characterized by a matching between two or more schools to disseminate practices that lead to school effectiveness. Staff from the effective schools serve in the role of external assisters.

Model schools are selected based on

- *Effectiveness:* They have outstanding student achievement and positive student and staff attitudes and behavior; they display a climate for learning including high expectations for students and staff, appropriate discipline, and strong instructional leadership.
- *Practices:* Model schools have a set of observable practices that are linked to their effectiveness. These practices are transferable or replicable in other contexts.
- *Commitment and Capacity to Disseminate:* Model schools have experience sharing their successful practices with others. They are willing to make staff time available for dissemination activities.

Once selected, teams from model schools are trained to disseminate the process and practices that made their schools successful. An external assister from the sponsoring organization conducts an extensive training program that helps the teams from the model schools to define the practices they will disseminate, practice public speaking and training skills, gather sample hands-on materials, and plan to host demonstration site visits and other events at their schools. Following the training, the model schools' teams refine processes for training they will offer for others and prepare awareness and training materials. The assisters help in this process while also planning such dissemination activities as conferences and presentations.

Model school staff help other schools improve while they spend most of their time maintaining the success of their own school. Because of these commitments, the sponsoring organization, whether it is a state department of education, a school district, or a private education service firm, takes major responsibility for initial dissemination activities. It arranges awareness events in which schools interested in improvement can hear about and experience the success of the model schools. It sets up visits to model schools as well as meetings with staff from the model schools. Through information sharing about the models and discussion of the potential partner schools' needs, staff from both model and partner schools determine where there is a fit. Once there appears to be a potential fit between a model and a partner school, a plan is developed to match the two schools. The plan outlines the areas within the partner school that require intervention and defines what the interventions will be.

The most effective strategy for building support within the adoption assistance model is to provide opportunities for the partner school staff to see the model school assisters operate within their own school. Teams of teachers and administrators visit the model school to see it in action. There they get answers to their questions about implementing such a model. A full day of observations and meetings helps develop a vision of what the partner school could become. Partner school staff later meet with the assisters to discuss what they observed and plan for the changes they will make.

This model is so comprehensive in scope that many different training programs can occur simultaneously. The school principal from the partner school is often paired with the model school principal for a week or more for shadowing, coaching, and training. Clusters of staff from the partner school are paired similarly with staff from the model school.

Frequent follow-up by phone and in person is subsequently provided by the model school staff. They may also serve a linking role by connecting the partner schools with the resources that the model used during its own reform.

Both the sponsoring organization and the model school, in their respective assister roles, take responsibility for establishing evaluation mechanisms to determine how well the model is being implemented in the new site. Instruments used in the model school are often put to use by the partner school to assess progress toward becoming more effective.

At the initiation of the partnership, long term written agreements are shared that describe what it will take to sustain the school improvements. Factors that affect institutionalization such as establishing policies, identifying funding, replenishing materials, and providing refresher training and training for new staff are built into the initial plan. The data from the implementation evaluation are continually fed back to help increase the chances that the changes will be sustained.

Common Elements

With an understanding, now, of the unique characteristics of each of the three models of technical assistance, a return to the common elements of technical assistance models shows how these three models relate to each other. Table 8–1 shows the three models of technical assistance and the relative importance of each of the six common elements within the models.

The planning and capacity-building and the training and follow-up assistance strategies or models of technical assistance have been the most frequently used within effective schools programs. But typically what happens in these models as depicted is that resources (including time and, less tangibly, energy and attention) are focused on the early stages of the program—identifying needs (context setting), determining how to address them (problem solving), and early implementation (establishing goals and plans)—and the much more difficult backend implementation tasks of allocation of resources, maintenance, and review and recycling are underresourced. External assisters who use the models need to help schools to balance their focus across the six critical elements so that energy and resources are available to promote sustained change.

The training and follow-up assistance model is often viewed as a "quick fix" for school problems. In this approach, there is not as thorough an assessment of the whole organization as is warranted, and often the wrong solution is attached to the problem. The strength of this model lies in the emphasis on building support for the change internally and helping to develop local facilitators to carry on the work that has begun. But this work is often a relatively small part of what is needed overall to organize the school for real improvement. External assisters working within this model need to define the problem clearly and connect the intervention for improvement to the more global goal of school effectiveness.

TABLE 8–1 Relative Importance of Critical Elements in External Assistance Models

ELEMENT	PLANNING AND BUILDING CAPACITY	TRAINING AND FOLLOW-UP ASSISTANCE	ADOPTIONS ASSISTANCE
Knowing the context	High	Low	Low
Problem solving	Moderate	Moderate	Moderate
Building support	High	Moderate	Moderate
Establishing goals/plans	High	Moderate	High
Allocating resources	Low	Low	High
Institutionalizing	Moderate	Low	High

The adoption assistance model is based on earlier development efforts that often came from schools that used the planning and capacity-building model. Thanks to these efforts, the adoption assistance model has a clear plan from the outset, with no surprises about what materials and resources are needed. The focus from the beginning is on how to institutionalize certain changes within the school. However, the external assister is challenged to address contextual factors and problem solving since model practices do not always fit directly into every situation without fine-tuning and customizing.

Summary

The three models highlighted in this chapter provide a description of some of the ways external assistance contributes to producing more effective schools. Unfortunately, there has not yet been much research on the role of external assistance in effective schools programs. Additional research is needed that examines how schools go through the improvement process while they achieve the characteristics of effective schools (MacKenzie, 1983; Purkey, Rutter, & Newmann, 1986–1987). However, a recent study of effective schools programs in urban settings (Miles et al., 1986) confirms and elaborates what has been learned to date through studies of assistance to general school improvement efforts. Among the study's learnings are

The success of improvement efforts is directly related to the amount of assistance received by schools. The assistance, most of which falls under our definition of technical assistance, helped reduce implementation problems and enhanced productive coping with them. This confirms the essential nature of assistance from without and the inadequacy of either print materials or wholly relying for help on those with other full-time responsibilities within the school (see also Crandall & Associates, 1982; Huberman & Miles, 1984).

Implementation success is directly related to receiving many types of external assistance from a variety of sources, both inside and outside the school. The desirability of complementary assistance from internal and external sources, and even redundancy (i.e., the same kind of assistance coming from more than one source) is confirmed in other research on assistance (Cox, Loucks-Horsley, & French, 1987).

Effective implementation requires long-term, sustained assistance. As discussed, one-shot workshops or visits by consultants are insufficient to nurture an effective schools program adequately. Other research on change supports this finding, particularly because the needs of the school and its staff change over time, and assistance that recognizes those changes and addresses them is required over the long term (Fullan, 1982; Hall & Loucks, 1978).

Minimal conceptions of school improvement and assistance lead to very limited provision of funds and time for assistance. One of the ways effective schools programs can fail is if they don't value and make accommodations for adequate levels of assistance and time to work with assistance providers. We know from other research as well that minimal conceptions of what it takes to improve, thinking that only small amounts of change, if any, are required on the part of school staff, reduces the likelihood of any change occurring at all (Crandall & Associates, 1982).

Assistance style, approach, and intensity need to fit the goals of the program involved and be reasonably congruent with staff's expectations about school improvement. Different kinds of programs are required by different school problems and conditions, while different kinds of assistance are called for by different kinds of programs. Tailoring the kind and intensity of assistance to the needs of the client, as noted in Watkins's definition of technical assistance, is both the challenge and the measure of good technical assistance.

It is clear from both the research and our experience in delivering technical assistance that good technical assistance for effective schools is not sporadic or episodic. The kind of changes that foster effective schools, and school improvement in general, require intensive and extensive assistance. And yet, many clients still crave the "quick fix," and technical assisters are pressured to provide it. There is still much work to be done to eliminate the misconception that schools can change from ineffective to effective overnight.

The challenge to external assisters working with effective schools programs is to help schools to do many things simultaneously: implement significant changes in everybody's work, ensure that some or all of those changes also equip school staff to address additional needs as they arise, and continue the intensity of the effort through at least two cycles of identifying needs and implementing changes. Without this multiple focus, effective schools programs fall far short of their potential impact.

There are at least two ways for the external assister to address this issue: one by encouraging decision makers to think long term and allocate resources for an adequate number of years and the other by shortening the early stages and encouraging participants to make and act on decisions quickly. This latter has its supporters in the school improvement literature (Loucks-Horsley & Hergert, 1985) as well as the literature that characterizes effective organizations as those with a propensity for action, as captured in the phrase, "Ready! Fire! Aim!" (Peters & Waterman, 1982). Quick action can be taken most effectively, when norms support experimentation, encouraging people to "suspend disbelief" and try something new with the agreement that they will participate fully in the review of its impact and planning of its future use (Crandall, 1983; Little, 1982). Or, as in the case of the adoption assistance model, the up-front planning and "trial-and-error" aspects have been completed by the initial model school which has had the opportunity to modify and refine its practices over time until they have tested out and proven themselves over the long run.

CONCLUSION

Effective schools programs currently receive assistance from a wide variety of people and organizations, representing different points of view and using different assistance models. In many cases, that assistance could be improved, given what is already known about assister abilities, assistance strategies, and successful improvement efforts.

One way to organize improvement is around the six common or critical elements of technical assistance. An effective assister needs to look at the assistance situation from all of those perspectives or vantage points and see how and where they interconnect within the school. Then he or she can help the school allocate resources and plans across all elements. Further, an understanding of what makes an external assister effective can provide useful information to best select and train external assisters.

R E F E R E N C E S

BAMBUR, J. D., & ANDREWS, R. L. (1988).   Implementing change in secondary schools using effective schools research. Paper presented at the annual American Education Research Association conference, New Orleans.

BERMAN, P., & MCLAUGHLIN, M. W. (1978). *Federal programs supporting educational change.* Vol. VIII, *Implementing and sustaining innovations.* Santa Monica, CA: Rand.

BERMAN, P., & MCLAUGHLIN, M. W., ET AL. (1977). *Federal programs supporting educational change* (8 vols.). Santa Monica, CA: Rand.

BUTLER, M., & PAISLEY, W. (1977). *Factors determining roles and functions of educational linking agents.* San Francisco, CA: Far West Laboratory.

CARLSON, R. V. (1987). School assessment and school improvement: A study of successful schools. Paper presented at the annual American Education Research Association conference. Washington, D.C.

CLARK, T. A., & MCCARTHY, D. P. (1983). School improvement in New York City: The evolution of a project. *Educational Researchers, 12*(4).

CLIFFORD, R. M., & TROHANIS, P. L. (1980). *Technical assistance in educational settings.* Columbus: Ohio State University.

COUNCIL OF CHIEF STATE SCHOOL OFFICERS COUNCIL. (1988). *State education indicators.* Washington, D.C.: CCSSOC.

COX, P. L. (November 1983). Complementary roles in successful change. *Educational Leadership, 41*(3), 10–13.

COX, P. L., LOUCKS-HORSLEY, S., & FRENCH, L. C. (1987). *Getting the principal off the hotseat: Configuring leadership and support for school improvement.* Andover, MA: The Regional Laboratory for Educational Improvement of the Northeast and Islands.

CRANDALL, D. P. (1977). Training and supporting linking agents. In N. Nash and J. Culberston (Eds.), *Linking processes in educational improvement.* Columbus, OH: University Council for Educational Administration.

CRANDALL, D. P. (November 1983). The teacher's role in school improvement. *Educational Leadership, 41*(3), 6–9.

CRANDALL, D. P., & ASSOCIATES. (1982). *People, policies, and practices: Examining the chain of school improvement* (10 vols.). Andover, MA: The NETWORK, Inc.

CRANDALL, D. P., EISEMAN, J., & LOUIS, K. S. (1986). Strategic planning issues that bear on the success of school improvement efforts. *Educational Administration Quarterly, 22*(3), 21–53.

CRANDALL, D. P., & LOUCKS, S. F. (1983). *A roadmap to school improvement.* Vol. X, *People, policies, and practices: Examining the chain of school improvement.* Andover, MA: The NETWORK, Inc.

CRANDALL, D. P., & WILLIAMS, M. (Summer 1981). *The maturation of technical assistance in the 1980's.* Chapel Hill, NC: TADS, Frank Porter Graham Child Development Center.

EMRICK, J., & PETERSON, S. (1980). *San Diego implementation study: Case study report and first-year measurement development.* Los Altos, CA: Emrick and Associates.

EMRICK, J., PETERSON, S., & AGARWALA-ROGERS, R. (1977). *Evaluation of the national diffusion network* (2 vols.). Menlo Park, CA: Stanford Research Institute.

FITZGERALD, J. P. (n.d.). *Survey of professional staff perceptions.* Albany: New York State Department of Education.

FUHRMAN, S., CLUNE, W. H., & ELMORE, R. F. (Winter 1988). Research on education reform: Lessons on the implementation of policy. *Teachers College Record, 90*(2).

FULLAN, M. (1982). *The meaning of educational change.* New York: Teachers College Press; Toronto: OISE Press.

HALL, G. E., & LOUCKS, S. F. (1978).   Teacher concerns as a basis for facilitating and personalizing staff development. *Teachers College Record, 80*(1), 36–53.

HAVELOCK, R. (1969).   *Planning for innovation*. Ann Arbor: Institute for Social Research, University of Michigan.

HORD, S. M., HYLING-AUSTIN, L., & HALL, G. E. (1987).   *Taking charge of change.* Alexandria, VA: Association for Supervision and Curriculum Development.

HUBERMAN, M., & MILES, M. B. (1984).   *Innovation up close.* New York: Plenum Press.

JOYCE, B., & SHOWERS, B. (1988).   *Student achievement through staff development.* New York: Longman.

LITTLE, J. W. (1982).   Norms of collegiality and experimentation: Workplace conditions of school success. *American Educational Research Journal, 19*(3), 325–40.

LOUCKS-HORSLEY, S., & HERGERT, L. F. (1985).   *An action guide to school improvement.* Andover, MA: The NETWORK, Inc.; Alexandria, VA: Association for Supervision and Curriculum Development.

LOUIS, K. S., & LOUCKS-HORSLEY, S. (1989).   *Supporting school improvement: A comparative perspective.* Leuven, Belgium: ACCO.

MACKENZIE, D. E. (1983).   Research for school improvement: An appraisal of some recent trends. *Educational Researcher, 12*(4).

MARYLAND STATE DEPARTMENT OF EDUCATION (1983).   *Process evaluation: A comprehensive study of outliers.* Baltimore: MSDE.

MILES, M. B. (November 1983).   Unraveling the mystery of institutionalization. *Educational Leadership, 41,* 14–19.

MILES, M. B., LOUIS, K. S., ROSENBLUM, S., CIPOLLONE, A., & FARRAR, E. (1986).   *Lessons for managing implementation.* Boston: Center for Survey Research, University of Massachusetts.

MILES, M. B., SAXL, E., & LIEBERMAN, A. (1988).   What skills do educational "change agents" need? An empirical view. *Curriculum Inquiry, 18*(2), 158–93.

MUNDRY, S. E. (1986).   *Technical assistance to successful schools annual report.* Andover, MA: The NETWORK, Inc.

PETERS, T., & WATERMAN, R. (1982).   *In search of excellence.* New York: Random House.

PURKEY, S. C., RUTTER, R. A., & NEWMAN, F. M. (Winter 1986–87).   U.S. high school improvement programs: A profile from the high school and beyond supplemental survey. *Metropolitan Education,* no. 3.

ROODY, D. (1989).   *Rehabilitation network of New England final report.* Andover, MA: The NETWORK, Inc.

ROSENBLUM, S. (December 1981).   *Title I Dissemination and program improvement.* Philadelphia: Research for Better Schools.

STEARNS, M., & NORWOOD, C. (1977).   *Evaluation of the field test of project information packages.* Menlo Park, CA: Stanford Research Institute.

SUDLOW, R. (1985).   *Application for recognition, Spencerport Public Schools.* Submitted to The NETWORK, Inc., Andover, MA.

UNITED STATES GENERAL ACCOUNTING OFFICE. (September 1989).   *Effective school programs: Their extent and characteristics.* Washington, D.C.

VILLANOVA, R. M., GAUTHIER, W. J., PROCTOR, C. P., & SHOEMAKER, J. (n.d.). *Connecticut school effectiveness questionnaire*. Hartford, CT: State Department of Education.

WATKINS, J. (1989). NEC*TAS staff stakeholder analysis, Unpublished draft manuscript. Andover, MA: The NETWORK, Inc.

9

NEW DIRECTIONS IN THE EFFECTIVE SCHOOLS MOVEMENT

Kent K. Peterson

Lawrence W. Lezotte

INTRODUCTION

Early research on effective schools and the many analyses that followed began a movement both in research and practice that focused on ways to improve schools for all children. The research on effective schools captured the attention and commitment of many practitioners and a number of researchers. Since the studies in the 1970s, many effective school projects based on the research were implemented in school districts, regional laboratories, and state departments of education. These projects used the ideas, values, and properties found in the effective schools research as ways to motivate, direct attention, and shape organizational direction. The most visible and long-standing approach to this effort has been the collective work of Wilbur Brookover, Ron Edmonds, Larry Lezotte, and others who provided technical assistance, training, and materials. These and others communicated a commitment to improving schools for all students. In 1987, this work was consolidated and served as the organizational focus for the National Center for Effective Schools Research and Development (NCESRD).

In this chapter we will describe the work of the National Center as well as the way new ideas and knowledge from practice and from research have become incorporated into its early programs. We will try to show how the center has taken on new ideas, knowledge, and practices useful to school improvement due to practical problems identified in change efforts and new theoretical concepts from the scholarly literature. Based on a variety of new research studies in organizations and the experience of practitioners, center staff elaborated on the early "correlates of effective schools" in order to serve field based change programs.

Specifically, the NCESRD has attempted to add knowledge and practical wisdom from experience to areas of concern that the early research did not address, inadequately elaborated, or simply ignored. This melding of new practical knowledge and current ideas regarding organizational improvement and change has added strength and identified concrete ways to combat problems faced in school improvement efforts. The evolution of the effective schools movement is detailed in other sections of this book and in a chapter by Lezotte (1989), so we will attempt to describe only some of those broad outlines of the evolution of the movement.

As Lezotte (1989) suggests, there appear to have been several stages of the effective schools movement. During the first stage, researchers sought to define what an effective school was. In the next stage, researchers studied a number of effective schools to specify their basic properties and characteristics. This was the time of the early research. Early research and its convincing findings promulgated around the country supported a period of action in school systems where educators attempted to create more effective schools, most often one at a time, using the available research. More recently, knowledge gained about the importance of the district in school improvement has shifted some of the emphasis to district-level school improvement effort rather than one school at a time. Finally, federal legislation and state policies in some regions have fostered more programs based on the effective schools research. While the direction of development has been toward larger programs, local schools and school districts continue to implement school improvement efforts based on the early research.

THE WORK OF THE NCESRD

Started in 1987, the NCESRD has been working with practitioners in an attempt to implement practical and research-based knowledge from several interrelated lines of inquiry. For example, the research on effective schools and organizational theory, knowledge about change and improvement, leadership and the school principalship, curriculum content, and staff development and adult learning are useful to change efforts. The use of new research and ideas from practice by the NCESRD is multifold and multiconceptual due to the complexities of school improvement. The center staff learned through actively working on programs of school improvement and through written accounts (Corbett, Dawson, & Firestone, 1984) that there is more to school transformation than simply seeking to increase the measures of the five correlates.

DEFINITION OF EFFECTIVE SCHOOLS

The early work in school improvement based on the effective schools research and the writings of Edmonds assumed that an effective school was one defined by both quality educational programs and equity of achievement across different subsets of students. As Lezotte and Bancroft (1985) note,

> Two outcome standards are anticipated in effective schools. First, the overall level of achievement to which the students rise on the outcomes measures must be sufficiently

high to signify acceptable mastery of the essential curriculum. Second, the distribution of achievement must not vary significantly across the major subsets of the student population (that is, middle socioeconomic students versus lower socioeconomic students). (p. 27)

Thus, schools should try to attain high levels of learning by students that is not predicted by socioeconomic background or race. More recently, educators have suggested that these subsets of students deserving equitable outcomes include subsets identified by gender and disabilities or family structure (e.g., single-parent versus dual-parent families). These newly identified subsets of students suggest the increased awareness by educators of potential negative stereotyping on other than racial or socioeconomic characteristics. In short, effective schools support academic achievement for all students.

Shifting Perspectives

The strict definition of an effective school has shifted slightly in some cases as educators seek to define their unique missions in their communities. While the early conceptualizations of effective schools were most concerned with the achievement of basic skills of minority students, some schools and districts in this movement have already reached a high level of effectiveness in basic skills. Working within this framework, some have redefined what they mean as basic to include higher-order thinking skills, problem solving, creativity, and other less basic, subject areas as part of their own local definitions of "effectiveness." For example, some suburban Chicago districts using the effective schools framework are closely examining the distribution of outcomes for various subsets of students, but also making what they consider "basic attainment" to mean achieving well above the fiftieth percentile and improving nonbasic skills. Thus, schools can define what they mean by mastery in ways that fit their particular context and community values. This is a substantial shift from the early focus on basic skills.

Similarly, some districts well above minimal mastery levels for most students have been encouraged (or perhaps pressured) by external environment to raise standards in response to local and national concerns about the need for more trained workers in the 1990s and the need to educate American students better due to the increased competition by foreign countries. More often than not, though, the impetus for change in many districts is for serving the local needs of individual students. Local needs seem the stronger concern and motivating force, in part because parents remain one of the most potent sources of external pressure.

CONCEPTUAL ADDITIONS TO THE INITIAL RESEARCH ON EFFECTIVE SCHOOLS

A number of conceptual additions have been incorporated into the NCESRD's work with school districts and schools as natural problems of school change efforts dictated them. While the core research on effective schools still provides the main support for improvement programs, it has been clear, both from research on school change and improvement and from programs with schools, that the effective schools' correlates in themselves provide only the underpinning for school success. Over time a number of different understandings have been added to enhance work with schools.

Why did this happen? The development of new ideas was an addition to and expansion of knowledge for two central reasons. First, the early conceptualizations of effective schools often did not specify the process by which schools *developed* and *maintained* effectiveness. More elaborate ideas of change processes were needed. Second, staff of the center and practitioners in the field identified useful new knowledge that was helpful in working with schools and school districts. Many new ideas sprung from the learnings of practitioners as they solved problems of change. The effective schools improvement efforts necessarily learned from practice and from research.

For example, the early programs of school improvement based on effective schools research emphasized the single school as the unit of change. As a result, the local board of education and central office were largely ignored. The experiences of local districts such as Jackson, Mississippi; Spencerport, New York; and Prince George's County, Maryland, taught us that school-by-school change will develop and be sustained if the school change process occurs in the context of districtwide programs and procedures that help to sustain the focus.

These districts and others also realized that special leadership training of building principals is essential to the success of the building-level improvement process. Preparation programs typically offered to principals do not generally give adequate attention to the research on organizational culture, visionary leadership and sustained change. As a result, districts incorporated extensive leadership training.

While it's not possible to include in detail all of the conceptual and practical additions to the early model, some key points should be highlighted. These additions are both complex and necessary to effective implementation of the earlier research.

IMPROVEMENT PROGRAMS

Perhaps the most significant shift in the effective schools movement has been the increased enactment of complex school and district improvement efforts. School improvement programs have been developed at the federally funded regional laboratories in the Northwest, Southwest, and midcontinent (as well as in the LEAD academies in many states). These improvement programs range from simple awareness sessions on the characteristics of effective schools to comprehensive, ongoing training programs designed to take schools and districts through sequential and cumulative experiences and activities to change basic school processes and learning outcomes. These programs, like the ones at NCESRD, apply the early research on effective schools as well as the current research and best practices to reshape schools that are not accomplishing their goals.

Perhaps the most powerful and important area of knowledge added to this work has been the research on organizational theory. First, it was clear from our work with schools that power and authority relations in schools did not always support the kind of collegial problem solving and teamwork that was necessary for schools to improve. Though many are using the term "empowerment" now, several districts for some time have sought ways that support the kind of influence teachers can have over what goes on in schools.

From the outset, we have argued that school-based planning for school improvement should be collegial in form and should be led by a trained school-based team. Anoka-Hennepin, Minnesota, Spring Branch Independent School

District, Texas; and the schools from the Michigan Middle Cities Education Association have all used school teams for several years. In each district the empowerment process has been supported by both teachers and administrators. The district, as well, must be committed, to a collaborative process that gives substantial authority to the schools' faculty and administration to foster change. This decentralization works well if two conditions are met. First, the school-based effort must be guided by a powerful and shared vision of what the school values. Second, the teams need to be trained in the processes of problem solving, reviewing research, and planning for complex, long-term change.

A second important area of organizational theory that has been incorporated has been the research on organizational culture (Deal, 1985; Purkey & Smith, 1983; Deal & Peterson, 1990). It is clear for much of this research that the underlining norms, values, and beliefs held by administrators and teachers are integral parts of school improvement and effective schools. Norms of performance and improvement (Little, 1982), and beliefs that all children can learn are key elements in establishing a school culture or ethos that supports the kinds of workplace conditions that were found in the early effective school research. These new conceptualizations and models are important additions to our understanding of effective schools and help guide work with school districts and schools. School districts using this research to foster change have tried to shape their cultures to support improvement. For example, the Spring Branch Independent School District, Houston, Texas, and Frederick County, Maryland, have had great success in affecting the culture of their organizations through elaborate districtwide opening school ceremonies. These ceremonies help to reinforce a culture of improvement, and the culture fosters success for all students.

In addition to the research on organizational theory, the comprehensive and useful research on school change and school improvement have been key in continuing the growth of the effective schools research model for school improvement (Corbett, Dawson, & Firestone, 1984; Fullan, 1982, 1985). The key findings here have been helpful in shaping work with schools and school districts. For example, much of the research notes that the most effective change occurs when it is viewed as process rather than an outcome (Fullan, 1985). Ongoing, steady improvement is critical to helping schools continuously improve.

A second important piece of knowledge from this literature notes the importance of developing a common technical language that makes it possible for educators to exchange information quickly and effectively throughout schools (Little, 1982). Practitioners have found the common language of the effective schools research useful to tie teachers and administrators together. Most of the districts that have been implementing effective schools research have programs that annually renew the language of effective schools for all their employees through staff development programs. Some schools require all new staff to attend district-sponsored training sessions. Others require new administrators to attend effective schools, conferences, or training programs.

Third, the research on school improvement and the parallel research in the business world on effective corporations shows that there is a need for a clear direction and a focused mission communicated regularly throughout the organization (see Waterman, 1987). Though it seemed obvious from the early research on effective schools that a clear school mission is important, this was reinforced by other research on change and improvement and change efforts in schools around the country. Norfolk, Virginia, has gone to great lengths to be sure that everyone is aware of the district's mission, using many routine and symbolic approaches to communicate the mission.

St. Louis, Missouri, has also emphasized the mission on charters, banners, stationery, and in other symbolic ways.

An education/school improvement program may involve an ongoing monitoring and evaluation system. This aids administrators to make school and district decision making more data driven and focused. Prince George's County, Maryland, uses a peer review and an effective schools audit to be sure that the practices maintain the intended effective schools focus. In Spencerport, New York, the superintendent and school teams meet twice a year to discuss the school's measured progress. Concrete ways of measuring student performance and disaggregating the data were developed in practice and implemented to improve schools.

A fourth set of conceptualizations involves the importance of educators' understanding and response to contextual factors in schools (Corbett, Dawson, & Firestone, 1984; Fullan, 1985). By understanding the contextual factors that shape school change and improvement, programs could be more successful. It was possible for those at the NCESRD to work more effectively with schools and districts facing differing sets of problems, opportunities, resources, and cultures when the notion of contextual differences was applied.

Many of the school districts that have been implementing the effective schools process have been experiencing rapid change in the demographic characteristics of student populations, especially rapid increases in the number of poor and economically disadvantaged students being served. When districts confront these changes head on, they seem to be more successful in managing changes. Helping districts analyze their contexts made change easier.

Fifth, the research on school change and improvement of Firestone, Wilson, and their associates (1985) points out the importance of varied organizational linkages in seeking changes in schools. The early research on effective schools did not conceptually separate the bureaucratic and cultural linkages as Wilson and Firestone (1985) did later. This conceptualization, though, has been helpful in articulating the usefulness for both cultural and structural change to occur in order to support effective schools efforts.

Most recently, the NCESRD has worked in collaboration with other agencies and organizations in Michigan to implement the statewide Leadership for School Improvement Program. This program is illustrative of what is happening across the country. First, it is aimed at a comprehensive, districtwide planning process designed to set the framework for school improvement as a district priority. Second, the program incorporates staff from the university, intermediate districts, and the state department of education. The focal point for the training itself is a vertical team from the local school district, and it must include the superintendent. But it also seeks to change basic underlying cognitive maps and educators' expectations.

LEADERSHIP

While there are no simple lists of characteristics of effective school leaders, it seems clear from research and descriptions of effective practice (Bennis & Nanus, 1985, Deal & Peterson, 1990; Firestone & Wilson, 1985; Taylor, 1990) that to achieve effectiveness, school and district leaders must have skills in administering the basic institution—technical skills—and skills in building a shared sense of mission and institutional culture—culture-building skills. Often, these schools and districts seeking to improve have leaders with a vision for their institutions, leaders who have a sense of what the organization can become (Peterson, 1985; Deal & Peterson, 1990; Schein, 1985). Thus, leaders may need both technical and culture-building skills. It appears that where administrative problems occur, the basic needs for coordination, resources, and personnel retard or restrict improvement. Where the culture either is not shared or does not support education for all children, this lack of cultural cohesion makes change and improvement problematic.

One of the reasons why the district-level planning model emerged was because the principals were often placed "at risk" in their own organizations if they attempted to create a change-oriented culture in their individual school. Work in the Michigan Middle Cities Association programs showed that without district-level support, only about one principal in three had the capacity to initiate and sustain planned change.

The research on leadership and school principals has also added useful new knowledge to work of the NCESRD. The initial conceptualizations of effective schools focused on the importance of school principals. The work on instructional leadership by Murphy and Hallinger (1985), Bossert and colleagues (1982), and Peterson (1982, 1985) has helped to refine, specify, and focus some of the actions that principals engage in to foster school effectiveness.

But the research on leadership and practical experience has also helped us understand that principals are not the only school leaders, especially in secondary schools (Peterson, 1985; Bird & Little, 1985; Hall & Hord, 1987; Pitner, 1986). While principals are still key players in individual school-improvement efforts, the leadership of others, especially teachers and superintendents, may be important as well. Teacher leadership, whether it is called empowerment, collegiality, or the informal culture of a school, seems an important aspect of effective schools improvement. The research on district-level leadership (Peterson, Murphy, & Hallinger, 1987; Lezotte, 1989) also points to the efforts that leadership from these other levels adds to school improvement. Programs in the Connecticut State Department of Education and elsewhere have identified the need for district support.

The early research on effective schools found strong instructional leaders, people who actively engaged in shaping the program. Increasingly, research and descriptions of practice are describing the ways school leaders act less directly and more collaboratively with teachers, acting in what Burns (1978) calls transformational leadership. This type of leadership gains much of its power by tapping the shared values of followers and building normative commitment to the mission of the school. These leaders focus on shaping the culture of the school as well as the professional and instructional structures of the organization. While this may seem different from the early findings, it may be that this more evanescent and subtle aspect of school leaders' actions was not identified. In short, more often than not, leadership for school improvement seems to be more transformational than coercive in nature. The research on leadership both from the public and the private sector has added greatly to our ability to describe to the practitioners what leadership can mean in schools. Peter and Waterman's (1982) notion of management by walking around, and Bennis and Nanus's (1985) approach to leadership as culture building have helped principals, teachers, and superintendents understand the ways they sometimes share leadership. Recent case studies, written by practitioners (Taylor, 1990) who have been trying to improve their districts, note that leadership from all levels is critical to shaping effective schools.

SCHOOL CULTURE

In working with schools and districts, it is clear that leaders using the effective schools framework also shape the culture or "ethos" (Purkey & Smith, 1983) of their institutions. Deal and Peterson (1990) describe the principal's role in culture building and provide illustrations in five case studies. These cases show how principals build the underlying norms, values, and beliefs of school members through a number of strategies. These include what they pay attention to; the ways they use traditions, rituals, and ceremonies to reinforce the culture; and the stories they tell in the course of their day. The specific ways these cultural events are important to school improvement are evident in many districts. For example, Prince George's County, Maryland, Frederick County, Maryland, and Spring Branch Independent School District, Texas, school districts hold massive beginning-of-school ceremonies with speeches, bands, and banners proclaiming the importance of educating all children. These ceremonies reinforce specific values and beliefs and help shape commitment to a culture of success.

One of the early criticisms of some of the writings on the effective school improvement was that teaching and curriculum content were often not addressed. Again, our understanding of schools as organizations makes it clear that the technical core of the school is the classroom and that, ultimately, what goes on in the classroom is what produces student learning. In the center's work with school districts, though, the NCESRD does not promote any particular approach to teaching or curriculum. Nonetheless, the center makes use of the research on teaching and curriculum. Practitioners in this movement moved quickly to incorporate instructional and curricular changes, through their own assessment of the literature. This took many forms.

Jackson, Mississippi, used vertical teams of teachers and parents and rebuilt the entire curriculum from K through 12. What emerged was what is known as the "Common Body of Knowledge" that details the essential learnings for every grade and subject taught. Similarly, the Glendale, Arizona, high school district has been developing a curriculum that clearly identifies, course by course, essential outcomes and has, like Jackson, developed a measurement system to monitor student learning. Other districts such as Norfolk, Virginia, and San Marcos, California, have developed plans by which all teachers will receive staff development in whatever that district has chosen as its basic model of teaching. These attempts to create the common curriculum serve to strengthen the process of change and the culture of the organization.

Curriculum alignment and curricular development have always been a focus in our work with schools and school districts. Initially the research and conceptualizations on the notion of "curriculum alignment" (Bossert et al., 1982) had been key to this effort. As one sees in Levine and Lezotte's (1990) synthesis on new directions in effective schools, curriculum that is not aligned and connected to some measurement of outcomes may not promote effective schools. Thus, while early research on effective schools did not specify or talk much about teaching and curriculum, our work with practitioners and other's research suggests attention to curriculum and teaching as necessary to promoting effective schools improvement.

Finally, the research on staff development and adult learning has been useful in technical assistance to schools and districts. The work on staff development and adult learning is voluminous (Joyce & Showers, 1983). That research suggests that adult learning occurs best when it meets certain criteria. In the center's technical assistance we have tried to help districts meet many, if not all, of the criteria for quality professional development. Many districts knew immediately that staff development had to be a cornerstone of school improvement.

St. Louis, Missouri, and Jackson, Mississippi, illustrate the level of commitment to staff development in "learning organizations." For years St. Louis teachers have received training on the effective schools and effective teaching research every summer. As a condition of employment in Jackson, Mississippi, board policy requires every employee of the district to receive 30 hours of training per year.

Thus, the National Center for Effective Schools Research and Development has taken the original characteristics of effective schools model and tried systematically and carefully to add elements of practical knowledge gleaned from our work in schools and districts to theoretical understanding and research knowledge on organizations and schools to provide a more comprehensive understanding of how schools can become more effective. While the initial correlates still provide an underpinning of our understanding of what makes for effective schools, under differing conditions in diverse schools and school districts, we find that a variety of other elements become important if school improvement is to be continuous and successful in helping all children learn.

CONCLUSION

Where do these new conceptualizations and additions place us relative to other new ideas? It seems clear that some practitioners and writers on effective schools have fallen into goal displacement, that is, focusing only on implementing the initial correlates of effective schools. We view our work as one of adding knowledge of effective practice and systematic knowledge to our understanding of this model. It seems clear that culture and leadership are critical; that improvement and renewal are continuous; that restructuring, site-based management, and decentralization may be key elements of improvement; that equity and quality ought to be sought concurrently; that the student monitoring system and assessment of outcomes are key; that curriculum and teaching must be understood and constantly refined; and that the norms, values, and beliefs of teachers, students, administrators, and central office personnel must be the basis for a culture of improvement focused on quality teaching and equity of learning outcomes. To maintain effectiveness, schools must constantly seek new knowledge and techniques from research and the new ideas from practitioners engaged in the process of school improvement.

REFERENCES

BENNIS, W., & NANUS, B. (1985). *Leaders: The strategies for taking charge.* New York: Harper & Row.

BIRD, T., & LITTLE, J. W. (1985). *Instructional leadership in eight secondary schools.* Boulder, CO: Center for Action Research.

BOSSERT, S. T., DWYER, D. C., ROWAN, B., & LEE, G. V. (1982). The instructional management role of the principal. *Educational Administration Quarterly, 18*(3), 34–64.

BURNS, J. M. (1978). *Leadership.* New York: Harper & Row.

CORBETT, N. D., DAWSON, J. A., & FIRESTONE, W. A. (1984). *School context and school change*. New York: Teachers College Press.

DEAL, T. E. (May 1985). The symbolism of effective schools. *The Elementary School Journal, 85*(5), 602–20.

DEAL, T. E., & PETERSON, K. D. (1990). *Symbolic leadership and the school principal: Shaping school cultures in different contexts*. Washington, D.C.: U. S. Department of Education, O.E.R.I.

FIRESTONE, W. A., & WILSON, B. L. (Spring 1985). Using bureaucratic and cultural linkages to improve instruction: The principal's contribution. *Educational Administration Quarterly, 21,* 17–30.

FULLAN, M. (1982). *The meaning of educational change*. New York: Teachers College Press.

FULLAN, M. (1985). Change processes and strategies at the local level. *The Elementary School Journal, 85,* 391–421.

HALL, G. E., & HORD, S. M. (1987). *Change in schools: Facilitating the process*. Albany: State University of New York Press.

JOYCE, B. R., & SHOWERS, B. (1983). *Power in staff development through research on training*. Alexandria, VA: Association for Supervision and Curriculum Development.

LEVINE, D. U., & LEZOTTE, L. (1990). *Unusually effective schools*. Madison: Wisconsin Center for Educational Research.

LEZOTTE, L. W., & BANCROFT, B. A. (March 1985). Growing use of the effective schools model for school improvement. *Educational Leadership, 42*(6), 23–27.

LEZOTTE, L. W. (1989). School improvement based on the effective schools research. In D. K. Lipsky and A. Gartner (Eds.), *Beyond separate education: Quality education for all*. Baltimore: Paul H. Brooks.

LITTLE, J. W. (1982). Norms of collegiality and experimentation: Workplace conditions of school success. *American Educational Research Journal, 19*(3), 325–40.

MURPHY, J. F., & HALLINGER, P. (1985). School effectiveness: A conceptual framework. *The Educational Forum, 49*(3), 362–74.

PETERS, T. J., & WATERMAN, R. N., JR. (1982). *In search of excellence*. New York: Harper & Row.

PETERSON, K. D. (1982). Making sense of principal's work. *Australian Administrator, 3*(3), 1–4.

PETERSON, K. D. (1985). Vision and problem finding in principal's work: Values and cognition in administration. In D. C. Dwyer (Ed.), The principal as instructional leader (Special issue). *Peabody Journal of Education, 63*(1), 87–107.

PETERSON, K. D., MURPHY, J., & HALLINGER, P. (1987). Superintendents' perceptions of the technical core in effective school districts. *Educational Administration Quarterly, 23*(1), 79–95.

PITNER, N. J. (1986). Substitutes for principal leadership behavior: An exploratory study. *Educational Administration Quarterly, 21*(2), 23–42.

PURKEY, S. C., & SMITH, M. S. (1983). Effective schools: A review. *Elementary School Journal, 83,* 427–52.

SCHEIN, E. N. (1985). *Organizational culture and leadership*. San Francisco: Jossey-Bass.

TAYLOR, B. O. (1990). *Case studies in effective school research*. Dubuque, IA: Kendall-Hunt.

WATERMAN, R. H. (1987). *The renewal factor*. New York: Bantam Books.

10

EFFECTIVE SCHOOLS
AND TEACHER PROFESSIONALISM:
EDUCATIONAL POLICY
AT A CROSSROADS

Barnett Berry and Rick Ginsberg
University of South Carolina

INTRODUCTION

Dissatisfaction with the public schools is long standing (Cuban, 1990). Over the last several decades, research studies have pointed to numerous inadequacies of schools and teachers. During the 1960s, Coleman and colleagues (1966) found that home background was the principal predictor of student achievement. Their research suggested that variation among schools did not affect what students learned. In the 1980s, other researchers pointed to the decline in teacher quality. Prospective teachers score lower on tests of academic ability than their counterparts in other professions. New teachers who are more academically able leave the classroom earlier and more often than do their "less able" counterparts (Schlecty & Vance, 1981; Weaver, 1983; Darling-Hammond, 1984). To compound these concerns, teacher shortages appeared in the 1980s, and there may be far more classroom vacancies in the future than certified teachers to fill them (Darling-Hammond & Berry, 1988).

Today, the shortcomings of the public schools are widely reported as both the popular and scholarly press lambast education programs, bureaucrats, and teachers. Educators and policymakers responded to these criticisms with a flurry of research reports and school improvement programs, bolstered by widely publicized rhetoric. In the 1970s, educators and policymakers used the effective schools literature to "prove" that schools can indeed produce results. As it became apparent that schools cannot produce without teaching talent, educators and policymakers coupled the drive for effective schools with a movement to professionalize teaching. Although supporters of both movements claim research support, the basis of both is more ideological than empirical. Advocates make normative claims for both administrator (effective schools) and teacher (teacher professionalism) control of public education. Still, both movements identify problem areas and offer viable solutions for American education. Given the considerable pressure for the restructuring of public education in the Unites States, the effective schools and teacher professionalism movements deserve attention.

This chapter argues that the ideological basis for the effective schools and teacher professionalism movements are not necessarily contradictory. However, effective schools programs generally emphasize top-down change within the existing structure and unidimensional measures of effectiveness. This approach runs head on into the current movement to professionalize teachers which emphasizes bottom-up change, restructured schools, and multidimensional measures of effectiveness. Thus, the effective school movement could stifle efforts to professionalize teaching beyond the level of rhetoric.

We develop our argument by reviewing the ideology of effective schools, the school reforms of the 1980s, the problems of teaching, the nature of professionalization, and the ideology of teacher professionalism. We show how school effectiveness-oriented reforms and calls for teacher professionalism are being transmitted in ways that do conflict. We conclude by asserting that educational reform is at a crossroads and that the likely outcome will not be a restructured teaching profession but a confirmation—in some form—of what teaching is today.

THE IDEOLOGY OF EFFECTIVE SCHOOLS

About two decades ago, researchers began pointing to ingredients found in some inner-city schools that substantially decreased (but rarely eradicated) basic skill achievement differences between socioeconomic groups. These included a six-ingredient formula: (1) strong instructional leadership by principals, (2) high student expectations, (3) clear goals, (4) an emphasis on basic skills, (5) an orderly and structured environment, and (6) frequent use of student achievement data to evaluate program success (Weber, 1971; Edmonds, 1979).

The effective schools research is widely accepted. As Darling-Hammond (1983) argued, the recipe for effective schools is quite "seductive," because of its "impeccable logic" and its "straightforwardness" (p. 1). No one could seriously argue that strong, instructionally oriented principals are not better than weak ones, that basic skills (and the assessment of them) should be ignored, that teachers should not have high expectations, and that turbulent schools are more appropriate than safe, orderly ones. To do so would be akin to defying Mom, apple pie, and (with apologies to Chevrolet), Lee Iaccoca.

Policymakers and educators popularized the six-factor formula with its emphasis on principal leadership and basic skill achievement. Policymakers moved quickly to remedy the ills of schools despite the fact that the effective schools research used questionable methodologies and produced inconsistent empirical findings (Ralph & Fennessey, 1983). For example, some critics point to research problems such as the overreliance on case studies, failure to control properly for socioeconomic status, the comparison of only extreme outlier schools, the overuse of correlational instead of causal designs, the lack of longitudinal design, and the sole use of elementary schools as the sampling unit (Stedman, 1987; Cuban, 1983; Rowan, Bossert, & Dwyer, 1983). Others point to empirical problems, including the failure of effective schools to enhance student achievement for *all* grade levels and actual variation of teacher expectations in schools with high achievement (Ralph & Fennessey, 1983).

Despite these flaws, analysts have searched the "best" effective schools research to identify the organizational factors that appear to decrease substantially (but not eliminate) the differences in basic skills achievement between socioeconomic groups in problematic, primarily inner city, schools (Purkey & Smith, 1983; Rosenholtz, 1985). From this beginning, the effective schools conclusions moved from the laboratory to the real world before research actually elucidated relevant and context-driven procedures of effective practices. For the most part, policymakers ignored the more difficult issues revealed by certain strands of the school and teacher effectiveness literature and developed policies and programs based on an inadequate data base.

For example, some analyses of the research point to broad and multifarious factors related to school effectiveness. In one review, Rosenholtz (1985) concluded that effective urban schools (1) use psychic rewards to mobilize teacher commitment; (2) use techniques to closely align the norms, values, and behaviors of principals and teachers; (3) elevate teacher selection as a critical activity for fostering shared values in the school; (4) "deisolate" teachers in order to develop collegial norms that drive improvement of instructional practices; (5) elevate principals as school leaders to foster teacher collaboration, buffer teachers from external pressures, and reduce uncertainty about teachers' success with students; and (6) facilitate joint administrative-teacher instructional decision making to transform isolated classrooms into coherent school programs. Such significant factors are difficult—at least at the state policy level—to operationalize for specific school settings.

Additionally, Pellicer and colleagues (1990), who studied effective high school leaders for the National Association for Secondary School Principals, concluded that principals in effective schools do not rigidly apply a single formula. Instead, effective school principals operate more like "Tom Cruise in *Top Gun*...on the edge of what can be allowed...(and) flying their jets upside down" (*The New York Times,* 1990).

Despite the complexity of creating competent schools, the effective schools movement "captured educators' and public's fancy by reducing a disparate literature to simple recipes for school improvement" (Purkey & Smith, 1983, p. 429). With an almost zealous intensity to implement the six-factor effectiveness formula, policymakers operationalized policies and procedures for educators to implement. These policies and procedures spread like wildfire. But in advocating the six-factor formula, policymakers and educators not only ignored the weaknesses in the research, but also one of the more critical tenets of the school effectiveness literature itself—school culture. As Purkey and Smith (1983) argued,

> The most persuasive (effective schools) research suggests that student academic performance is strongly affected by school culture. This culture is composed of values, norms, and roles existing within institutionally distinct structures....Successful schools are found to have cultures that produce a climate or "ethos" conducive to teaching and learning. As dynamic social systems, school cultures will vary in part to the composition of the staff and student body and to the environment in which the school exists...(thus) school effectiveness is *not* likely to result from a small number of discrete changes imposed on schools by external agents. (pp. 356–57)

Interestingly, this synthesis of the "best" of the school effectiveness research which spurned simple policies and procedures also points to contextual variables that influence school success, implying that no single set of prescriptions will cure all school ailments (i.e., see Teddlie & Wimpelberg, 1987). Instead, effective school practices are as much a "means" as they are an "end." It follows that the process of creating effective schools should be viewed as a continuous cycle of improvement and renewal.

Within this interpretive framework, effective schools do not consist of static qualities, nor do they necessarily require instructional leadership by the principal. The importance of the teacher-principal collaborative relationship suggests strongly that teachers—who know most intimately the pedagogical needs of their students—could become instructional leaders, and principals—who understand and can respond to internal and external demands placed on the school—could become the leaders of leaders. While this notion is soundly rooted in the effective schools literature, it has been rarely evident in the implementation of the 1980s-styled school reform.

SCHOOL REFORM OF THE 1980S

For many policymakers and practitioners, the effective school movement could not have come at a more auspicious time. The six effectiveness ingredients were readily consumed by reformers and transformed into policy mandates and training programs. Programs to train instructional leaders are especially easy to provide. At the same time, the emphasis on narrowing educational goals to focus on basic skills acquisition, monitoring test scores carefully, and exhorting students to do well coincided with the national mood to get tough on the basics by increasing the number and visibility of high-stakes tests, increasing high school graduation requirements, and emphasizing traditional "3Rs" subjects. During the 1980s, when policymakers and business leaders did not trust educators to reform themselves, these policies proliferated. The effective schools six-factor formula helped implement those policies and ensured that the narrow, basic skills agenda would be met (Stedman, 1987). In fact, according to a recent report, approximately 50 percent of the nation's schools with effective school programs were required to have them (U.S. General Accounting Office, 1989).

With mounting pressure for schools to change and produce, the effective schools formula provided a legitimate framework for school improvement. And with basic skills achievement data as the dominant dependent measure of effectiveness, the linkage between what is taught and what is tested tightened—with a rigid vengeance. Many school districts that adopted effective schools formula have returned to a pre-1900 notion of a uniform curriculum with a singular textbook and prespecified worksheets (Cuban, 1983) at the expense of a liberal arts curriculum and higher-order thinking skills (Resnick & Resnick, 1985).

While the effective schools formula did not directly speak to teachers and pedagogy, researchers in the late 1970s began to reveal discrete sets of teaching behavior which led to increased student performance (Medley, 1979; Stallings, 1977). This research primarily investigated the behaviors of teachers who taught math and language arts to elementary school students. In turn, teachers were more systematically trained, certified, and assessed for their ability to deploy direct instruction—a peda-gogical practice that increases students' basic skill achievement. Consequently, new teacher evaluation systems began to emerge—with the purpose of measuring as many as 50 to 100 generic indicators of effective direct instruction in a single 50-minute class period (Popham, 1987; Wise et al., 1987). In doing so, this latest attempt to monitor teacher performance drew upon a tradition of research on direct instruction that was used in early effective schools programs.

These monitoring efforts ignored a different strand of teacher-effects literature suggesting that effective teaching behaviors varied considerably for students with different socioeconomic, mental, and psychological characteristics (e.g., Brophy & Evertson, 1977; Cronbach & Snow, 1977; Teddlie & Stringfield, 1987) and for different grade levels and subject areas (Gage, 1978; McDonald & Elias, 1976).

Furthermore, with the drive for school accountability, many states began to utilize commercially developed and teacherproof curriculum packages (e.g., "Scoring High") that were *directly* linked to the content of such standardized achievement tests as CAT and CTBS (Putka, 1989). Thus, policymakers established quality control in the profession by relying very heavily on a limited conception of teachers and teaching and, in doing so, posited simplistic, overly standardized, unidimensional indicators of teacher and student quality. However, this conception of teaching was compatible with the six-factor school effectiveness formula which did not speak at all to the question of what constituted good teaching. It was also considerably easier to implement than other models which would allow for inclusion of variables such as subject matter and student differences as well as professional judgment.

By most accounts, the school reforms of the 1980s have played to "mixed reviews" (Plank, 1988). While some consider these "first-wave" policies to be "the most sustained and far-reaching reform effort in modern times" (Boyd, 1987), others assert that many of these promulgated policies have been more symbolic than substantive (Rossmiller, 1986) and have not significantly altered the structure and functioning of the nation's public schools (Plank, 1988). Some have argued that the effects of these first-wave efforts may be more insidious. These critics lament that state governments have become more involved in the details of teaching, testing, and curriculum than ever before (Airasian, 1987) and, consequently, have reduced the discretion of *teachers* while enhancing the bureaucratic conception of schooling with its "legislated learning," "rigid rules," and "pseudoscientific processes" (Wise, 1979, 1989). While centralization and teacherproof curricula preceded the effective schools movement for decades, the testing mania of the 1980s made the effective schools formula very popular. In this view, shrinking teacher discretion has contributed to many of the problems currently recognized in teaching. It is to these problems we turn next.

THE PROBLEMS OF TEACHING

As previously discussed, policymakers in the 1980s enacted and implemented a plethora of teacher certification and compensation policies. By sheer volume of legislation, it is clear that state policymakers have "reformed" teaching. But tallies of legislation—that is, the numbers of new certification requirements, teacher evaluation systems, increases in average pay, new merit pay programs—do not tell the whole story. When one peers inside the recent statutes and regulations, what is most evident is the ignorance and confusion that many policymakers display about the nature of teaching and the roles of teachers. On one extreme is a view of teachers as semiskilled laborers who must follow cookbook recipes for practice. On the other is a view of teachers as professionals who must rely on a complex knowledge base to serve the diverse needs of students. If they are semiskilled laborers, teachers need only basic skills and rudimentary abilities to manage a classroom. If they are professionals, they must understand learning theory and pedagogy as the basis for informed educational decision making (Darling-Hammond & Berry, 1988).

If one looks at teachers' working conditions, their lives are closer to the "teacher as laborer" conception than the professionalized view. First, the Carnegie Study, a national survey of 13,500 teachers, revealed that teachers have a conflicted view of their occupation. On the one hand, they noted improvements in principal leadership, technology for teaching, instructional materials, and school discipline since 1983. On the other, they lamented increased classroom interruptions, noninstructional duties, teaching loads, and class size; *significant increases* in political interference, state regulation, and burdensome paperwork; and declines in fiscal resources, time for preparation and collaboration, and overall morale (Carnegie Foundation, 1988).

Second, in a study of urban schools conducted by the Institute of Educational Leadership, researchers found, for the most part, working conditions which could best be described as "bleak," "substandard," and "intolerable" (Corcoran, Walker, & White, 1988). Case studies of 31 elementary, middle, and high schools revealed working conditions that would not be tolerated in true professions. The researchers pointed out that many teachers worked in dilapidated buildings (dirty and in very ill repair) without basic instructional materials like textbooks and paper or classrooms of their own. These teachers had little confidence in district-level leadership and complained of the lack of respect they received from district officials. Even in districts that had recently allowed more school-based decision making, teachers perceived these "reforms" as top-down, ambiguous, and inadequate for their efforts to reach students (Corcoran, Walker, & White, 1988).

Finally, in South Carolina—which has mandated effective schools programs for its schools and has been highly touted for its omnibus South Carolina Education Improvement Act (EIA)—a recent study of teacher working conditions and burnout reveals the problems and concerns related to and associated with overly prescriptive, top-down–oriented reforms (Ginsberg & Berry, 1990). Ginsberg and colleagues (1989) specifically link recent reforms to the declining condition of teaching. They surveyed over 4,000 South Carolina teachers and interviewed an additional 108 about their working conditions, burnout, and the impact of the EIA passed in 1984. While certain aspects of the reform such as improvements in inservice, leadership of principal, and clarity of goals and expectations were well received, teachers reported extraordinarily high levels of emotional exhaustion. This exhaustion was linked to several internal aspects of teaching, including (1) excessive paperwork, (2) lack of time to prepare for classes and to meet with other teachers, (3) lack of opportunity for creativity in the classroom, (4) excessive nonteaching duties, and (5) role conflict from having to do unnecessary job tasks. Interview data disclosed teacher concerns about overly prescriptive and rigid state and district mandates, especially related to standardized curriculum and testing. One teacher summed up the problem in the following manner:

> I am being made into a machine and my students are being made into machines....I am a factory worker, that is what I feel like here....I guess I went to college to become a file clerk [referring to the required documentation related to the curriculum and testing]....Each day I have to come in with their objectives and the skills I must

teach....Sometimes I know I am pushing it down their throat—just like pumping gasoline. (Ginsberg et al., 1989, p. 68)

Policy analysts have suggested that in order to determine the success of any school reform, some exploration of the impact on school culture must be undertaken (Timar & Kirp, 1989). Specifically, it is necessary to examine how those who work in schools are affected by the many changes being mandated. Both the Carnegie study (1988) and Ginsberg and colleagues (1989) concluded that recent reforms had undermined organizational culture. Both studies asked teachers if morale had improved or worsened as a result of school reform. In the Carnegie study (1988), 49 percent of the teachers from around the United States indicated that morale had worsened as a result of the education reform movement. In spite of the praise the South Carolina reforms have received (Inman, 1987; Chance, 1986; Timar & Kirp, 1989), over 60 percent of the teachers surveyed said the reforms had reduced morale. Such findings suggest a pessimistic outcome for reform in terms of the culture of the schools.

In sum, recent curriculum, certification, and evaluation policies based on the view of teaching as unskilled labor compounded the negative effects of top-down implementation of the school effectiveness formula with its emphasis on standardized achievement. Many teachers lamented that they were not only told what to teach, but to how to teach it. Teachers—such as those in South Carolina—claim that "teaching and testing programs" gave them no choice but to defer to the central authorities (e.g., legislators, state department of education personnel, central office supervisors, or principals). To remedy these concerns, a new movement has been building to professionalize teaching. Before addressing the ideology of teacher professionalism, we will speak to the nature of professionalization itself.

THE NATURE OF PROFESSIONALIZATION

In American Society, professionalism is a concept that is usually applied in a morally evaluative manner—that is, one occupational group is better (e.g., medicine) than another (e.g., teaching). Becker (1962) suggests that a profession is nothing more than an "occupation which has been fortunate enough in the politics of today's work world to gain and maintain possession of that honorific title" (p. 33). While professionalism may be more a folk concept than a scientific one (Turner, 1957), sociologists usually speak to several characteristics which distinguish professions from other "less lofty" occupations. For Becker (1962) the distinguishing characteristics of a profession are: (1) the possession of an esoteric and abstract body of knowledge, (2) peer control over admitting new members, (3) lengthy training, (4) a monopoly of services, (5) a code of ethics, (6) the trust of clients, and (7) an esteemed position in society. Of all these characteristics, the development of and control over professional knowledge may be the most critical. As Barber notes (1984),

> An essential attribute of professional role is autonomy and self-control regarding the development and application of the body of generalized knowledge in which they alone are expert (p. 15).

Since professional knowledge is indeterminate, effective practice cannot be reduced to checklists of specific behaviors, nor can effective practice be determined by outsiders. A profession develops its status, in part, by its arcane knowledge which cannot be applied routinely and, in part, by the knowledge base which defines the nature of profession itself. In the "established" legal profession, lawyers define meaning and substance of justice while in the medical profession doctors define the meaning and substance of health (Darling-Hammond, 1985). However, teachers—without question—do not define the nature of education.

THE IDEOLOGY OF TEACHER PROFESSIONALISM

Today's calls for school reform build on the ideology of teacher professionalism (e.g., see Carnegie Foundations, 1986; National Governor's Association, 1986; Holmes Group, 1986). Much like the early 1980s "first-wave" reform reports (e.g., the National Commission on Excellence on Education's *A Nation at Risk*), the more recent reform wave responds to economic imperatives. Asserting that our schools are still inadequately preparing students for an increasingly technological labor market, reform leaders call for schools to do better—to facilitate more than just the transfer of basic skills to students. To do so, teachers must be professionalized—that is, empowered to convey highly technical knowledge and stimulate students to think critically about the widening range of complex issues they will face in their lives and careers. Devaney and Sykes (1988) argue that teacher professionalism is imperative because schoolwork should be more complex and that students need to be educated in solving ill-structured problems—that is, the kind they will most likely face in the workplace. Thus, schools should not employ teachers who spoonfeed students, but those who can enable students to understand what they have come to know. This means that for students and teachers, getting the right answer may be less important than understanding why certain answers may or may not fit certain questions. However, this type of teaching and learning is most likely suppressed with the current press for basic skill achievement and its measurement by standardized multiple choice tests.

Simply stated, the new rhetoric of reform suggests the need for a new breed of teachers for reconceptualized schools. This new breed could be identified in part by the norms of excellence that may be set by the National Board for Professional Teaching Standards (NBPTS). Such teachers would need to be empowered to recreate the conditions for their work and that of their students. With the right mix of training, socialization, and organizational structure, these new school reforms are expected to empower teachers to bring about higher-order thinking and social learning to empower students (Lanier & Sedlak, 1989).

Despite this pervasive (and, to what some argue, persuasive) teacher professionalism ideology, there is virtually no research on teacher professionalism and its potential impact on improving school outcomes. The little research evidence supporting teacher professionalism is found in the curriculum implementation literature. Researchers such as Berman and McLaughlin (1978) present data suggesting that teacher participation in the implementation process facilitates organizational and individual change. Loucks and Lieberman (1983)—at least indirectly—link teacher professionalism with the whole notion of adult development. This literature notes that successful curriculum implementation hinges on teachers' opportunities to engage in experiential learning within an open climate of trust and affirmation. Rosenholtz's (1985) review of the "best" of the effective schools literature confirms the importance of teacher involvement and collaboration. She asserts that in effective schools, teachers are less likely to work in isolated settings and that collegial norms drive improvement in instructional practices.

Nonetheless, today's calls for teacher professionalism usually point to the dismal (e.g., the 1988 Carnegie Study) and isolated (McLauglin & Yee, 1988) conditions of teacher work or to the studies which point to bright young people who choose not to teach because of the lack of control and flexibility in the profession (Page & Page, 1984; Mangieri & Kemper, 1987; Berry, McCormick, & Buxton, 1989). Perhaps, the most persuasive argument (although nondata based) is offered by Darling-Hammond (1988b) who suggests that professional accountability is the most efficient form of regulation in teaching. Since students are not sufficiently standardized and they will not respond to predictable treatments, bureaucratic monitoring of teaching is much too expensive and cumbersome as well as ultimately ineffective. She notes that

> Professionals are obligated to do what is best for the client, not what is easiest, most expedient, or even what the client might want. (p. 12)

This does not mean that professional teachers should teach just the way they want or the way they were once taught. Instead, through rigorous standards for entry into teaching, protracted internships where theory becomes intimately linked with practice, and collective decision making about evolving definitions of best practice, teachers can assure a suspecting public that they can police their own.

While the limited research base (as well as the centralized controls of the 1980s school reforms) have diminished the prospects for teacher professionalism, so have other numerous, long-standing structural impediments. First, even today, policymakers and administrators continue to view teachers as females who are incapable of mature judgment (see Boston Women's Teachers' Group, 1983). Despite the gains of the feminist's movement, teaching continues to be shackled by its label of low-status women's work.

Second, teachers may not want the responsibility associated with teacher professionalism (see Devaney & Sykes, 1988). One could argue that the brightest and most aggressive women and minorities no longer choose to teach—leaving the occupation to those who are passive, more likely to accept the status quo, and deferent to the present authority structure. A study of a high school teacher recruitment program revealed that the individuals who did *not* choose teaching were more likely to seek power and authority as well as opportunities for flexibility and creativity in their future careers than those who did (Berry, Kijai, & Hare, 1990). Additionally, those who did *not* choose teaching also scored higher on the SAT than their counterparts who intended to teach.

Third, schools of education continue to suffer from low-status, unstable leadership, and an increasingly narrow and technocratic view of teaching (Olsen, 1990). Teacher training programs focus on substrata of the occupation (e.g., secondary, guidance, vocational), not on a unified discipline (Sykes, 1983). The lack of member control over access to and induction into teaching looms as specter over the prospects for teacher professionalism (Wise, Darling-Hammond, & Berry, 1987). Until teacher selection, from recruitment to retention, becomes controlled by teachers themselves, the old adage that "no one has ever died of a split infinitive" will continue to beset teaching.

Finally, despite the growth of knowledge in teaching (Schulman, 1988), teachers, by and large, tend to shy away from new research on either teaching practices, school improvement, or the politics of education. In fact, the words "research indicates" frustrate teachers since they seldom have opportunities to link theory and practice carefully. These words become an euphemism for ivory tower academics (who have not been in classroom for 20 years) telling teachers what to do. Teachers have long been socialized to work independently in their "egg-crate" classrooms (Lortie, 1975) and have little time for reflection, analysis, or collaboration (Fullan, 1982). Without systematic collaborative interchange and analysis, professional norms of excellence cannot emerge to drive the development of the field. Knowledge utilization and dissemination is critical to teachers' capacity to become socialized to compete in the politics of education.

The development of the National Board of Professional Teaching Standards (NBPTS)—and its efforts to certify teachers who demonstrate high levels of *context-specific* knowledge in their fields and articulate professional standards of practice—has some potential for uplifting the field and undoing many damning perceptions of teaching and teacher education. Yet the NBPTS is not part of any state's certification or training program, and it remains unclear as to what impact, if any, it will have. At the time of this writing, teacher education institutions, teacher organizations, and the NBPTS are in a political squabble over whether or not a candidate for national certification must have graduated from an accredited program of teacher education. Some analysts anticipate that the NBPTS will lead to the creation of analogous state boards, comprised of outstanding teachers and education professionals. The state boards would be charged with identifying critical knowledge and skills, constructing evaluation mechanisms, and restricting entry of the unqualified and the incompetent (Wise, 1989). However, for this to happen, states must first abandon many teacher policy mandates of the 1980s, and most of the previously mentioned structural impediments to teacher professionalism must be tackled. Such obstacles seem overwhelming! Thus, we conclude that educational reform is at a crossroads. One road may be to heed the "best" of effective schools literature—with its emphasis on school culture and collaboration—and merge it with the emerging teacher professionalism literature. The other road may be to continue the top-down, highly centralized, school reforms of the 1980s—which fed on the simplistic school effectiveness formula.

EDUCATIONAL REFORM AT A CROSSROADS

As we enter the 1990s, consensus grows among business leaders, education-oriented governors, certain segments of the education community, and policy analysts that school improvement requires the professionalization of teachers. Without substantive changes in the occupational structure of teaching, public schools will not attract and retain talented individuals, nor will these talented individuals have the mandate to exercise the teaching methods required to meet the complex needs of the students of the twenty-first century. However, efforts to professionalize teaching are running head on with numerous first-wave policy reforms with their emphasis on "hyperrationalizing" the curriculum (Wise, 1979), routinizing teaching, and deskilling (or deprofessionalizing) teachers (McNeil, 1986). The school effectiveness formula with its narrow focus on basic skills instruction, underdeveloped conceptualization of what constitutes good teaching, and excessive reliance on testing and administrative leadership aids and abets these developments.

The curriculum required for the twenty-first century cannot be prescribed by formula nor can it be created by totally autonomous teachers. No longer can teachers be tellers of facts nor can students be only passive recipients of teacher talk. Even the blue-collar jobs of today and tomorrow require students to be "knowledge workers" who must think critically and solve ill-structured problems (Devaney & Sykes, 1988). To understand this point, all one has to do is look at the engine under the hood of any 1990 model of Mazda, Toyota, or Chrysler.

School culture, history, and environment are critical determinants of the activities and behaviors of teachers. Thus, school context has a major effect on student outcomes and school effectiveness (Cuban, 1984; Teddlie & Wimpelberg, 1987). However, the realities of school life and teacher and student work severely limit the likelihood of significant changes using the effectiveness antidote. Current rhetoric and proposed reforms will work only to the extent that they are responsive to the demanding realities of teaching and learning. Sadly, the realities of teacher and student work are unsettling. Today's educators (especially teachers) are frustrated and "exhausted" from their work, and without their energy and vision, school *reform* may go wanting. Consequently, teachers cannot present the positive role models for bright young people to choose teaching as a prospective career. Without an influx of young talent into teaching, the prospects for teacher professionalism remain dim.

For teacher professionalism to occur, many first-wave policy reforms must be significantly altered or abandoned. These include the rigid adherence to the standardized curricula, the assessment of student learning through basic skills tests, the assessment of teachers through simplistic evaluation tools, and certification loopholes which denigrate the emerging knowledge base for teaching. Huge state bureaucracies have been built on the basis of a first-wave definition of school effectiveness.

The school effectiveness literature has a subtext that emphasizes cultural norms and collaboration. This subtext could provide a strong justification for second-wave conceptions of restructuring and professional accountability. As developed by Rosenholtz (1985) and Stedman (1987), this newer scenario (not formula) provides an argument against the bureaucratic accountability systems that are presently driving teaching and learning and pulling teachers and students away from complex assignments. For professionalism to occur, teachers must come up with new forms of accountability that will assure policymakers and the public that teachers should have the autonomy, responsibility, obligations, and status associated with modern professionalism.

At the heart of teacher professionalism is the creation and utilization of a knowledge base to advance student learning. If teacher professionalism is not going to disintegrate into self-aggrandizement, then the focus of the teachers' efforts must be on the student. However, socializing, educating, and rallying a "dispirited" teacher work force to focus on student learning is only one small piece of the puzzle. Governors, state legislators, state department of education bureaucrats, state and local boards of education, local superintendents, and principals have to commit organizational resources and space for the vision of teacher professionalism to be fulfilled.

CONCLUSION

The challenge for the future is to transform the *typical* school classroom, with a single teacher lecturing to large numbers of students who are then required to do seatwork and use "dumbed-down" textbooks, to *new* classrooms, with teams of teachers helping students making complex constructions of knowledge. In these new classrooms, students would be expected to organize and monitor their own learning and engage in collaborative and situation-specific learning activities (Devaney & Sykes, 1988).

The present reality of schools—with its rote learning, seatwork, lecturing, and testing—is intensified by the popular interpretation of the effectiveness movement (also known as improving test scores). First-wave modes of accountability exacerbate the long-standing tension between the contradictory goals of educating students and processing them. McNeil (1988) found that when school resources, personnel, and policies focus on processing students, "Many teachers lapse into a pattern of boring, mechanical teaching that shows little evidence of their full knowledge of a subject or of their ideas of what students need to know" (p. 334). Unfortunately, when states such as South Carolina implement the six-factor school effectiveness formula in ways that emphasize narrow definitions of accountability and control rather than collegiality and professionalism, they reinforce this pattern of teaching and intensify rather than alter the present realities of schools. We are deeply concerned that—given these realities of schools—organizational renewal and the development of a professional culture of teaching will be just that more difficult to realize. Without systemic and dynamic changes in those stifling school realities, frustrated teachers will stagnate, bright young people will choose other occupations, and policy will continue to limit teachers' judgments and capacities. The professionalization of teaching remains only as rhetorical splendor and academic debate. Policy analysts such as us make a good living, but children suffer.

REFERENCES

APPLEBEE, A. N., LANGER, J., & MULLIS, I. (1989). *Crossroads in American education: A summary of findings*. Princeton, NJ: National Assessment of Educational Progress and Educational Testing Service.

AIRASIAN, P. (May 1987). State mandated testing and educational reform: context and consequence. *American Journal of Education*, 393–412.

BARBER, L. W. (1984). Teacher evaluation and merit pay. Paper prepared for the Task Force on Education for Economic Growth (TF-83-5).

BECKER, H. (1962). The nature of a profession. In *Education for the professions*. Chicago: University of Chicago Press.

BERMAN, P., & MCLAUGHLIN, M. (1978). Implementation of educational innovation. *Educational Forum, 40*, 345–70.

BERRY, B., KIJAI, J., & HARE, R. D. (1990). Professional attitudes and deprofessionalized working conditions: The impact of a teacher recruitment program. Paper presented at the 1990 Annual Meeting of the American Educational Research Association, Boston.

BERRY, B., MCCORMICK, C., & BUXTON, T. (1989). *Recruiting the next generation of teachers: Conversations with high school sophomores*. Research Triangle Park, NC: Southeastern Educational Improvement Lab.

BOSTON'S WOMEN'S TEACHERS' GROUP. (1983). Teaching: An imperiled profession. In L. Schulman and G. Sykes (Eds.), *Handbook of teaching and policy.* New York: Longman.

BOYD, W. L. (1987). Public education's last hurrah: Schizophrenia, amnesia, and ignorance in school politics. Paper presented to the Annual Meeting of the American Political Association, Washington, D.C.

BROPHY, J. E., & EVERTSON, C. (1974). *Process-product correlations in the Texas teacher effectiveness study: Final report.* Austin: Research and Development Center for Teacher Education, University of Texas.

THE CARNEGIE FOUNDATION FOR THE ADVANCEMENT OF TEACHING. (1986). *A nation prepared: Teachers for the 21st century.* New York: Carnegie Foundation.

THE CARNEGIE FOUNDATION FOR THE ADVANCEMENT OF TEACHING. (1988). *Report card on school reform: The teachers speak.* New York: Carnegie Foundation.

CHANCE, W. (1986). *The best of education: Reforming America's public schools in the 1980s.* Chicago: The John D. and Catherine T. MacArthur Foundation.

CLARK, D., LOTTO, L., & ASTUTO, T. (1984). Effective schools and school improvement: A comparative analysis of two lines of inquiry. *Educational Administration Quarterly, 20,* 41–68.

COLEMAN, J. S., CAMPBELL, E., HOBSON, C., McPARTLAND, J., MOOD, A., WEINFELD, F., & YORK, R. (1966). *Equality of educational opportunity.* Washington, D.C.: Government Printing Office.

CORCORAN, T. B., WALKER, L., & WHITE, J. L. (1988). *Working in urban schools.* Washington, D.C.: Institute for Educational Leadership.

CRONBACH, L. J., & SNOW, R. E. (1977). *Aptitudes and instructional methods: A handbook for research on interactions.* Irvington, NY: Basic Books.

CUBAN, L. (1983). Effective schools: A friendly but cautionary note. *Kappan, 9,* 695–96.

CUBAN, L. (1984). Transforming the frog into a prince: Effective schools research, policy, and practice at the district level. *Harvard Educational Review, 54,* 129–51.

CUBAN, L. (1990). Reforming again, again, and again. *Educational Researcher, 19,* 3–14.

DARLING-HAMMOND, L. (1983). The seduction of central office administrators by effective schools research. Paper presented to the Superintendent's Roundtable Seminar, Washington, D.C.

DARLING-HAMMOND, L. (1984). *Beyond the commission reports: The coming crisis in teaching.* Santa Monica, CA: Rand.

DARLING-HAMMOND, L. (1985). Valuing teachers: The making of a profession. *Teachers College Record.*

DARLING-HAMMOND, L. (1988a). Policy and Professionalism. In Anne Lieberman (Ed.), *Building a professional culture in schools.* New York: Teacher College Press.

DARLING-HAMMOND, L. (1988b). Accountability and teacher professionalism. *American Educator,* Winter, 8–13, 40–43.

DARLING-HAMMOND, L., & BERRY, B. (1988). *The evolution of teacher policy.* Santa Monica, CA: Rand.

DEVANEY, K., & SYKES, G. (1988). Making the case for professionalism. In Anne Lieberman (Ed.), *Building a professional culture in schools.* New York: Teachers College Press.

EASTON, J., & GINSBERG, R. (1985). Student learning processing...How poor prepared students succeed in college. *Research and Teaching in Developmental Education, 1,* 12–38.

EDMONDS, R. (October 1979).   Effective schools for the urban poor. *Educational Leadership,* *37,* 16.

EDUCATION COMMISSION OF THE STATES. (1983).   *A Survey of State School Improvement* *Efforts.* Denver, CO: ECS.

EDUCATION WEEK. (February 7, 1990).   The teacher's workweek, p. 3.

FULLAN, M. (1982).   *The meaning of educational change.* New York: Teachers College Press.

GAGE, N. L. (1978).   *The scientific basis of the art of teaching.* New York: Teachers College Press.

GINSBERG, R., ET AL. (1989).   Teaching in South Carolina: A retirement initiative. Report prepared for the South Carolina Education Association. Columbia: The South Carolina Educational Policy Center.

GINSBERG, R., & BERRY, B. (March 1990).   Experiencing school reform: The view from South Carolina. *Kappan, 67,* 549–52.

THE HOLMES GROUP. (1986).   *Tomorrow's Teachers: A Report of the Holmes Group.* Lansing, MI: The Holmes Group, Inc., April.

INMAN, D. (1987).   The financial impact of educational reform. Paper presented at the Annual Meeting of the American Educational Research Association, Washington, D.C.

LANIER, J., & SEDLAK, M. (1989).   Teacher efficacy and school quality. In T. Sergiovani & J. T. Moore (Eds.), *Schooling for tomorrow.* Boston: Allyn & Bacon.

LORTIE, D. C. (1975).   *Schoolteacher: A sociological analysis.* Chicago: University of Chicago Press.

LOUCKS, S., & LIEBERMAN, A. (1983).   Curriculum Implementation. In F. English (Ed.), *Fundamental Curriculum Decision.* Alexandria, VA: Ass. for Supervisor & Curriculum Dev.

MANGIERI, J. N., & KEMPER, R. E. (1987).   America's future teaching force: Predictions and recommendations. *Phi Delta Kappan, 64,* 393–95.

MCDONALD, F. J., & ELIAS, P. (1976).   *Executive summary report: Beginning teacher evaluation study, phase II.* Princeton, NJ: Educational Testing Service.

MCLAUGHLIN, M., & YEE, S. (1988).   School as a place to have a career. In Anne Lieberman (Ed.), *Building a professional culture in schools.* New York: Teacher College Press.

MCNEIL, (1986).   *Contradictions of Control: School Structure and School Knowledge.* New York: Routledge Books.

MCNEIL, L. (1988).   Contradictions of control, part I: Administrators and teachers. *Kappan, 70,* 334.

MEDLEY, D. M. (1979).   The effectiveness of teachers. In P. L. Peterson & H. J. Walberg (Eds.), *Research on teaching.* Berkeley, CA: McCutchan.

NATIONAL EDUCATION ASSOCIATION. (1987).   *Status of the American public school teacher:* *1985–86.* Washington, D.C.: NEA.

NATIONAL GOVERNOR'S ASSOCIATION. (1986).   *Time for results.* Washington, D.C.: NGA.

THE NEW YORK TIMES. (February 21, 1990).   The good principal: A tradition breaker, p. 25.

OLSEN, L. (February 28, 1990).   Goodlad on teacher education: Low status, unclear mission. *Education Week,* p. 1.

PAGE, J. A., & PAGE, F. (1984).   *High school seniors perceptions of teaching as a career opportunity.* Statesboro: Georgia Southern College.

PELLICER, L. O., ANDERSON, L. W., KEEFE, J. W., KELLY, E. A., & MCCLEARY, L. (1990).   *High school leaders and their schools. Vol. II, Effectiveness profiles.* Reston, VA: National Association for Secondary School Principals.

PLANK, D. (1988).   Why school reform doesn't change school: Political and organizational perspectives. In W. L. Boyd & C. T. Kerchner, *The politics of excellence and choice in education*. Philadelphia: Falmer Press.

POPHAM, W. J. (1987).   The shortcomings of champagne teacher evaluations. *Journal of Personnel Evaluation, 1*, 25–28.

PURKEY, S. C., & SMITH, M. (1983).   School reform: The district policy implications of the effective schools literature. *The Elementary School Journal, 85*, 353–89.

PUTKA, G. (November 2, 1989).   School tests closely match material in commercial practice kits, booklets. *The Wall Street Journal*, p. 22b.

RALPH, J. H., & FENNESSEY, J. (1983).   Science or reform: Some questions about the effective schools model. *Kappan, 60*, 689–94.

RESNICK, D., & RESNICK, L. (1985).   Standards, curriculum, and performance: Historical and comparative perspectives. *Educational Researcher, 14*, 5–20.

ROSENHOLTZ, S. (May 1985).   Effective schools: Interpreting the evidence. *American Journal of Education*, 353–88.

ROSSMILLER, R. (1986).   Some contemporary trends and their implications for the preparation of educational administrators. *UCEA Review, 27*, 2–3.

ROWAN, B., BOSSERT, S., & DWYER, D. C. (1983).   Research on effective schools: A cautionary note. *Educational Researcher, 12*, 24–31.

SCHLECHTY P., & VANCE, V. (1981).   Do academically able teachers leave education? The North Carolina case. *Kappan, 63*, 106–12.

SHULMAN, L. (1988).   A union of insufficiencies: Strategies for teacher assessment in a period of educational reform. *Educational Leadership, 46*, 36–41.

STALLING, J. (1977).   How instructional processes relate to child outcomes. In G. D. Borich (Ed.), *The appraisal of teaching: outcomes*. Reading, MA: Addison-Wesley.

STEDMAN, L. C. (1987).   It's time we changed the effective schools formula. *Kappan, 69*, 215–24.

SYKES, G. (1983).   Contradictions, ironies, and promises unfulfilled: A contemporary account of the status of teaching. *Kappan, 65*, 87–93.

TEDDLIE, C., STRINGFIELD, S., WIMPLEBERG, R., & KIRBY, P. (1987).   A time to summarize: six years and three phases of the Louisiana School Effectiveness Study. ED 286272. Paper presented at the Annual Meeting of the American Educational Research Association, Washington, D.C.

TEDDLIE, C., & WIMPELBERG, B. (1987).   The issue of differentiated context in school effectiveness studies. Paper presented at the Annual Meeting of the American Educational Research Association, Washington, D.C.

TIMAR, T., & KIRP, D. (1989).   Education reform in the States: Lessons from the States. *Kappan, 66*, 505–11.

TURNER, R. H. (1957).   The normative coherence of folk concepts. *Research Studies of the State College of Washington, 25*, 125–36.

U.S. GENERAL ACCOUNTING OFFICE. (1989).   *Effective schools programs: Their extent and characteristics*. Washington, D.C.: GAO.

WEAVER, T. (1983).   *America's quality teacher problem: Alternatives for reform*. New York: Praeger.

WEBER, G. (1971). *Inner city children can be taught to read: Four successful schools.* Occasional Papers, No. 18. Washington D.C.: Council for Basic Education.

WISE, A. E. (1979). *Legislated learning.* Berkeley: University of California Press.

WISE, A. E. (January 11, 1989).   States must create teaching standards boards. *Education Week,* p. 48.

WISE, A. E., DARLING-HAMMOND, L., & BERRY, B. (1987).   *Teacher selection: From recruitment to retention.* Santa Monica, CA: Rand.

WISE, A. E., DARLING-HAMMOND, L., BERRY, B., & KLEIN, S. (1987).   *Liscening teachers: A design for a profession.* Santa Monica, CA: Rand.

11

PERESTROIKA
FOR AMERICAN EDUCATION

Charles L. Glenn
Office of Educational Equity
The Commonwealth of Massachusetts
Department of Education
Quincy, Massachusetts

INTRODUCTION: THE MASSIVE REALITY OF PARENT CHOICE

Parent choice of schools has become the most hotly debated element in the education reform agenda. While endorsed by presidents Reagan and Bush, by the nation's governors, by Albert Shanker, and by many business leaders, parent choice is strongly resisted by the National Education Association, many civil rights leaders, and the sheer inertia of the public education system.

Much of the discussion of parent choice is abstract, based upon speculations about what might happen, for good or ill, if public policy were to encourage parent choice. Economists have offered a variety of scenarios—positive and negative—for how school choice might function. Yet there has been insufficient attention to the actual functioning of parent choice, already a massive reality in American education.

One hundred twenty thousand pupils in Massachusetts attend public "schools of choice" in 15 cities; 8 of these cities, including Boston, have made parent choice— not geography—the only basis for assignment to a school. Other states and cities have similar programs to promote school choice for desegregation, often adopted as an alternative to mandatory assignment plans.

Publicly sponsored choice is only the tip of an iceberg; it is likely that most pupils in Massachusetts and elsewhere in the nation attend schools that have in some sense been chosen by their parents. Parent decisions are always an important element in how pupils are sorted out among schools. Middle-class parents commonly decide where they will live in part on the basis of the availability of the kind of education they want for their children. A 1984 study in Minnesota

found that 62 per cent of public school parents reported being "active choosers" as compared to only 53 per cent of private school parents. Although less likely than private school parents to have considered other schools at the time of current school choice…most of them had considered public school quality as an important factor in determining residential location. (Darling-Hammond and Kirby, 1988, pp. 247–48)

The real estate section of *The Boston Globe* noted recently that

many home buyers pay more for homes in a pricey community—and sacrifice some space, too—because such towns often have good schools for their children. [One family interviewed] have justified going over their budget by saying, "Now, we don't have to send the kids to private school." In fact, there seems to be a correlation between pricey towns and good schools. (Koppel, 1989, p. 41)

This reality was even used—rather cynically—by officials of an urban teachers' union in Massachusetts as grounds for opposing, as unnecessary and damaging to public education, legislation that would have provided equal access to out-of-district schools.

[M]ost parents select and choose the public schools their children attend because, excepting conditions of poverty and discrimination, parents select and choose the communities where they reside; and, more often than not, they choose communities which boast excellent public schools. It logically follows then that parents already have the opportunity to select their schools, and, to increase parental choice, in most cases, is to either choose to change one's residence, therefore one's public schools, or choose to pay the additional cost for private or out-of-district education. (Kasparian, 1988)

Other middle-class parents find ways of "working the system" to get their children into the school they want. Thus it is common, in the liability phase of a school desegregation suit, to find that large numbers of white pupils are attending predominantly white schools rather than integrated schools in their racially changing neighborhoods.

Massachusetts has moved beyond tolerating—as of course it must—the individual choices that middle-class parents already make, to promoting choice actively in the name of equal educational opportunity. Four out of five black and Hispanic pupils in the state now attend schools that have achieved integrated enrollments through parental choice. Over the past 15 years, the state has provided $500 million to support such desegregative choices.

The focus of these efforts has shifted from promoting individual magnet schools to establishing policies under which every school enrolls its pupils through a process of parental choice. Magnet schools, as many critics have noted, while providing significant benefits for the pupils fortunate enough to be enrolled, are not so positive in their overall effect on urban school systems and on the pupils who do not participate. The concerns raised by some critics of choice, that it can produce new inequities even as it improves education for some, have been confirmed in Boston and other cities.

How can we put parent choice to work for integration and school improvement while minimizing its negative side effects? Cambridge was the first city to universalize choice; since 1981, parent choice has been the *only* means of enrolling in a school, and thus every school has come under pressure to become distinctively attractive to minority and majority parents (Alves and Willie, 1986; Rossell and Glenn, 1988). Other cities in Massachusetts and across the nation have since followed suit.

Reporters often call to ask me for evidence of the impact of choice upon educational results. Does allowing parents to select schools make schools more effective?

It's a question I answer with another: What is an effective school in our society? What kind of schools do we want to have? Failure to be clear about our goals for education leads to taking the easy but misleading course of measuring effectiveness exclusively by scores on standardized tests. An appreciation of the complexity of what a good school—or a bad school—accomplishes and of the divergent goals of different parents and pupils should warn us against seeking a simple and unitary definition of effectiveness.

> To put it very schematically, a good school for our pluralistic democracy must exhibit and develop our core values of justice and liberty, as well as teaching academic skills and knowledge efficiently.
>
> The appropriate question about the impact of parent choice, then, is: How do different policies for publicly supported choice of schools protect and advance justice, liberty, and instructional efficiency? How do other policies for choice, while serving private ends, undermine our public goals as a society?

CHOICE SERVING JUSTICE

Those who support parent choice as an effective means of advancing educational justice stress that it is an effective way to achieve desegregation and to break the link between residence and access to educational opportunities; under a well-designed choice plan, geography (and the income that largely dictates residence) is no longer destiny.

In what continues to be the best book available on parent choice, Coons and Sugarman insist that it "can create opportunities for integration that lie beyond the reach of legal compulsion; it is in many instances the only hope for integration....Integration that occurs by choice is stable and enduring" (1978, pp. 109, 116). It has been through seeking to achieve stable and productive integration that we have come to support a continuing expansion of parent choice among Massachusetts schools.

While desegregation mandates have forced hundreds of public school systems into developing magnet schools as a lesser evil than mandatory reassignments, other dimensions of educational equity could also be served by an intelligent use of parent choice. As Jencks concluded in his influential *Inequality: A Reassessment of the Effect of Family and Schooling in America* (1972),

> we will have to accept diverse standards for judging schools....A school system that provides only one variety of schooling, no matter how good, must almost invariably seem unsatisfactory to many parents and children. The ideal system is one that provides as many varieties of schooling as its children and parents want and finds ways of matching children to schools that suit them. (p. 256)

The access of black pupils to a wide range of educational opportunities, Jencks and his associates concluded after a major policy study, would be expanded by a system of parent choice (Areen & Jencks, 1972, p. 56).

The Massachusetts experience has been that effective use of parent choice to advance educational equity for poor and minority pupils requires attention to three elements:

1. A share of the seats available in each school must be set aside for minority pupils, and a share for majority pupils; parental preferences are accommodated within limits set by the need to maintain stable integration and equal access.

2. All enrollment of pupils new to the school system must occur through a parent information center which counsels parents individually (in their native languages) about the options available and how to be active participants in the schooling of their children. My office is currently funding 14 parent information centers in Massachusetts cities.

3. Every school must be stimulated and helped to become distinctive as a means of becoming more attractive to parents. This is the most difficult task associated with promoting parent choice, since it runs counter to the "common school" orthodoxy of American public education (Glenn, 1988).

CHOICE SERVING SCHOOL EFFECTIVENESS

Recently, diversity and choice among schools have received support from new thinking about the requirements of educational effectiveness. Not that choice of itself improves schools, but that the active exercise of choice by parents changes for the better—so the argument goes—the environment within which schools operate.

For years, the voices advocating public policies supporting parent choice of schools have come largely from the ranks of Catholic and Protestant nonpublic education (Blum, 1972, McCarthy et al., 1981), occasionally joined by libertarians with no stake in the religious content of schooling but objections to state control (Friedman, 1962; Arons, 1986). Recently, however, they have been joined by a new group of supporters whose primary concern is with the effectiveness of American education. The discipline of the market, they argue, would force many schools to become more effective or to go out of business. Interest in extending the market to popular education (since elite education has always operated in a free market) has been debated periodically among economists, but the impetus to move it to the center of the education policy debate has come in large part from state governors and business leaders, who have seen it as a way to stimulate individual schools to become more effective. Perhaps the most influential exponent of this view has been David Kearns, head of the Xerox Corporation:

> By any measure, today's educational system is a failed monopoly....The monopolist is free to ignore the legitimate needs and interests of both the consumer and the worker, a picture that describes the reality of today's educational system. Teachers and students are the losers.
>
> An economic model of education is both more democratic and more responsive than a political model. The essence of democracy is choice, and this frame of reference permits the public to think about schools and deal with them constructively. (Kearns and Doyle, 1988, pp. 16–17)

From this perspective, which could be called the "blunt weapon strategy," choice will help to render schools more responsive to demand and thus force them to improve in quality or to go out of business. The public education system is seen as analogous to the command economies of the Soviet bloc, in need of a *perestroika* more fundamental than new curriculum or increased teacher pay (Brimelow, 1985, p. 351).

There is a more benign version of the argument for a link between parent choice and school improvement, stressing that properly designed choice fosters those behaviors and that sense of purpose in schools essential to effectiveness.

The effect—indirect but powerful—of parent choice through changing the environment within which public schools function is difficult to demonstrate with reading scores, but has been confirmed beyond question to those working in Massachusetts school systems that have made choice the only basis for attending school. Similarly, the National Governors' Association, in its comprehensive report on school reform, concluded that "[c]arefully designed programs permitting choice among public schools can increase student achievement, educator morale, and parental satisfaction" (1986, p. 86). But how is this effect mediated?

Parent choice permits, indeed requires, diversity among schools, and diversity in turn allows the faculty of each school to have a clear educational mission and requires them to align their efforts closely to accomplish that mission. Such consistency among teachers (arrived at through cooperation, rather than imposed) is one of the conditions necessary to effective schooling. Early proponents of "effective schools" relied too heavily upon exhorting principals to adopt a single model of organization and instruction, comparable to the "one best system" sought by earlier education reformers (Tyack, 1974).

The influential Carnegie Task Force proposal for the reform of American education, *A Nation Prepared: Teachers for the 21st Century,* called for a "new framework" for teaching:

> Bureaucratic management of schools proceeds from the view that teachers lack the talent or motivation to think for themselves....Within the context of a limited set of clear goals for students set by state and local policymakers, teachers, working together, must be free to exercise their professional judgment as to the best way to achieve these goals. (Task Force on Teaching as a Profession, 1986, p. 57)

Talk about restructuring of education, however, has too often assumed that teachers are eager to make the additional effort required to turn their schools into dynamic centers for learning. This is as unrealistic as to believe that Russian workers are yearning to accept the effort and the risks of managing their own factories.

If—as almost everyone now seems to agree—improved school effectiveness requires freeing principals to be educational leaders and freeing teachers to work as professionals, we need to determine what will stimulate such behaviors. Old habits die hard, particularly when the reward structure itself is not fundamentally changed; a Russian historian has noted that the reforming autocrat Peter the Great believed he could order slaves to act boldly and freely in ways that would benefit the state, and in no other. Some urban superintendents suffer from a similar illusion about their teachers.

Despite the current fashion for granting waivers of bureaucratic requirements to support school restructuring efforts, Susan Fuhrman found that the waivers actually requested tended to be timid and marginal (Fuhrman, 1989).

Parent choice and the diversity which it stimulates can free teachers to develop distinctive approaches to education in which they—and the parents who are their "customers"—believe strongly and thus will implement with conviction. A Dutch researcher found a connection between the distinctive identity of nongovernment schools and their effectiveness and deplored the colorless quality of schools which seek to be neutral (Marwijk Kooy-von Baumhauer, 1984). Similarly, one of the best recent books on the culture of American schools noted that

> [s]tudents of all kinds usually thrive by participation in institutions with distinctive purposes and common expectations. Magnet schools, examination schools, and schools-within-schools are expressions of the desire for communities of focused educational and often moral purpose. Because they are special places to begin with, teachers and students feel more special in them. Both are more likely to be committed to a purpose and the expectations that flow from it is they choose—and are chosen by—schools and sub-schools than if they are simply assigned to them. The existence of a common purpose has an educational force of its own, quite independent of the skills of individual teachers. It also helps good teachers do a better job and may soften the impact of less able teachers. (Powell, Farrar, & Cohen, 1985, p. 316)

Perhaps the strongest formulation of this link between choice and the characteristics of effective schools has been advanced by John Chubb and Terry Moe, drawing upon the high school and beyond data. Their study concluded that "[p]rivate schools appear to have intrinsic advantages over public schools because they operate in environments that, for a variety of reasons, promote the development of 'effective school' characteristics" (1986a, pp. 4, 9).

Several ways in which private schools tend to differ from public schools, they found, were definite advantages from the perspective of the effective schools research:

> private schools have simpler, friendlier, less constraining environments of administrators, school boards, and parents;
>
> they are more autonomous and more strongly led;
>
> they have clearer goals, more rigorous requirements, and place greater stress on academic excellence;
>
> relations between principals and teachers, and among teachers themselves, are more harmonious, more frequent, and more directly concerned with teaching;
>
> teachers are more integrally involved in policy-making, have greater control over their job situations, and are more satisfied with their jobs. (Chubb and Moe, 1986a, pp. 42-43)

Current school reform efforts cannot work, the authors concluded, because they fail to change the environment in which public schools must function.

As we have labored, in Massachusetts, to improve the effectiveness of urban education, several things have become clear. One is that programs can generally be no better than the schools that house them. Rather than concentrate on enforcing program guidelines for bilingual education, for example, it is more valuable to work on strengthening the entire school, with bilingual instruction as an aspect of how the school does business. With Carter and Chatfield, "[w]e doubt that bilingual programs acting independently of an effective school environment are sufficient to produce sustained positive student outcomes....Characteristics or attributes associated statistically with effectiveness are not what make an effective institution; rather, such schools are produced by a set of dynamic interrelationships and processes" (1986, pp. 201–3).

We have found that systems of parent choice that include all (not just elite or alternative) schools stimulate such creative experimentation, with accountability for results, by requiring each school to develop clarity of educational mission and strategy, a method of direct accountability for results, sufficient specialization of climate, and theme or pedagogy to serve some pupils very well. Such schools are free to serve some pupils very well precisely because they do not have to aim for the lowest common denominator of a geographical catchment area.

Successful parent choice requires schools that are diversely effective, and this cannot happen without strong leadership that can evoke collegiality and shared responsibility on the part of staff. Like the prospect of hanging in Johnson's celebrated aphorism, the threat of not being chosen concentrates the mind wonderfully and evokes the energy—in principal and teachers alike—essential to real school improvement.

This strategy is inconsistent with belief that there is one best way of teaching any subject or of developing a school climate that encourages learning and develops civic virtue. It reflects a conviction that top-down reforms—while necessary to achieve greater clarity about our educational goals—are incapable of stimulating creative problem solving in schools. We are convinced of the wisdom of Firestone's suggestion that "it may be useful to develop policies that allow several models of practice to develop simultaneously, and then let local practitioners experiment with these models to see which works best for them" (1989, p. 22).

RESPONDING TO THE CRITICS

Critics of parent choice do not usually challenge the claim that some pupils will end up in schools that are better for them. Sometimes they even concede that some schools may become more effective under the pressure of the market or through the opportunity to draw pupils who will be well served by a particular emphasis. Their fundamental criticisms are (1) that choice will benefit the few at the expense of the many, sorting pupils on the basis of social class and academic ability (Snider, 1987, 1988) and (2) that choice—even limited to public schools—will somehow undermine public education.

Perhaps the most effective criticism of parent choice policies is that made by the Chicago advocacy group, Designs for Change:

> In school districts with a substantial number of low-income, minority, and low-achieving students, public school choice programs have almost always resulted in maintaining or increasing the isolation of these students at risk in separate schools and programs. Thus, in practice, public school choice typically becomes a new form of discriminatory tracking....Public schools of choice in big city school systems have a number of detrimental effects on non-selective neighborhood schools, which include taking their most capable teachers, parents, and students from them. To the extent that school choice motivates changes in neighborhood schools, these changes are almost always focused on attracting and serving high-achieving students, not on overall school improvement. (Moore, 1989, p. 32)

These conclusions are entirely consistent with my own in 1983, when I prepared a report on magnet schools and assignments in Chicago for the city's Monitoring

Commission. Parent choice, even if restricted to the public schools of a single community, will tend to work against equity unless it is appropriately organized and supported. Selective secondary schools (Moore cites Boston Latin School, among others) echo and reinforce social class and racial stratification—what else is new?

A consistent antichoice position driven by equity concerns would have to insist upon forbidding alternatives to and within public education and break completely the link between residence and school attendance. There is no nation on earth where those with resources and power do not insist upon choosing the schools their children will attend. If we want to achieve class as well as racial integration, it must be on the basis of persuading those who have other alternatives to volunteer their children.

Done right, parent choice does not produce the negative side effects described by Moore; Massachusetts has found it an extremely powerful means of advancing educational equity.

Does justice require the common school to be a Noah's ark, with two of everything and no more common purpose than the need to get on board? Surely not. Misunderstanding the demands of democratic education has given us the "shopping mall high school" where

> pluralism is celebrated as a supreme institutional virtue, and tolerating diversity is the moral glue that holds schools together. But tolerance further precludes schools' celebrating more focused notions of education or of character. "Community" has come to mean differences peacefully coexisting rather than people working together toward some serious end....
>
> Agreement about school purpose is especially important for average students. But many teachers accept as inevitable and desirable the neutrality of the shopping mall high school....One teacher admitted that his school had no clear commitment to learning, only a clear commitment to accommodating student diversity. (Powell, Farrar, & Cohen, 1985, pp. 3, 199)

The fact is, that the "common school" preached by Horace Mann, the school bringing together in shared purpose the sons and daughters of the elite of commerce and the professions (not to mention the academic and policy elite) with those of the immigrant and the manual laborer has never been the norm in American society, and is less so than ever with the decline of economically diverse residential communities. This has led some to call for a "new common school," one based upon voluntary choice and shared goals for education (Glenn, 1987b).

Sociologist James Coleman insists that a recovery of coherence of purpose— possible only on the basis of parent choice—is essential to real educational effectiveness under contemporary conditions. Coleman shifts the emphasis from how efficient a particular institution—the urban school—may be in relation to limited and quantifiable goals and asks how well our common interests as a society are served by the overall socialization of urban youth.

> [T]here appear to be two alternatives for the role of families in the socialization of children. One is to accept their demise, and to substitute for them new institutions of socialization, far more powerful than the schools we know, institutions as yet unknown. A second is to strengthen the family's capacity to raise its children, building upon the fragments of communities that continue to exist among families, and searching for potential communities of interest....for the school to be such an institution requires abandoning the assumption of the school as an agent of the state, and substituting an

assumption closer to that in the private sector of education: the school is properly an extension of the family and the social community or value community of which that family is a part....It implies a nurturance, by the school, of those fragile social norms that the families of a school will support. (Coleman, 1985b, pp. 21–22)

There is no remedy for the ills of urban education to be found in insisting upon the lowest–common denominator school. Schools can be different and respond to teacher and parent goals, can build a sense of community and educational purpose, without accepting racial or class segregation.

The most consistent institutional critic of expanded parent choice has been the National Education Association (NEA), in concert with its state affiliates. The position of these organizations, as expressed by the NEA, has been that parent choice poses a threat to public education—if it is extended to those who cannot afford private schools:

[I]ndividuals, at their expense, should be free to choose, to supplement, or to substitute education in privately supported, nonpublic schools. The Association believes that tuition tax credits and vouchers could lead to racial, economic and social isolation of children and undermine our commitment to the public school system. (National Education Association, 1985)

This seems to say that parents who can afford to pay for private education, who are to an overwhelming extent white and middle class, should be free to choose, even though the impact of those choices is demonstrably to promote racial, economic, and social isolation, but that parents who must use publicly funded education should not be free to choose, even though such choices might expand their access to integrated schools. This seems to be an example of

lobbying groups who assert that the best chance for children lies in the government buying some of whatever service each group has to sell. While these groups may differ somewhat over policy, they seldom lobby for increased family authority, tending to view parental independence more as the problem than as a potential solution. (Coons & Sugarman, 1978, p. 222)

CHOICE AND EFFECTIVE SCHOOLS IN BOSTON

The impact of a system of universal controlled choice on the climate for school improvement can be illustrated by the current experience of the Boston public schools, long battered by controversy over a desegregation plan based upon mandatory assignment. The Boston School Committee adopted a controlled choice assignment plan for implementation in September 1989, similar to that in Cambridge and other Massachusetts cities.

Although Boston had operated more than 20 magnet schools under its desegregation plan, it was only in the spring of 1989 that enrollment by choice became the norm in kindergarten and grades one and six; after refinements based upon the first year's experience, controlled choice is expected to become universal for all grades in 1990.

In a July 1983 report to the federal district court on Boston's earlier desegregation plan then in effect, I included a detailed analysis of preferences expressed by pupils entering high schools. As I noted,

[o]ne of the most valuable sources of information on how the Boston student desegregation plan is "working" is the functioning of student choices built into the plan. Contrary to the general impression, adoption of this plan has greatly increased the amount of choice for students in the public schools....no system under a mandate to remedy past unconstitutional racial segregation can fail to control student assignments with great care to assure that they have a positive effect. Over time, however, it is reasonable to seek to increase the proportion of students who *do* receive their first (or second or third) choice....A large school system, after all, is not static; programs are created, and others phased out, school facilities are built or closed....It is reasonable, and indeed obligatory, to ask whether these changes are made with a consistent design: to expand relevant opportunities, to make access more equal, to respond to the educational goals of students and their parents, and to assure stable desegregation. The data available in Boston as a result of the annual assignment process could be very valuable in guiding this process, and especially so at a point when basic questions are being raised about the shape and structure of the education which will be offered in the decades ahead. In effect, the assignment applications constitute an annual referendum on desired educational opportunities, and indeed more than a referendum, since each student (or parent) is in fact indicating a choice which may well translate into a commitment. These decisions are not lightly made, and they deserve to be listened to attentively.

Unfortunately, the school system did not make effective use of the information available from school selections under its mandatory assignment plan to strengthen secondary education. The controlled choice plan adopted in 1989 was a second chance to put a sense of urgency into school improvement. This would only be the case, of course, if parents made choices at least in part on educational grounds rather than simply selecting the nearest school.

Despite a very inadequate outreach effort in the spring of 1989, the applications received for sixth grade in Boston's middle schools amounted to 80 percent of the current sixth-grade enrollment, with 2,838 first preferences expressed. The return rate was solidly respectable and an indication that parents took the process seriously. Ranking all middle schools by the number of preferences in relation to number of pupils in sixth grade currently, by racial/ethnic group, the most popular across racial/ethnic groups were not concentrated in white areas.

The two most popular (Timilty and Taft), the two next most popular (Lewenberg and Rogers), the two that followed those in popularity (Thompson and Edison), and the four that followed those (Curley, Edwards, Irving, and McCormack) were evenly distributed between white and minority areas. The least popular schools included the Gavin in white South Boston as well as the Lewis and Wilson in minority areas and the Cleveland in a racially mixed area.

It was clear that certain schools would need substantial assistance in becoming attractive to all groups, minority as well as white pupils. To minimize involuntary assignments in 1989, however, these schools were assigned fewer sixth graders than currently, with more assigned to other schools that were popular with all racial/ethnic groups. The size of the entering sixth grade at the Timilty, located in the heart of the minority residential community, was increased to 334, in comparison with 190 the previous year. The Lewis school, located half a mile from the Timilty, attracted so few applications that its sixth grade was assigned only 65 pupils, in contrast to 99 the year before.

Through responding in this way to parent choices, the school system was able to limit involuntary assignments to under 15 percent of the sixth-grade total, while actually achieving more desegregation than the previous year, under the mandatory assignment plan.

GRADE 6	BLACK		WHITE		OTHER	
First choice	1,151	58%	512	61%	785	62%
Second choice	199	10%	59	7%	91	7%
Third choice	66	3%	22	3%	22	2%
Fourth choice	21	1%	5	1%	5	0%
Fifth choice	8	0%	1	0%	6	0%
Special ed	132	7%	59	7%	83	7%
Nonpromote	140	7%	56	7%	83	7%
Involuntary	279	14%	123	15%	171	14%

The rate of involuntary assignments was even lower for first graders.

GRADE 1	BLACK		WHITE		OTHER	
First choice	1,445	60%	866	62%	1,013	71%
Second choice	98	4%	42	3%	56	4%
Third choice	20	1%	18	1%	8	1%
Fourth choice	21	1%	11	1%	4	0%
Fifth choice	4	0%	6	0%	0	0%
Special ed	140	6%	86	6%	73	5%
Nonpromote	428	18%	99	7%	213	15%
Involuntary	231	10%	222	16%	54	4%

During the 1989–90 school year a major focus of the school system and the state has been to assist those schools that were not able to attract a sufficient number of applicants under the first year of controlled choice. School improvement efforts are of course no novelty in Boston as in other urban school systems, but the prospect of "facing the voters" again in early 1990—and 1991 and 1992—is lending urgency to the task of looking honestly at what must be changed in the way in which each school operates.

Twenty-four elementary and middle schools were identified that had failed to attract a sufficient number of parent applications; 18 of these volunteered to participate in a process of fundamental self-examination and change. A modest increase in state funding was provided to these schools for the costs of a planning process involving staff and parents. A single proposal form was developed to access funds from six state and federal programs, so that the school planning teams would be encouraged to think in a coherent way about their shared responsibility for all of the pupils.

More than a dozen models of "restructuring," each worked out with staffing and other implications, were developed by state and university specialists, but it was left up to the school teams to decide which—if any—of these they would adopt. It was not optional, however, whether to involve bilingual and special education staff in the process, and a number of schools decided that integration of these programs would be a priority.

Meanwhile, the system's four parent information centers (funded with $850,000 in state desegregation funds) have begun the process of outreach to parents with information about every school. All parents new to the system must register through these centers, with individual counseling in their native languages, and those considering a transfer request or selecting a school at the next higher level are encouraged to visit the centers as well. "School fairs" have been held in the different sections of the city, with exhibits, teachers, and parents to answer questions about each school, and on days set aside for visits, a shuttle bus network has been arranged to encourage parents to take a look at more than one school.

Controlled choice in Boston has been a powerful stimulant to schools that had tended to take their clientele for granted. It is no longer possible to shift responsibility for educational failure to parents, or to social conditions, or to "downtown"; the staff of each school, while entitled to outside assistance, are ultimately responsible. Some will respond with energy and imagination to their new freedom to shape the educational experience that they will provide; others will seek ways to avoid the challenge. The power of parent choice is that the challenge will be unavoidable.

CONCLUSION

Parent choice is no cure-all for American education, but it can operate powerfully along several dimensions. Well-designed choice, with appropriate controls, will provide more equal access to educational opportunities. Choice that is tied to increased diversity among the schools available will increase the freedom of parents to take responsibility for the nature of the schooling that their children receive and provide a powerful stimulus to doing so (Glenn, 1987a).

Choice can also create space for school-level reform, through allowing and indeed compelling schools to begin to exhibit the characteristics that are associated with effective education: staff cooperation based upon clarity of mission, strong leadership (less hampered by "downtown"), open accountability for results, and strong involvement of parents in the learning process.

This school reform effect—like the enhancement of justice and liberty through choice—is by no means automatic. Poorly designed programs of choice can simply increase the opportunity for sophisticated parents to get their children into the more effective schools, thus reducing the pressure to improve the others.

The fact that poorly designed choice programs can have a negative impact should not serve as an excuse to fail to employ such a powerful force for educational reform as well-conceived and well-organized parent choice. For all the social and economic difficulties experienced today by Poland and the Soviet Union, does anyone seriously doubt that the long-term health of those societies depends upon more rather than less freedom? Despite controversy and uncertainty, over the past year, around Boston, there is a strong sense in the community that better times for education lie ahead as a result of the decision to break out of the old protective routines.

It is up to policymakers and educators to assure that the impact of more freedom upon American education is to improve its quality and to serve the most vulnerable children more effectively.

REFERENCES

ALVES, M. J., & WILLIE, C. V. (1987). Controlled choice assignments: A new and more effective approach to school desegregation. *Urban Review,* 67–88.

AREEN, J., & JENCKS, C. (1972).   Education vouchers: A proposal for diversity and choice.   In G. R. LaNoue (Ed.), *Education vouchers: Concepts and controversies*.   New York: Teachers College Press.

ARONS, S. (1972).   The peaceful uses of education vouchers.   In G. R. LaNoue (Ed.), *Educational vouchers: Concepts and controversies*.   New York: Teachers College Press.

ARONS, S. (1982).   Educational choice: Unanswered questions in the American experience.   In M. E. Manley-Casimir (Ed.), *Family Choice in Schooling*. Lexington, MA: D.C. Heath.

ARONS, S. (1986).   *Compelling belief: The culture of American schooling*. Amherst: University of Massachusetts Press.

ARONS, S. (1989).   Educational choice as a civil rights strategy.   In N. E. Devins (Ed.), *Public values, private schools*. New York: Falmer Press.

BLANK, R. K. (December 1984).   Effects of magnet schools on the quality of education in urban school districts.   *Phi Delta Kappan, 66*(4), 270–72.

BLANK, R. K., DENTLER, R. A., BALTZELL, D. C., & CHABOTAR, K. (1983).   *Survey of magnet schools: Analyzing a model for quality integrated education*.   Chicago: James Lowry Associates.

BLUM, V. C. (1972).   Freedom of choice in education [1958].   In G. R. LaNoue (Ed.), *Educational vouchers: Concepts and controversies*. New York: Teachers College Press.

BREDO, E. (1988).   Choice, constraint, and community.   In W. L. Boyd & C. T. Kerchner (Eds.), *The politics of excellence and choice in education: 1987 yearbook of the politics of education association*. New York: Falmer Press.

BRIDGE, R. G., & BLACKMAN, J. (1978).   *A study of alternatives in American education*. Vol. IV; *Family choice in schooling*. Santa Monica, CA: Rand.

BRIMELOW, P. (1985).   Competition for Public Schools.   In B. Gross & R. Gross (Eds.), *The great school debate: Which way for American education*. New York: Simon & Schuster.

BUREAU OF EQUAL EDUCATIONAL OPPORTUNITY. (1977).   *Schools and programs of choice: Voluntary desegregation in Massachusetts*. Boston: Massachusetts Department of Education.

CARTER, T. P., & CHATFIELD, M. L. (November 1986).   Effective bilingual schools: Implications for policy and practice.   *American Journal of Education, 95*(1).

CHUBB, J. (1987).   Effective schools and the problems of the poor.   In D. P. Doyle, J. S. Michie, & B. I. Williams (Eds.), *Policy options for the future of compensatory education: Conference papers*. Washington, D.C.: Research and Evaluation Associates.

CHUBB, J. E. (Winter 1988).   Why the current wave of school reform will fail.   *The Public Interest, 90*.

CHUBB, J. E., & MOE, T. M. (1986a).   Politics, markets, and the organization of schools.   Governmental Studies Discussion Paper 1, The Brookings Institution, Washington, D.C.

CHUBB, J. E., & MOE, T. M. (Fall 1986).   No school is an island: Politics, markets, and education.   *The Brookings Review*.

CHUBB, J. E., & MOE, T. M. (1989).   Effective schools and equal opportunity.   In N. E. Devins (Ed.), *Public values, private* schools. New York: Falmer Press.

CITYWIDE EDUCATIONAL COALITION. (1978).   *Survey of magnet school parents in three cities*. Boston: Massachusetts Department of Education.

CITYWIDE EDUCATIONAL COALITION. (1985).   *A study of attitudes among parents of elementary school children in Boston*, prepared by Martilla and Kiley Associates. Boston: Citywide Educational Coalition.

COLEMAN, J. S. (April 1985).   Schools and the communities they serve. *Phi Delta Kappan.*

COLEMAN, J. S. (1985b).   Schools, families, and children. The 1985 Ryerson Lecture, University of Chicago, 1985.

COLEMAN, J. S., & HOFFER, T. (1987).   *Public and private high schools: The impact of communities.* New York: Basic Books.

COONS, J. E., & SUGARMAN, S. D. (1978).   *Education by choice: The case for family control.* Berkeley: University of California Press.

DARLING-HAMMOND, L., & NATARAJ KIRBY, S. (1988).   Public policy and private choice: The case of Minnesota. In T. James & H. M. Levin (Eds.), *Comparing public and private schools.* Vol. 1; *Institutions and organizations.* New York: Falmer Press.

EDMONDS, R. (1979).   Effective schools for the urban poor. *Educational Leadership, 37.*

ELMORE, R. F. (1988).   Choice in public education. In W. L. Boyd & C. T. Kerchner (Eds.), *The politics of excellence and choice in education: 1987 yearbook of the politics of education association.* New York: Falmer Press.

FIRESTONE, W. A. (October 1989).   Educational policy as an ecology of games. *Educational Researcher, 18.*

FRIEDMAN, M. (1962).   *Capitalism and freedom.* Chicago: University of Chicago Press.

FUHRMAN, S. (1989).   Diversity amidst standardization: state differential treatment of districts, typescript.

GLENN, C. L. (1978).   *Magnet schools and programs.* Boston: Massachusetts Department of Education.

GLENN, C. L. (Winter 1985).   Analysis of 1983 Boston student assignments: Preferences for ninth grade. *Equity and Choice, 1*(2).

GLENN, C. L. (Spring 1985).   The significance of choice for public education. *Equity and Choice, 1*(3).

GLENN, C. L. (May 1986).   Putting choice to work for public education. *Equity and Choice, II* (special issue).

GLENN, C. L. (1986).   *Family choice and public schools.* Boston: Massachusetts Department of Education.

GLENN, C. L. (1987).   Letting poor parents act responsibly. *Equity and Choice, 3*(3), 52–54, Spring.

GLENN, C. L. (December 1987b).   The new common school. *Phi Delta Kappan, 69*(4), 290–94.

GLENN, C. L. (1988).   *The myth of the common school.* Amherst: University of Massachusetts Press.

JENCKS, C., SMITH, M., ACLAND, H., BANE, M., COHEN, D., GINTIS, H., HEYNS, B., & MICHELSON, S. (1972).   *Inequality: A reassessment of the effect of family and schooling in America.* New York: Harper & Row.

KASPARIAN, M. (1988).   *Response to "Choose-a-School" draft legislation.* Springfield, MA: Springfield Education Association.

KEARNS, D. T., & DOYLE, D. P. (1988).   *Winning the brain race: A bold plan to make our schools competitive.* San Francisco: Institute for Contemporary Studies.

KOPPEL, D. (September 16, 1989).   Compromise is key to buying a house in a pricey town. *The Boston Globe.*

MARWIJK KOOY-VON BAUMHAUER, LIESBETH VAN. (1984).   *Scholen verschillen.* Groningen, Netherlands: Wolters Noordhoff.

McCARTHY, R. M., OPPEWAL, D., PETERSON, W., & SPYKMAN, G. (1981). *Society, state, and schools: A case for structural and confessional pluralism*. Grand Rapids, MI: Eerdmans.

McCARTHY, R. M., SKILLEN, J. W., & HARPER, W. A. (Eds.). (1982). *Disestablishment a second time: Genuine pluralism for American schools*. Grand Rapids, MI: Eerdmans.

MOORE, D. R. (1989). *Voice and choice in Chicago*. Typescript. University of Wisconsin: Control and Choice in American Education. Madison, WI.

MOORE, D. R., & DAVENPORT, S. (1990). "School Choice: The New Improved Sorting Machine." *Choice in Education: Potential and Problems*. In William Lowe Boyd & Herbert J. Walberg (Eds.), Berkeley: McCutchen.

NATHAN, J. (1984). *Free to teach: Achieving equity and excellence in schools*. Minneapolis: Winston Press.

NATIONAL EDUCATION ASSOCIATION. (1985). *Choice and education: A discussion paper*. Typescript.

NATIONAL GOVERNORS' ASSOCIATION. (1986). *Time for results: The governors' 1991 report on education*. Washington, D.C.: NGA.

POWELL, A. G., FARRAR, E., & COHEN, D. K. (1985). *The shopping mall high school: Winners and losers in the educational marketplace*. Boston: Houghton Mifflin.

RAYWID, M. A. (April 1984). Synthesis of research on schools of choice. *Educational Leadership*.

RAYWID, M. A. (1985). The choice concept takes hold. *Equity and Choice, 2*(1).

RAYWID, M. A. (Winter 1985). Family choice arrangements in public schools: A review of the literature. *Review of Educational Research, 55*.

RAYWID, M. A. (1990). Contrasting strategies for restructuring schools: Site-based management and choice. *Equity and Choice, 6*(2), 26–28, Winter.

RAYWID, M. A. (1989). *The case for public schools of choice*. Bloomington, IN: Phi Delta Kappa Educational Foundation.

ROSSELL, C. H., & GLENN, C. L. (1988). The Cambridge controlled choice plan. *The Urban Review, 20*(2).

SNIDER, W. (June 24, 1987). The call for choice: Competition in the educational marketplace. *Education Week*.

SNIDER, W. (May 18, 1988). School choice: New more efficient sorting machine? *Education Week*.

TALBERT, J. E. (1988). Conditions of public and private school organization and notions of effective schools. In T. James & H. M. Levin (Eds.), *Comparing public and private schools*. Vol. 1; *Institutions and organizations*. New York: Falmer Press.

TASK FORCE ON TEACHING AS A PROFESSION. (1986). *A nation prepared: Teachers for the 21st century*. New York: Carnegie Forum on Education and the Economy.

TYACK, D. B. (1974). *The one best system: A history of American urban education*. Cambridge, MA: Harvard University Press.

12

SITE-BASED MANAGEMENT: RESTRUCTURING DECISION MAKING FOR SCHOOLS

Rafael Ramirez, Florence R. Webb, and James W. Guthrie
University of California at Berkeley

INTRODUCTION

The effective schools literature asserts that the school is the logical place to begin improving instruction. However, individual schools often are constrained by district, state, and federal regulations that preclude making necessary changes. To implement effective schools prescriptions, school personnel require a degree of autonomy. This chapter suggests means by which site-based school management may promote the autonomy needed to design and operate more effective schools.

Large schools in large urban districts are characterized by a large number of organizational problems. These big operating units function amid awesome complexity. There are literally thousands of local district, state, and federal government rules and expectations to which they are subject. What is the most effective set of connections or links and what is the most effective way to cope with this complexity and meet these intergovernmental constraints? What are the most effective ways to coordinate discrete units of an organization in the face of ever-increasing intergovernmental and organizational diversity? At the technical core of schooling are the knowledge and experience of teachers. For the most part, they teach in individual classrooms but with less professional autonomy than needed. How can a balance be struck between professional discretion, the desire to build a cooperative culture at the school site, and the governance and accountability expectations of local school districts and states?

Generally, the effective schools model proposes conditions intended to enhance student achievement. This body of knowledge emphasizes strong school leadership; clearly articulated goals; high expectations for students; clear, cohesive, firm, and fair discipline policy; and alignment of the curriculum with the frequent evaluation of student performance. Implementing and sustaining these conditions has been a continuing challenge for policymakers and practitioners.

In an attempt to address this challenge, much of the latest effective schools literature is concerned not only with the individual school but also with the school within the context of the entire educational system. It is this emphasis on context and implementation that has shifted the focus of much of the effective schools research from student outcomes to system change.

As outlined elsewhere in this book, effective schools research has drawn from organizational theory, change theory, leadership practices, curriculum and context, staff development, school change, and improvement literature. Just as this research has influenced the effective schools movement, so the effective schools movement has influenced how schooling is viewed and practiced.

A more complex and extended understanding of the concept of leadership is emerging from the research on teaching. For example, it is now considered important that a sense of leadership and responsibility be developed not only in principals but also in teachers and district staff. This requires a rethinking of appropriate authority and power relationships within and between schools.

This new organizational view translates in the classroom to a concern for establishing collegial problem solving and a shared set of norms, values, and beliefs. Collegial problem solving is seen as necessary for achieving a clearly articulated mission and set of goals.

The central question of leadership has been how to allocate decision authority. There is almost always a tension in an organization between the "center" and the "periphery" regarding decision discretion. How much authority should reside with central managers and how much decision discretion should be accorded to "technical operators" in more remote locations of an organization? For example, early effective schools programs often tried to bypass the district or communicate directly with individuals at sites. However, reformers found that the district central office could not be ignored overall; district support was necessary for successful change.

These observations challenge the appropriateness of extremist schemes for vesting exclusive power either in central district operations[1] or at individual school sites. We will argue for a careful rebalancing of decision-making authority between the center and the periphery in the current educational structure.

Site-based management can be seen as a way of addressing in a comprehensive fashion the need for schools and educational communities to reinvent themselves with a new sense of purpose and motivation. Redesigning decision making can be expected to enhance teamwork and promote cohesiveness in handling personnel, student discipline, and curricular issues. Brown (1990) examines school effectiveness within the context of decentralization and concludes,

> ...any restructuring of schools and districts which requires more leadership from the principal, increases the extent of school planning, offers more support for decisions made, and requires that school activity be more closely monitored should make those schools more like effective schools on the administrative dimension. (p. 82)

DEFINITIONS, DESCRIPTIONS, AND THEORIES

The focus of this chapter is "site-based management," a concept for restructuring the decision-making processes of public school districts. Site-based management is defined as a set of organizational arrangements in which the balance of authority to make operational decisions is located at school sites. There are several ways for authority to be allocated within a site-based structure; these will be discussed at some length throughout the chapter. First, however, this chapter describes typical decision-making structures in today's schools and considers the theoretical constructs from which they have evolved. Next, the chapter examines the hypothetical basis for restructuring reform of school districts and describes site-based management proposals and projects. Finally, issues that must be addressed for effective reform will be identified, and implications of various options for reform are discussed.

Structural Reform in Education: Evolving Policy Context

As recently as the beginning of this century, site-based management was the norm in American education. Before that time, most school districts contained only one school. Fueled by industrial models of centralization, the flames of the school consolidation movement were fanned by administrators who had much to gain in power, prestige, and pay if school districts became larger and more complex (Guthrie, 1979).

The consolidation movement dominated education for much of the twentieth century. As a result, the average school district today consists of over 3,000 students, compared with a 1930s mean district size of 200 (Guthrie, 1979). New York City schools with nearly 1 million students and Los Angeles Unified with more than 600,000 are extreme examples of a basic truth: many school districts today are gigantic organizations that bear little resemblance to their predecessors for which our current governance and management systems were designed.

The result of these changes, according to many critics, is a structure that succeeds in some places but fails in others (Benveniste, 1986; Berman & Weiler, 1988; Carnegie, 1986; Wise, 1979). The school consolidation movement has left many school districts with the rigidity and unresponsiveness of a large centralized system and the lack of uniform standards of a completely localized system (Guthrie, 1985). In short, some districts are seen as just too big to be responsive or even knowledgeable about local schools' needs.

Much of educational reform implemented since the early 1980s has been directed at classroom activities. As Boyd (1989) observes, the "first wave" of reform following *A Nation at Risk* was concerned with intensifying what was already being done: longer school day and year, tougher graduation requirements, more rigorous basic instruction, and beefed-up teacher credentialing requirements and evaluation procedures. The emphasis was on raising standards and requirements, and centralizing the control of schools at the state level was advocated in order to mandate policy.

The United States has entered a "second wave" of reform and interest is now directed at reform of the decision-making balance among governance, management, and operations in education. Among state-level policymakers, there is a contention that schools are not meeting expectations in educating students. In an attempt to improve student performance, states have continued the trend of exercising their authority over schools by demanding and legislating more accountability measures in conjunction with increased standards.

At the same time that state policymakers attempt to impose improvement on schools and school districts, there is growing concern that school districts are too centralized, and many contend that more discretion should be devolved onto the school site or classroom teachers.

As Boyd (1989) states, "Remarkably, we now have simultaneous efforts to increase both the centralization (to the state level) and decentralization (to the school level) of governance arrangement in education." To understand how school-site management fits into this framework of opposing pressures on the public educational system, it is necessary to examine this concept and its theoretical justification.

School-Site Management: Variations on a Theme

School-site management is a term which encompasses at least two converging trends. "Decentralized decision making" involves moving the locus of selected district operations from the central office to the school site or to satellite administrative or planning units. "Participatory management" (or inclusive management) is being practiced when teachers and other employees, parents, or even students are given a voice in the operations of the district.

Decision processes can be made more participatory without being more decentralized, as when decisions are made by districtwide employee or citizen committees. Likewise, decentralization can occur without participation if the site administrator has ultimate authority.

Discussions of educational governance and management are apt to proceed as though organizational characteristics are bipolar in nature: a district has either centralized or noncentralized management, decision making is either inclusive or noninclusive of professional staff and community.

In fact, each of these dimensions can be conceptualized as a continuum, with the functioning of a given district falling anywhere along the scale. The two factors are somewhat orthogonal; that is, they are independent of one another although they may be related. Falling nearer to one end or the other on either of these scales is connected with identifiable advantages and disadvantages. In the next section we will detail these implications of various organizational structures.

Centralization: Roles, Locations, and the Locus of Decision Making

One definition of centralization comes from organizational theory. The more decision-making authority is held by those lower in a vertical authority structure, the less centralized the organization is (Etzioni, 1964). This definition stems from the assumption—not altogether accurate in the case of school districts—that the "central office" invariably contains the highest ranks and the peripheries the lowest ones. In fact, low-level administrators, managers, or practitioners (for example, project directors) may be assigned to the district office while higher-ranking individuals (principals or regional directors) manage school sites or multischool regions within a district.

Given this distinction, it is useful here to assign a narrower meaning which concentrates only upon location, not relative rank or hierarchy. The more decision-making authority is reserved by those (of whatever rank) at the district office and withheld from those (of whatever rank) at the school sites, the greater the degree of centralization in a school district. The issue of hierarchy is treated separately, under the heading of inclusiveness.

Proponents of a high degree of centralization (such as that found in most overseas national school systems) assert that it makes it possible to develop, implement, and enforce systemwide achievement standards, renders it easy to direct resources, and permits rapid establishment of a new course of action for a whole system (Guthrie, 1985). Those who believe that public schools can and should show rapid measurable improvement in their outputs frequently favor centralization as a strategy for these reasons (Wise, 1979).

Certain tasks, such as curriculum coordination over a K–12 span of influence, staff development related to adoption of a large-scale program, equity-based resource allocation, facilities planning, and deployment of specialized personnel, are most effectively accomplished at a level involving several schools if not a whole district.

However, strong central direction involves a loss of discretion by those at the periphery—in the case of schools, the school site and the classroom teacher. Etzioni (1964) states, "...centralized organizations allow for less local experimentation and grant less unit flexibility, although they are more likely to be able to provide facilities that independent units could not afford, and to enforce "labor relations" standards, such as tenure, more efficiently."

According to Benveniste (1983), it is particularly necessary for peripheral discretion to be preserved in cases where (1) local conditions are highly variable and (2) the tasks of individual practitioners require invention and problem solving. In a multisite organization, central control can be maintained only by routines (control through detailed regulations) of daily operations; such routinization is appropriate only when the technology (what works and what does not work) is well understood, and inputs (i.e., students and student needs) are routine and predictable.

Likewise, the needs of children are unpredictable, particularly in heterogeneous urban settings. Therefore, routinization and detailed regulation are inappropriate strategies for controlling the process of teaching (Benveniste, 1983).

Another disadvantage cited for excessive centralization is that participants on the periphery of a centralized bureaucracy (teachers and parents) may have little access to or connection with the controlling center. This can lead to a sense of isolation which interferes with the development of the community commitment crucial to the functioning of a public service organization.

Centralization, then, offers the opportunity to plan and to implement large-scale operations such as construction projects, core curriculum planning, specialized training and service delivery, and major reforms. At the same time, however, centralization may interfere with the day-to-day problem-solving activities of classroom teachers, responsiveness of a school to localized conditions, and a sense of autonomy and ownership on the part of a school community.

Participation in Decision Making: Hierarchies and Professional Organizations

The issue of relative rank or hierarchy comes into play when inclusiveness is considered as a facet of management structure. Inclusiveness means participation of classroom teachers, site administrators, parents, and even students in planning and decision-making functions. A connected concept is departmentalization; if only those assigned to administrative roles are included in decision making, there may be a strict grouping of tasks based on rank or role (Scott, 1981).

Etzioni (1964), however, described a departmentalized, hierarchical organization as follows: "...the whole organization can be viewed as an efficient tool with general policy-making concentrated at the top, policy specification carried out by the middle ranks, and actual work performance carried out by the lower ranks." This division of policy-making and performance is a common (but by no means the only) model of efficient allocation of decision making and work.

A hierarchy has been viewed as a rational organizational arrangement in private business, and the standard of business frequently spills over into expectations for educational organizations. However, Etzioni himself has proposed a very different standard for the structure of *professional* organizations: "...in professional organizations administrators are in charge of secondary activities; they administer *means* to the major activity carried out by professionals. In other words, to the extent that there is a staff-line relationship at all, professionals should hold the major authority and administrators the secondary staff authority." Depending, then, on the extent to which one views teaching as a profession,[2] one may be applying an inappropriate structural model to school districts.

Many who believe that teaching should be elevated to the status of a full profession find in site-based management the opportunity to advance toward that goal. Teachers are uniquely positioned to understand classroom conditions, issues, and trends which affect teaching and learning. The tendency for managers to hold personnel accountable through an extensive regulatory process is one of the dangers of a compartmentalized, centralized structure. Regulations, particularly those written by ex-practitioners or nonpractitioners with little exposure to site conditions, may be unsuited to conditions which call for on-the-spot professional judgment.

Teachers must use their own judgment daily to synthesize and to improvise from within the weak technology of education, developing classroom environments, and behaviors that help children learn. It is logical, then, for classroom teachers to advise or even guide decision making in areas connected to school and classroom operations.

Issues of alienation can arise in a hierarchical structure. Teachers generally do see themselves as professionals, and may resent reward and punishment systems which they view as encroaching on their necessary autonomy. On the other hand, substantial responsibility for planning and policy-making could prove a burden as well as a boon. As with centralization, ease of decision making is facilitated by a noninclusive approach; roles are clearly delineated, and a high degree of specialization is made possible.

Some organizational analysts have proposed yet another model for "semiprofessional" organizations. In this scenario, management functions would be "split" according to whether they were or were not directly connected with the professional activities of the organization. That is, instruction, curriculum functions, training and staff development, and teaching personnel functions might be in a separate organizational structure from administrative tasks such as supplies, facilities, compliance paperwork, and so on.

The professional side would be governed by a collegial professional team, while the administrative side would run in a traditional hierarchy. The two would be integrated by a superintendent who possesses skills, training, and aptitude for both administrative and professional roles (Benveniste, 1987; Etzioni, 1964).

In summary, decision making can be much more rapid in a departmentalized, noninclusive structure and can benefit from the full-time attention of specialists. But teacher morale and the quality of decisions may suffer if district decision making excludes classroom teachers. Districts need to acknowledge that teaching is increasingly seen as a professional field in which practitioners may be the best informed participants about many facets of their practice.

Community members, too, may benefit from a sense of access to decision making affecting their local school. In a large school district, each board member may represent many thousands of constituents (Guthrie, 1979). Thus, provision of a point of access to policy determination at the site level effectively enfranchises many.

In studying a group of schools in Canada and the United States which have adopted principal-centered structural reforms, Brown (1990) discusses several intended outcomes of decentralization in education. Three of these are referred to as flexibility, accountability, and productivity. These intended outcomes are consistent with the basic correlates of the effective schools model and should be addressed in any site-based management approach.

Flexibility refers to the authority of schools to control resources. Accountability refers to the measures of performance to be used and actions are to be taken when results are below expectation. Productivity refers to the ability of site-based management to increase school effectiveness, promote school efficiency, and provide a greater level of student equity. The following conclusions from Brown's work (1990) are germane to this discussion:

> Schools under decentralization are considered to be much more responsive than when they were under centralized management. School based management may be a viable avenue for school improvement because of the flexibility it accords schools. Boards become more concerned with policy matters than school administration. Principals see themselves as solely accountable for their schools. Decentralization was not introduced to cut costs. Certain outputs, as measured by parental and student satisfaction, have increased under school based management. Schools under school based management may have some administrative similarities with effective schools. (p. 99)

The foregoing conclusions indicate that leadership of the principal, school planning, support for decision making, and student monitoring are common elements of both effective school research and many school-based management proposals. However, as with effective schools research, site-based management discussions still do not address the basic issue of how schools produce learning. Nonetheless, it is important to note variables that consistently appear related (whether causally or not) to school achievement.

The Structures of Site-Based Management

Depending on the needs of the district, plans to implement site-based management will vary in content. As already discussed, there is no need to assume that implementing site-based management will force a district to choose either complete decentralization or complete centralization. Centralized administration has an important role at the district level. The district frequently must conduct a variety of tasks, from establishing criteria for promotion, attendance, and graduation to collective bargaining.

Decentralized administration has a different role at the site level. As the earlier discussion suggests, classroom instruction can benefit from providing teachers with discretion sufficient to develop implementation plans, engage in problem solving, collaborate with peers, and develop curricular initiatives in concert with site administration.

A number of recent educational reform reports have contained specific proposals regarding site-based management. They tend to follow one of three general tracks: those primarily aimed at empowering teachers, those primarily aimed at empowering parents and community members, and those that focus on the authority of the site administrator.

Guthrie, Garmes and Pierce (1988) have suggested a political decentralization model which incorporated site-based collective bargaining and site-based parent committees. These parent committees would have authority over school policy and the hiring and firing of principals. An alternative model is one in which power is devolved from the district to the school administratively. It is essentially an organizational decentralization involving an administrative shift of certain powers to the school site and not an abdication of control of school policy.

A teacher-oriented proposal comes from the Carnegie Forum on Education and the Economy, in *A Nation Prepared: Teachers for the 21st Century* (1986). This report proposes a "lead teacher" model, using collegial decision-making processes to establish specific school goals and agree on standards of performance.

In *Restructuring California Education* for the California Business Roundtable, Berman and Weiler (1988) emphasize the community. This report proposes an elected governing board for each site, to consist of parents and community members. The site board would have responsibility to approve the school's educational program, expenditures of school discretionary budget, and hiring and replacement of all school employees.

The Association of California School Administrators (1988) proposes the site principal as the central figure in site management. In the site-based proposal contained in *Return to Greatness,* principals, with advice from "key instructional staff," would be given authority for resource allocation, program development, hiring, and evaluation. Though a collegial process is urged, the proposal is clearly aligned with the school effectiveness model which emphasizes the importance of the principal's leadership role.

SITE-BASED MANAGEMENT: MAKING IT WORK

It is possible to balance the benefits of local discretion while actively pursuing central unifying goals. Murphy (1989) notes that there appears to be an inherent paradox evident in well-run decentralized organizations: "successful decentralization depends on strong centralization in certain facets of the organization." With respect to schools, "The implicit assumption is that schools can be trusted and that, while they need help, they do not need control." It is the district's responsibility to provide services to those schools which need it the most and to provide more freedom to those schools less in need. Schools need technical assistance, staff development, and staff released time.

Murphy has argued that a system of checks and balances is needed. For this system to perform effectively, there needs to be a relationship of trust between the district and site professional. This trust implies room for discretion and tolerance for risk taking, experimentation, and (above all) mistakes.

If one accepts that site-level operations in a given district require more discretionary power, a process must be established to identify and transfer those authoritative functions that are inappropriately placed. Through a dialectic process, the discretionary powers given to sites must be consensual. Clearly, there will be a need for establishing mechanisms and training to effect this transfer of power. Since rebalancing decision-making authority is intended to allow for customizing instructional programs at the local level, there is no one right way to effect this rebalancing. There are, however, some consistent issues and concerns which must be addressed if restructuring is to enhance school effectiveness.

Site-Based Management: Issues, Implications, Implementations

This section examines restructuring reform in terms of the methods which have been proposed and the issues that must be addressed in planning and implementing a new kind of system. The first part of this discussion is divided according to the previously described themes of decentralization and inclusiveness. Though the two approaches may be overlapping in a given proposal, there is value in analyzing them separately and combining them according to the desired result.

To determine the optimal location for each kind of management activity, it is necessary first to establish the ground rules for district functioning. Each operational area may have a different "best" balance of power. Consider the following example.

Instructional planning and implementation can most directly reflect the needs of students if it takes place at individual sites or between sites within a particular community. Since the learning styles, social needs, and skills of children vary considerably from one school or classroom to another, inflexible regulation of instructional practices from the district level may inhibit teachers' ability to operate effectively within their classrooms.

Curriculum planning must be articulated across all the schools a given child will attend between kindergarten and twelfth grade; as children from different schools move from one level to another, they must be assured of equivalent preparation for educational advancement. At the same time, program frameworks must be flexible to allow for local interpretations, variations, and innovations. Professional development planning and implementation must occur at three levels. The individual classroom teacher may desire activities to upgrade or maintain specific skills, school sites must be able to operate as units to improve on identified weaknesses or develop site-specific programs, and activities connected with K through 12 core curriculum may require inservice preparation which is consistent across many schools. Some types of training activities are too costly or too specialized to provide locally and will only occur if several sites or a whole district function together.

Personnel decisions must accord with district policy. Hiring, evaluating, and firing practices must be coordinated so that no site is "stuck" with another's mistake. While substantial participation from sites in selecting staff may improve morale and teamwork, the actual hiring entity (usually the district) may need the flexibility to redeploy personnel as sites' needs change. Conversely, teacher morale may suffer if the possibilities for voluntary transfers among district sites are limited or curtailed by site-based policies. Facilities construction, site acquisition, and other activities related to the major physical assets of a school district may require the resources of a larger community than is encompassed by a single school. District, county, or even state-level allocations may be required to ensure equity in the provision of physical assets to school communities. Because neighborhoods are unequally endowed, some enhancement or redistribution of local resources may be required to adequately provide for all.

Centralization and Inclusiveness

We have mentioned before that management can be decentralized without being participatory (e.g., by giving total discretion to site principals); it can also be participatory without being decentralized, if districtwide committees or teams are empowered within the district's management patterns. For a district to develop a management program which is both decentralized and participatory may require more than the design and adoption of a structure, by whatever process. It may be necessary to rework the entire framework of relationships and regulations by which the district has operated.

The role of the elected school district governing board must not be neglected. The child is the client of both the district and the school. It is the district's responsibility to ensure that each child receives a continuity of instruction. The district provides the overarching structure and the general direction for the entire set of schools under its auspices. The district provides programs and services to children that would not be feasible at the site level alone. As the policy-making body for the district, acting on behalf of the total district community, the lay governing board is literally the voice of the community which "owns," funds, and operates the school district.

In determining its role and that of the district office, the governing board might keep in mind the question: "When is it inappropriate for the site to do X for the child?" As one example, it might be dysfunctional to the child if the district's curriculum coordination functions failed to assure equivalent preparation to all students entering a given school. As mentioned earlier, some organizational analysts support the "splitting up" of functions to assign various levels of authority to different organizational levels, based on efficacy (Benveniste, 1987; Etzioni, 1964; Scott, 1981).

Implications for Equity

As the craft of policy research has evolved, there has been a shift in thinking about equity issues. Once seen as a simple matter of providing equal access to undifferentiated services for all children, the concept of educational equity had broadened to include equity of outcome (Guthrie & Reed, 1986). With this redefinition of equality has come recognition of the need for specialized services to be provided to certain populations; compensatory education programs, nutrition, child care, special day classes, language instruction, and the like.

Clearly, the allocation of fiscal and professional resources for site management programs must provide appropriately for special-needs populations. In addition, site management must not be allowed to serve as a rationale for allowing racially desegregated schools to resegregate themselves in the name of local autonomy. In this as in other dimensions of restructuring, the district must establish sound policy direction to act as a framework for site decision making.

Implications for Accountability

One issue raised in the preliminary evaluations of existing site-based projects is that of accountability. Some principals at sites have expressed concern that they are to be held solely accountable for outcomes at their schools, but they no longer had sole authority over key decisions.

Obviously, it will be necessary, when considering decision-making processes in a district, to restructure accountability measures accordingly. It is relatively easy to design for school sites incentives that have the potential to be effective "carrots." It is more challenging to envision appropriate "sticks" for dealing with a professional group decision-making process.

In designing an accountability component within a site-based management plan, issues such as the following should be addressed: In what way can the district accurately assess student progress and achievement? Commonly used are standardized or customized achievement tests, with their known limitations (Oakes, 1986); student knowledge and problem-solving ability can be compared against a population norm (as in the SAT) or against some body of knowledge (as in the New York State Regents). Many other outcome measures exist and decision makers must decide among them. In what way can a district accurately assess quality of teaching? Teacher evaluation methods may need to be examined site by site to provide continuity with each site's goals and needs. Will sites be held accountable only for results, or will methods be evaluated? How will adherence to district policy be monitored if districts take a "hands-off" approach to site management? An administrator who fails to perform can be demoted, transferred, or fired. Likewise, a school staff which does not measure up could be disbanded or placed under an authoritarian administrator to ensure improvement. Like the trusteeship arrangements occasionally invoked against school districts, individual schools which fail to meet expectations could be divested of their autonomy until appropriate standards are achieved.

One of the stickier issues related to site management proposals is that of principal accountability. On the one hand, in a site plan which emphasizes administrative responsibility and declares the site principal to be a "chief executive officer" of the school, the hierarchical chain of accountability—and therefore the functional chain of command—may be little different than in today's typical centralized district. On the other hand, some existing arrangements hold principals supremely accountable for operations over which they may cease to have administrative control.

Under a "split operations" model like Etzioni's, a separate accountability mechanism could be established for each set of functions: perhaps a traditional hierarchy supervising administrative operations and a "trusteeship" arrangement enforcing instructional standards.

Whatever arrangements are devised for ensuring accountability, they will promote greater school effectiveness only to the extent that they accurately pinpoint and reinforce new allocations of authority.

Program Implications

Coordination, flexibility, and accurate communication are keys to successful site-based educational programs for effective schools.

If discretionary license is not to result in managerial chaos, a broad and diffuse system of management will require development of a sharp and focused program of communication and coordination. Any site-based curriculum planning process must include significant provisions for coordination between sites and between grades so that children from different schools and different classrooms are offered equivalent preparation for educational advancement. An overall framework may be developed by site teachers and administrators but should be coordinated and adopted at the district level to promote program articulation.

At the same time, program frameworks must be sufficiently flexible to allow for local variations in interpretation and implementation. If there is room for innovation within the system, opportunities for improvement will be as numerous as the district's capable teachers.

In order to maximize improvement opportunities, schools and districts must develop networks for sharing information. For ideas to become well known and used, someone must convey them from place to place and pass them from mind to mind. Communications across grade levels at each school, between different schools, and even across district lines can enhance the continuity and quality of each student's total educational experience.

Personnel Implications

If a district chooses to reorganize to include teachers, parents, or citizens in a broad decision-making capacity, it will be important to differentiate their roles from that of the elected school board. The Institute for Educational Leadership describes local boards as "...the only means through which the community expresses itself in respect to education. Boards are the legally authorized interpreters and translators of need and demand. They mediate between and among conflicting interests. They sort out contending values, and they initiate and enact policies to govern locally" (Carol et al., 1986).

Implementing a school-based management program may mean creating new roles for teachers, other staff members, or parents. New avenues for conflict resolution may be needed, as the traditional ones may no longer fit. It may be necessary to train participants in needed new skills and to encourage new ways of thinking about leadership for effective schools.

For teachers in particular, being actively responsible for decision making at the site may be a new experience. Group process is a time-consuming endeavor; development of policies or plans may take longer under a more inclusive system. In addition, the expectation may arise that those who put in extra hours on site councils or committees should be compensated incrementally for their leadership activities.

For central administrators, too, the new process may require adjustments. The district office staff which previously made decisions for schools must now provide information and support services, perhaps coordinating between sites or areas, overseeing program articulation, or acting as consultants or facilitators for site or regional councils.

As with the teachers, the change in focus may necessitate retraining or reorganizing administrative staff. Additional staff may ultimately be needed at the site level, and reductions may be possible at the district office.

In a decision-making process that includes parents or citizens, these individuals will need to be educated in school law and program considerations in order to represent their schools responsibly.

If school site councils are empowered to hire teachers, provision must be made to ensure that hiring and tenure decisions are made in accordance with overall district policy. Fluctuating enrollment patterns and district-based employment laws may necessitate teacher transfers between schools; principles of equity, attention to specific needs at other sites, and some degree of flexibility for deployment of specialized staff should be guiding factors in fashioning site-based hiring processes, for they have the potential to affect an entire district.

Empowerment of the Community

Advocates of site-based management frequently seek to enhance community control over school. Most proposals involve the use of site management teams composed of staff and community members. It is unclear to what extent parental empowerment will actually follow site-based management, especially among these most disenfranchised groups. Malen and colleagues suggest that in early experiments with site management, teams were sometimes dominated by teachers at the expense of parental or public influence (Malen, Ogawa, & Kranz, 1989).

In addition, there is a danger that site-based programs could encounter the pitfall experienced by the California School Improvement Program: the resources provided to site councils might be inadequate to effect genuine improvement at the site. This could be due to inadequate overall resources available to a district or to a district's failure to allocate fairly to some or all sites.

These concerns raise the possibility that what begins as an honest attempt to empower participants in the educational process could be diverted in either of two directions to undermine efforts to create more effective schools.

Those charged with the responsibility for governance and management may use site-based management as an excuse to abdicate, dumping insoluble problems into the laps of teachers and parents. The whole system may lack the resources to deal with a given problem or adequate reallocation of resources may not take place. In these cases a shift in the balance of responsibility could result in the demoralization of the very individuals for whom empowerment is sought.

The potential for teacher dominance of site-based structures can be seen as a desirable outcome to the extent that lack of sufficient professional discretion has hampered effective teaching. However, those seeking a stronger community voice through this type of reform may be disappointed if parents, formerly voiceless in the face of a monolithic bureaucracy, are now muted by a new power of the classroom teacher. The task of designing a structure that will accommodate both of these values will be a delicate balancing act.

CONCLUSION

The functioning of a school system can be characterized in terms of governance, management, and operations. Identifying the most efficacious balance of power among these three is the essence of the current "second wave" of reform. States are attempting to impose more centralized controls on education, while at the same time public and community pressure at the local sites are attempting to decentralize the governance of education.

Centralization can be useful for planning of large-scale operations, especially those involving specialized and costly training. But overcentralized planning may neglect specific needs and therefore may be less responsive to local conditions and to change. Centralization can provide a more rapid decision making process. However, efficient decision making which fails to reflect unique conditions at the local level may hamper instructional improvement.

Noninclusive decision making in education occurs when teachers and parents have only a minimal role. Like centralization, efficiency can be a driving factor in a system where management tasks are performed by specialized managers. But as with centralized decision making, insufficiently inclusive decision making may lead to unresponsive management. Teachers as professionals desire greater management involvement in many districts.

If a centralized, noninclusive district management denies teacher and site administrators sufficient discretion to respond to the needs of children, effective schools will remain a concept that will fall short of attainment. There is evidence that the commitment, goal orientation, leadership, and responsiveness to children's needs which are central to the effective schools prescriptions for instructional improvement require a sense of personal authority and flexibility to deal with local condition.

The basic assumption of site-based management is that site-level administrators, teachers, and parents are the most knowledgeable individuals when it comes to identifying and establishing the most effective learning environments for particular students at a particular school. Site-based management is one way of reorganizing the decision-making process within a school system. It is an approach that can be used to increase responsiveness to children's needs. Proponents assert that site-based management can also positively affect teacher morale and teacher professionalism in ways which would benefit both staff and students.

As discussed, the concept of site-based management has taken on many forms; different sites within districts as well as particular districts will have different needs which should be addressed individually. Restructuring is a complex process which will require a long-term commitment to a carefully planned, integrative approach.

In a decentralized model it will be necessary to coordinate curricula within a districtwide program that will allow for articulation across sites and make for smooth transitions from elementary school through high school. This will require coordination, flexibility, and communication.

If a district chooses to grant broad decision-making powers to the site level, there will be a need to differentiate new roles of the school board, parents, administrators, and teachers. Districts will need to examine the costs and types of training and or retraining that will be required to ensure that everyone knows the responsibilities of each role and is enabled to carry them out.

Empowerment of the site and community in the educational process could have unintended consequences if issues such as curricular articulation and allocation of resources are not discussed and handled properly. If realignment of authority fundamentally alters the decision-making process, it must do so within a framework of flexibility, accountability, equity, and communication. Particularly for the large urban districts that are the most specific targets of pressure for restructuring reform, a well-designed shift in the balance of decision-making authority may be the key which unlocks the door to greater school effectiveness.

REFERENCES

ASSOCIATION OF CALIFORNIA SCHOOL ADMINISTRATORS. (1988). Return to greatness: Recommendations from the Commission on Public School Administration and Leadership. Sacramento, CA: CSA.

BALDRIDGE, V. J. (1983). Strategic planning in higher education: Does the emperor have any clothes? In V. J. Baldridge & T. Deal (Eds.), *The dynamics of organizational change in education.* Berkeley, CA: McCutchan.

BENVENISTE, G. (1983). *Bureaucracy.* San Francisco: Boyd and Fraser.

BENVENISTE, G. (1986). School accountability and the professionalization of teaching. *Education and Urban Society, 18*(3), 271–89.

BENVENISTE, G. (1987). *Professionalizing the organization.* San Francisco: Jossey-Bass.

BERMAN, P., & WEILER, P. T. (1988). Restructuring California education: A design for public education in the twenty-first century, recommendations to the California Business Roundtable. Berkeley, CA: Berman, Weiler Associates.

BOYD, W. L. (1989). The governance of school based management. *The State Board Connection: Issues in Brief, 9*(6), 7–9.

BROWN, D. J. (1990). *Decentralization and school-based management.* New York: Falmer Press.

CALIFORNIA SCHOOLS BOARDS ASSOCIATION. (1989). *Analysis of site based management: Issues in shared decision making.* Sacramento, CA.

CARNEGIE FORUM ON EDUCATION AND THE ECONOMY. (1986). *A nation prepared: Teachers for the 21st century.* New York: CFEE.

CAROL, L. N., DANZBERGER, J. P., MCCLOUD, B. A., CUNNINGHAM, L. L., & CLINCHY, E. (1986). Chicago's great experimentation begins: Will radical decentralization bring school reform? Equity and choice. *Network News and Views VIII, 7.*

ETZIONI, A. (1964). Modern organizations. Englewood Cliffs, NJ: Prentice Hall.

GUTHRIE, J. W. (1979). Organizational scale and school success. *Educational Evaluation and Policy Analysis, 1*(1), 17–27.

GUTHRIE, J. W. (1985). *Administrative innovations: Redistributing decision between the center and the periphery.* Las Termas de Catillo, Chile: Organization of American States.

GUTHRIE, J. W., & REED, R. J. (1986). *Educational administration and policy: Effective leadership for American education.* Englewood Cliffs, NJ: Prentice Hall.

GUTHRIE, J. W., GARMS, W. I., & PIERCE, L. C. (1988). *School finance and education policy: Enhancing educational efficiency, equality, and choice,* 2nd ed. Englewood Cliffs, NJ: Prentice Hall.

HILL, P. T., WISE, A. E., & SHAPIRO, L. (1989). *Educational progress: Cities mobilize to improve their schools,* R-3711-JSM/CSTP. Santa Monica, CA: Rand.

KANTER, R. M. (1983). *The change masters.* New York: Simon & Schuster.

KIRST, M. (1984). *Who should control our schools.* New York: W. H. Freeman & Company.

KIRST, M. W., & USDAN, M. D. (1986). *School boards: Strengthening grass roots leadership.* The Institute for Educational Leadership, Washington, D.C.

KOPPICH, J. E., & KERCHNER, C. T. (1989). *Educational policy trust agreements: Connecting labor relations and school reform.* Policy Analysis for California Education (PACE): University of California at Berkeley.

LIEBERT, D. (1989). Early evidence from two districts piloting school based management. *The State Board Connection: Issues in Brief, 9*(6), 4–6.

MALEN, B., OGAWA, R. T., & KRANZ, J. (1989). *An analysis of site based management as an education reform strategy.* Graduate School of Education, The University of Utah, Salt Lake.

MARBURGER, C., & HANSEN, B. (1989). School based management: An overview. *The State Board Connection: Issues in Brief, 9*(6), 1–3.

MURPHY, J. T. (1989). Paradox of decentralizing schools: Lessons from business, government, and the Catholic Church. *Phi Delta Kappan, 70*(10), 808–12.

OAKES, J. (1986). *Educational indicators: A guide for policymakers.* Center for Policy Research in Education, Rutgers University, The Rand Corporation, University of Wisconsin-Madison.

PETERSON, J. L., PURKEY, S. C., & PARKER, J. B. (1986). *Productive school systems for a nonrational world.* Alexandria, VA: Association for Supervision and Curriculum Development.

PURKEY, S. C., & SMITH, M. S. School reform: The district policy of the effective schools literature. *The Elementary School Journal, 85*(3), 353–89.

SCOTT, W. R. (1981). *Organizations: Rational, natural, and open systems,* 2nd ed. Englewood Cliffs, NJ: Prentice Hall.

WISE, A. W. (1979). *Legislated learning: The bureaucratization of the American classroom.* Berkeley: University of California Press.

ENDNOTES

[1]The authors recognize that this is the unfortunate reality in many of today's large urban school districts and in some smaller, nonurban districts.

[2]Benveniste describes characteristics of professions to include the following: specialized knowledge base; control over access to the profession, frequently through a licensure process; existence of codes of conduct or ethics; existence of professional organizations; and the existence of a sense of calling or public responsibility. He refers to teachers as "semiprofessionals," noting that teaching meets some of the criteria-specialized knowledge base, sense of public responsibility, but lacks others, such as control over licensure and a formalized code of ethics (Benveniste, 1987, p. 17).

13

POSTSCRIPT: RETHINKING EFFECTIVE SCHOOLS

Craig E. Richards
Teachers College, Columbia University

INTRODUCTION

Most of the research and discussion about effective schools is implicitly a discussion about mass production (factory) technique. It answers the unspoken question: "What can we do to overhaul public education, particularly for urban school children?" Yet it may be that the elusive nature of "good schooling" is elusive precisely because it is so context sensitive that production functions are the wrong metaphor. When technologies are poorly specified, as they are in education, then it may make more sense to control the outcome quality and allow local entrepreneurship to furnish and organize the inputs. This is at the heart of devolution experiments like site-based management. But we intent to sweep the production function into the dustbin of history; then we need a new metaphor. One such metaphor is experimentalism.

If the invention of effective schooling is as much a consequence of art and experiment as it is of organizational science, then an alternative to the factory model for producing effective schools should be a model consistent with the meanings and methods of artisans and experimentalists.

What are the tools and media of this artisan/experimentalist that we might call the inventive educator? Answer: mastery of a variety of intellectual media, including reading, writing, and calculating in the visual mode; listening and speaking in the auditory mode; dance and athletics in the kinesthetic mode. What are the methods of training artisan/experimentalist educators? Answer: apprenticeship under a master teacher is still the primary method of instruction among experimentalists of all types, from musicians to scientists. Apprentice artists and scientists sign on at research laboratories, where they work on research of interest to their mentor, eventually acquiring the skills, knowledge, and financial support to pursue research agendas of their own.

Take the example of mathematics instruction. Good and Brophy's review (1986) of the RISE project in Milwaukee suggests that the greatest gains that could be enjoyed by urban students would be precisely in mathematics and science. It seems that the middle- and upper-middle-class household does not provide a very large out-of-school advantage in mathematics and science. And these are the areas of study in which the United States is most in need of students with high ability. It is apparently more difficult for urban children to acquire the cultural and linguistic advantages that accrue to students in middle-class homes. Assuming that intelligence is randomly distributed among the social classes, it follows that urban schools have a comparative advantage in pursuing educational programs designed to enhance the mathematics and scientific skills of their students.[1]

Teachers and administrators who would view their chosen profession from an experimentalist perspective would need to possess a prodigious capacity for autonomous learning and self-direction. These qualities are anathema to the bureaucratic organization of schooling where loyalty is valued more than competence.

The method of technology transfer could stray some distance from traditional institutions of higher education. (Have we met the enemy and, like Pogo, found him to be us?) We might fund at a respectable level organizations like the National Diffusion Network or create state legislation (or national where appropriate) to require all prospective principals (those about to be hired by school districts) to spend one year as an apprentice in a model school with a master administrator. Teacher training might follow a similar pattern within a single district or regional cluster of districts.

If the first-grade class of 1990 is to learn what it needs to function in the twenty-first century, much will have to change in our public schools. It will be a century dominated by computers, worldwide communication, and a global economy (Steen, 1989).

The Office of Technology Assessment (1988) reports that the American workplace will increasingly rely on intelligent devices (e.g., computers, imaging systems, laser video disks). Consequently, the goals, content, and required outcomes of public education will change dramatically. Because such technology will be organized to facilitate open-ended problem solving, users will require a capacity for creativity, flexibility, and decision making with incomplete data. Students will need to learn complex pattern recognition; develop the capacity to seek new information, analyze, evaluate and synthesize; and demonstrate a capacity for holistic thinking and learning while doing. At least one futurist argues that these skills may become the basis of a new definition of human intelligence (Dede, 1988). It is in this context that the poverty of the effective schools movement as it was defined in the 1970s becomes self-evident.

What are the implications of an experimentalist approach to effective schooling for accountability? If we are searching for a kind of school system that meets the early criteria of effectiveness, then we will of necessity have an accountability system focused on a narrow set of achievement outcomes. If, on the other hand, we are seeking to reinvent effective schooling for the future, then we must forgo the kind of reductionism that controls for a few "critical" inputs and outputs. Schools will need to be fundamentally restructured if the way we hold them accountable is to change. The test reflects the way instruction is delivered and simultaneously reinforces a curriculum that reflects the test. The current practice of partialing knowledge into specific disciplines of study like English literature, history, economics, and civics is predicated on an obsolete Cartesian-Newtonian world view. This problem is not lost on the business community. Peter Drucker wrote 20 years ago that

> The fact that we are shifting from a Cartesian view of the universe, in which the accent has been on parts and elements, to a configuration view, with emphasis on wholes and patterns, challenges every single dividing line between areas of study and knowledge. (1969, p. 13).

Does this mean we must abandon accountability in the name of the inventive educator? Not necessarily. It might mean, however, that we abandon the simplistic half-dozen achievement outcomes that dominate most models at present and the kind of school systems they measure. Not only do we need better tests of student learning such as those currently under development in Connecticut and elsewhere[2] (Prowda, 1988), but it also means that we must work at developing measures of competencies of generic intellectual and social skills like autonomous learning and cooperative problem solving.

REFERENCES

DEDE, C. J. (1988).   The probable evolution of artificial intelligence based educational devices. *Technological Forecasting and Social Change, 34,* 115–33.

DRUCKER, P. (1989).   *The age of discontinuity.* New York: Basic Books.

GORRY, G. A., BURGER, A. M., CHANEY, R. J., LONG, K. B., & TAUSK, C. M. (September 26–28, 1988).   Computer support for biomedical workgroups. *Proceedings of the Conference on Computer-Supported Cooperative Work.* Portland, Oregon, pp. 39–51. New York: Association for Computing Machinery.

GOOD, T. L., & BROPHY, J. E. (1986).   School effects. *Handbook of research on teaching,* 3rd ed., pp. 570–602. New York: Macmillan.

OFFICE OF TECHNOLOGY ASSESSMENT, U.S. CONGRESS. (1988).   *Technology and the American economic transition: Choices for the future.* Washington, D.C.: U.S. Government Printing Office.

PROWDA, P. M. (1988).   *Connecticut's accountability programs: Improvement through state-wide and district reporting.* Washington, D.C.: OERI Study Group.

STEEN, D. (September 18–22, 1989).   Teaching mathematics for tomorrow's world. *Educational Leadership, 7*(1).

ENDNOTES

[1]I recognize that this proposal sidesteps the question of where we will find teachers capable of leapfrogging the current system. It may be that interactive computer software will

ABOUT THE CONTRIBUTORS

Barnett Berry received his Ph.D. from the University of North Carolina-Chapel Hill in Educational Administration and Policy Studies. His research interests focus on teacher professionalism, teacher labor markets, and school restructuring. Presently, he is the associate director of the South Carolina Educational Policy Center (and assistant professor of curriculum) in the College of Education, University of South Carolina. A former public school teacher in South Carolina, Berry has served as a social scientist at the Rand Corporation in Washington, D.C., and has served as a consultant to numerous foundations, educational policy research centers, social service agencies, and school districts.

James R. Bliss is assistant professor in the Department of Educational Theory, Policy, and Administration at Rutgers University. Bliss has several years of experience as an urban practitioner. He received his undergraduate degree from Cornell University, his M.S. from Syracuse University, and his Ph.D. from Cornell University. Recent articles have appeared in *Educational Administration Quarterly* and *Planning and Changing* with C. John Tarter and Wayne K. Hoy.

William A. Firestone received his Ph.D. from the University of Chicago. He now teaches at Rutgers University where he is also a senior research fellow at the Center for Policy Research in Education. His research interests include the relationship between school organization and teacher, policy implementation, and research utilization. His work has appeared in *Educational Leadership, Educational Evaluation* *and Policy Analysis,* and *Educational Researcher.* He is on the editorial board of *Educational Administration Quarterly.*

Rick Ginsberg, Ph.D., is an associate professor in the Department of Educational Leadership and Policies, University of South Carolina. He did his graduate training at the University of Chicago in the program of Administrative, Institutional and Policy Studies. He co-edited the 1988–89 volume of the *Administrator's Notebook* in a joint venture between the University of Chicago and the Politics of Education Association. He serves on the editorial board of the *Urban Review,* and reviews manuscripts for several other journals. Ginsberg is co-editor of *Southern Cities, Southern Schools,* a collection of essays on southern school reform published by Greenwood Press. He had published widely on the area of educational reform and public policy, and recently directed several large scale analyses of the impact of various aspects of South Carolina's 1984 school reform legislation. Currently, he is completing a federally funded study on vocationally successful learning disabled adults.

Charles Glenn received his Ed.D. from Harvard and his Ph.D. from Boston University. Since 1970 he has been responsible for equity and urban education policies for the Massachusetts Department of Education. He has published extensively on parent choice, desegregation, and religion and public education, including *The Myth of the Common School* (1988) and *Choice of Schools in Six Nations* (1990). Glenn is currently writing a book on the education of immigrant children in 12 Western democracies.

James W. Guthrie is professor of education at the University of California at Berkeley and codirector of Policy Analysis for California Education (PACE). He has written extensively on educational policy, school finance and governance, including major books on school finance, educational administration, and teacher education. Currently a vice president of the American Educational Research Association, he has served as editor of *Educational Evaluation and Policy Analysis.* Before joining the University of California faculty, Guthrie was the educational specialist in the U.S. Senate and a special assistant to the secretary of the Department of Health, Education, and Welfare.

Lawrence W. Lezotte received his Ph.D. from Michigan State University, where subsequently he was professor of education for 18 years. At present, he is senior consultant at Effective Schools, an educational publishing and consulting firm. Lezotte served with Ronald Edmonds and Wilbur Brookover as a member of the original team of Effective Schools' researchers conducting the initial equity studies. Over the past two decades, Lezotte has conducted workshops and conferences on effective schools research and practices. He is the coauthor of many works that include *Creating Effective Schools.*

Susan Loucks-Horsley is program director for teacher development at The Regional Laboratory for Educational Improvement of the Northeast and Islands and associate director of The National Center for Improving Science Education. Her research and development interests include innovation and change, staff development, and program improvement, and she was codeveloper of the concerns-based adoption model while at the Texas Research and Development Center for Teacher Education. Her focus on narrowing the gap between research and practice has resulted in two recent publications: *An Action Guide to Improvement* and *Continuing to Learn: A Guidebook for Teacher Development.*

Karen Seashore Louis received her doctoral degree in sociology from Columbia University. Most of her research focuses on how to improve schools through organization design and development, research utilization, and better planning and implementation processes. Recent publications include *Supporting School Improvement: A Comparative Analysis* (with Susan Loucks-Horsley) (Acco, 1989), "Knowledge Use and School Improvement," (with Robert Dentler) (1988), "The Role of the School District in School Improvement," (1989), "Social Values and Teacher Quality of Work Life" (1990), and *Improving the Urban High School: What Works and Why* (with Matthew B. Miles) (1990). She is currently associate professor in the Department of Educational Policy and Administration at the University of Minnesota.

Matthew B. Miles received his Ed.D. from Columbia University. He has been senior research associate at the Center for Policy Research, New York, since 1970. He has carried out research, development, and consulting in the field of planned change in education for over 30 years, heading up major studies of leadership and intensive group training, school organizational renewal, educational innovation, program implementation, design of new schools, and the work of "change agents." Recent books include *Improving the Urban High School: What Works and Why* (with Karen Seashore Louis), *Assisting Change in Education, Lasting School Improvement, Qualitative Data Analysis,* and *Innovation Up Close.*

Peter Mortimore received his Ph.D. from the University of London, England. Since September 1990 he has been deputy director of the Institute of Education, University of London. His previous posts have included that of professor of educational research and director of the School of Education at the University of Lancaster, England, and director of research and statistics for the Inner London Authority. He has also been a high school teacher, school inspector, and central office administrator. Since 1975 he has been involved in a series of research studies on school effectiveness and has published widely in this and other related areas. He is a coauthor of *Fifteen Thousand Hours* (Harvard University Press), a study of effective British high schools, and of *School Matters* (University of California Press), a study of effective British elementary schools.

Susan E. Mundry is the associate director of The NETWORK, Inc., in Andover, Massachusetts, where she oversees school improvement projects and the development and marketing of products and services. Her prior position was director of the National Network of Successful Schools, a group of schools identified for their exemplary curriculum, staff development, leadership, and instruction, with the goal of helping other schools adopt their effective practices. Mundry's numerous publications in the areas of school improvement, dissemination, and technical assistance include *Making Change for School Improvement,* a training tool that simulates the process of change in schools.

Fred M. Newmann directs the National Center on Effective Schools, one of several national research centers funded by the U.S. Department of Education. The center conducts research on how to enhance student engagement in school work in order to boost achievement. A professor of curriculum and instruction at the University of Wisconsin—Madison, Newmann majored in American studies at Amherst College and received masters' and doctoral degrees in education at Harvard. He has extensive experience in teacher education, research, and curriculum development in secondary social studies. His publications deal with curriculum for citizenship, education and the building of community, and alternatives to standardized testing.

Kent D. Peterson is associate professor in the Department of Educational Administration and the director of the National Center for Effective Schools, Research and Development at the University of Wisconsin–Madison. He received his Ph.D. in administration, institutional and policy studies from the University of Chicago. His major research interests include the principalship, organizational theory, and effective schools. He is widely published on principalship, including research on work life, instructional leadership, evaluation, and the technical and symbolic aspects of leadership. His most recent works focus on the role of the principal in building school culture and how culture can enhance commitment in schools.

Rafael Ramirez received his M.A. degree from the University of London. He has most recently been associated with Policy Analysis for California Education (PACE) at the University of California, Berkeley, where he is completing work toward his Ph.D. in policy and management research. He has just been appointed education analyst at the U.S. Senate working for Senator Jeff Bingaman. He has been a teacher (K–8) as well as a college lecturer. His research interests include education policy, teacher research, and school governance.

Craig E. Richards currently is associate professor of education at Teachers College, Columbia University. Richards received his M.S. in educational administration from University of Wisconsin–Milwaukee, and his M.A. in economics, and Ph.D. in education from Stanford University. His current research interests are in economics of education and educational policy. He is author of *Microcomputer Applications for Strategic Management in Education: A Case Study Approach.*

Florence R. Webb received her M.A. degree from the University of California at Berkeley, where she is now completing her Ph.D. in educational policy analysis. Her research interests are education policy, school governance, and the social-emotional development of students in schools. She is serving her third term as president of the Dixie School District Board of Trustees in California and serves on the Board of Directors of the California School Boards Association.

INDEX